"CAUFFIEL KNOWS HOW TO DRAMATIZE TRUE CRIME!"
—Elmore Leonard,
bestselling author CUBA LIBRE

CRITICS RAVE ABOUT CAUFFIEL'S HOUSE OF SECRETS:

"A balance and grimly engaging {true crime} account of the weirdest domestic situation this side of the HOUSE OF USHER!"

Publishers Weekly

"An odyssey into American pathology . . .
Deeply disturbing!"

Detroit Free Press

"Incest, rape, murder, infanticide, torture, psychological abuse . . . HOUSE OF SECRETS is bedtime reading for devoted true crime fans!"

Booklist

Other Works by Lowell Cauffiel

Nonfiction

Masquerade
Forever and Five Days
Eye of the Beholder

Fiction:

Dark Rage
Marker

HOUSE OF SECRETS

Lowell Cauffiel

Pinnacle Books
Kensington Publishing Corp.

http://www.pinnaclebooks.com

For Paul Dinas, who appreciates all it takes.

PINNACLE BOOKS are published by

Kensington Publishing Corp.
850 Third Avenue
New York, NY 10022

First Kensington Hardcover Printing: November, 1997
First Pinnacle Printing: October, 1998

20 19 18

Printed in the United States of America

AUTHOR'S NOTE

House of Secrets employs no "fictionalization" to tell its story. It is told with court and police records, interviews with key participants, and nearly three years of research using proven methods of journalistic discovery.

The names of a few individuals in this account have been changed to help protect their safety and privacy. The pseudonyms are: Anne and Gerry Greene; Walter and Kathleen Dundee; Augusta Townsend; Tuck, Colleen and Bonnie Carson, and Tommy Sexton. Also, the accounts by Estella May Sexton, Sr., were taken from taped interviews, her quotes organized for clarity but kept in context. Also, like other secondhand accounts, Machelle Sexton Croto's disclosures to Anne Green were also confirmed and explored in many hours of taped interviews with Machelle.

Some of the victims in this book are minor children. Certain agencies, juvenile courts, and some news organizations keep the names of minors confidential. The intent is to protect children from embarrassment or ridicule. But the perpetrators in this story further exploited these children by manipulating the well-intentioned confidentiality maintained by these agencies for their own criminal purposes. Some child experts also believe this secrecy only contributes to the stigma of certain types of abuse, and fails to alert good citizens to the predators who walk among them.

Aspects of this case eventually were tried in the adult court system. There, the names of minors and the crimes committed against them found their way into publicly available police files, sworn depositions, testimony, and other material available under state freedom of information laws.

Some news organizations also publish the names of the entire Sexton family. Though part of the family's story was made public in the courts and news media, many details continued to remain secret simply because others lacked the time, resources, or interest to discover them—until this book.

Nevertheless, my interviews with workers for the Stark County Department of Human Services were limited to material already on the public record, in keeping with the agency's standard of confidentiality. The DHS provided no material to me directly from its interviews with the children. Human services reports, psychological evaluations, and summaries cited in this work were already available in public court files in Ohio and Florida.

8149 Caroline Street Northwest

Outside near the ascending walkway, a statue of Jesus stood with outstretched arms—amputated at the wrist, as if to deprive the Savior from offering any comfort and hope.

At the front door, somebody had tacked a small metal cross to the clapboards, inscribed with the words: "Peace to All Who Enter Here." But some people were already saying it: In the house on Caroline Street, there had been no peace at all.

These contradictions and others struck Bob and Edie Johnson when they first inspected the house during the short days of the winter of 1994.

The Stark County sheriff was offering the property for back taxes, bank foreclosure, and various other debts. A year earlier, the original owner had tried to auction it, but title liens had sabotaged the sale.

An auctioneer's one-column ad in the *Canton Repository* read:

SPACIOUS 9 ROOM CAPE COD HOME ON ONE ACRE
STOCK POND-TANDEM 4 CAR GARAGE
CONTENTS-APPLIANCES-FURNITURE

The home was perched on a hilltop, its front deck over-looking the pond. A weathered split-rail fence bordered the property. Beyond it, across Wales Avenue, the gable of the New Covenant Christian Church poked through the treetops.

Better Homes & Gardens featured the home in an article not long after it was built in the late 1950s, the Johnsons were later told. There were anecdotes about backyard barbecues in the summer and hot chocolate in the winter for kids coming in with their skates from the frozen pond.

It was one of the largest properties in the old Highland View Farms sub, easy to find. Coming from woodsy suburbs north of Canton, you drove south on Wales past the clubhouse and 18th green of Shady Hollow Country Club. Caroline was another mile south. Or, you could drive two miles north on Wales, out of the rusty rail town of Massilon. The property was in Jackson Township, the Canton-Massilon area's hottest suburb. First-rate schools. A half dozen lakes. Four golf courses. A well-equipped and smartly uniformed police department. And Belden Village, a mall and shopping district that featured so many upscale franchise restaurants it looked like the proving grounds for America's newest chains.

The auctioneer's ad promised a spacious family home. The large garage was below grade, opening to Caroline Street. On the first floor there was a large living room with a fireplace, its sliding doors opening to a fenced area shaded by nine tall pines. A family room, kitchen, dinette, formal dining and master bedroom with full bath were also on the first floor. Three more bedrooms, a full bath and ample closet space were located upstairs.

The contents were listed in the first auction ad as well: Three chest-type freezers and one upright. A Maytag washer and dryer, and another set by Whirlpool, too. Two sets of bunk beds. A three-piece French Provincial bedroom suite. Bookcases. Three couches. Tables and chairs. There were rods and reels and a 15-foot Coleman canoe. There were ten ladders, most of them aluminum. Six lawn mowers. Chains saws. A snow blower. A '77 Suzuki motorcycle. There was a wheelchair, hardly used, and a shiny new hospital bed.

There was a hint of even more. "Family is moving out of state and decided to sell everything, loads of contents not seen," the ad read.

Bob Johnson knew that owner. His name was Eddie Lee Sexton. Sexton was a long-time customer at his used car lot, Johnson Motors. Sexton showed up one day 15 years before at his first lot on 7th Street in Canton, and Johnson kept his business as the lot moved to other city locations over the years. Sexton bought cars in the $1,500 to $4,000 price range, usually paying cash. Johnson had sold him a Ford van and a '76 black Cadillac.

Johnson remembered Sexton as a striking figure. His hair receded deeply above the temples. He had a long weathered face and penetrating eyes, which he softened somewhat with a full beard. Early on, he told Johnson he was "retired," but he hardly looked old enough to qualify for a military pension, let alone one from a forge plant where he said he once worked.

But Eddie Sexton also was the most polite man Bob Johnson had ever met.

"Yes, sir."

"No, sir."

"Thank you very kindly. I appreciate that very much."

And bright, too. Knew his cars. Knew how to make a deal. Not one to argue or get anxious or be indecisive. He shopped the lot methodically, in no hurry. He seemed to be a regular guy with common sense.

Bob Johnson also had met Sexton's wife, Estella May, and several of the children. The wife always waited in the car. She sat patiently on the passenger's side, the door closed, her feet never touching the lot.

Sexton told him he had a dozen children at home—seven boys and five girls. He never brought the girls to look at cars, only the older boys. They walked the lot with him, then came into the sales shack. They sat quietly in chairs, their backs straight, listening to their father conduct his business. When they reached their late teens, they began stopping by on their own, checking out the inventory. They always had something to say about their father, particularly his namesake, Eddie Lee Sexton, Jr. Dad's doing this. Dad's doing that.

"Man, did his kids love him," Johnson would tell me. "You know, you could just tell."

One of those big, old-fashioned happy families, Bob Johnson thought. Not a lot of money, but a measured mix of love and discipline. You'd have to really love kids to have 12 of them. You'd have to have some discipline to survive living with them under one roof. And you'd need bunk beds and four freezers and two washers and dryers and everything else the auctioneer promised in the house.

At the auction for the house's contents, the appliances and the canoe and the tools were snatched up by the small crowd that gathered at the home on February 18, 1993. One of Sexton's older daughters, now married and a mother, stood silently as the bids rolled off the auctioneer's tongue. She passed on bikes and beds and household heirlooms. She bought a refrigerator, her only purchase that day.

The Johnsons, Edie in particular, were interested in real estate. She ran the family's construction business. The couple had bought and remodeled almost 50 houses with their small firm. Edie envisioned turning 8149 Caroline Street into a $150,000 property—a handsome homestead by Ohio's reasonable real estate values. If her suspicions proved correct, 8149 Caroline was going to auction for much less than that. Dark headlines and TV reports could do that to a property. At the 1994 real estate auction on the courthouse steps, Edie Johnson and a lot of other people in Stark County knew that Eddie Lee and Estella May Sexton had not only "left the state."

They'd been on the wanted list of the FBI.

There was only one other bidder for the homestead. When the bidding was over, the Johnsons purchased the property for $56,000. It was enough to pay off the Sextons' $46,000 mortgage balance and $7,200 in back taxes. It was not enough to satisfy a list of other creditors, one of whom was Eddie Sexton, Jr. He no longer talked lovingly of his father. He claimed his father stole nearly 8,000 bucks from him.

When they took title, a policeman friend said, "Bob, watch closely when you're digging out that little lake."

After they took possession, a friend in Edie Johnson's office said, "My God, what have you done? I'm going to bring over holy water and sprinkle it."

Edie said, "Leave the holy water and bring some Spic & Span."

But as the work began, the house seemed to whisper secrets. The Sextons liked to hide things. Underneath the deck, they found a stash of everything imaginable. Bicycles. Paint cans. Wood. Old tools. Newspapers. Weathered lumber. Rusty toys. It took eight men an entire day to fill a Dumpster with items. It was the first of eight Dumpsters they would need to clean up 8149 Caroline.

As the couple became more familiar with the property, the back part of the lot intrigued them. An eight-foot stockade fence shielded the home on three sides. Neighbors had no view of the lower windows. Privacy was one thing, but it seemed like overkill, considering the shrubs and trees that already shielded the lot.

One by one, the neighbors began to drop by, telling stories.

An old woman showed up. "Is there a Weed Wacker in

that garage?" she asked. "They borrowed mine and never brought it back."

Bob Johnson hadn't seen a Weed Wacker.

"I thought it might be here," the woman said, wandering off.

He wondered why she'd never simply asked the Sextons for it back.

The Johnsons soon befriended a retarded woman in her 40s who lived behind them. Her voice quaked with terror at the mention of the Sexton name. Years of harassment by the Sextons had killed her disabled father, she claimed.

There were a spate of stories about fires in the neighborhood. Fires in trash cans and Dumpsters. Fiery attacks on neighborhood homes. One neighbor said she'd taken a nap after returning from a family funeral one afternoon, only to be woken by the sounds of Sexton children trying to set fire to her awning. Another claimed the Sexton boys tried to burn down her garage.

There also had been two blazes at the Sexton home. One neighbor brought over photographs, showing fire trucks arriving at 8149 Caroline as flames leaped from an upper dormer. It was a bedroom where the Sexton children slept, but no one was home that day. It was said the fires were caused by bad wiring and careless smoking.

They heard other versions of the children's behavior, particularly how well-behaved they were. In the later years, Estella May Sexton was no longer having babies, but two of her teenage daughters did. They didn't have husbands. They didn't move out of the house. Neighbors said Eddie Sexton had a certain way with children. They would follow the patriarch as he walked the grounds, or took them to the pond to fish and swim. They clustered around him, hanging onto his words. One neighbor had nicknamed him "The Bellhop," because of the way his children jumped at his commands.

Inside the home, the Johnsons found evidence of a certain chaos. There were four wallpaper patterns in the living room, none of it really matching the gold carpet that covered the first floor. The window moldings all had nail holes, as if they'd been boarded up from the inside. The kitchen stove was caked with deposits inside. Edie was convinced it hadn't been cleaned in 10 years or more.

The Johnsons were struck by the doors. The locks were dysfunctional on every interior door in the house. The strike plates were busted out, as if someone had kicked in every one.

Up the narrow stairs to the second floor, 9-x-13 bedrooms and one 18-x-12 seemed inadequate for 12 children. The smell of cigarette smoke pervaded one of the bedrooms. Along the walls of the children's rooms, the Johnsons found small trapdoors, the kind used for access to the hidden attics under the lower roof of a Cape Cod.

As Johnson opened them, she found small human nests between the ceiling rafters. There were children's blankets and toys and stuffed animals.

Edie said, "These look like they were some kind of place for punishment."

"Or hiding," Bob Johnson said.

Throughout the property, they found other disturbing signs. In the basement they found a twin bed mattress covered with graffiti, done in magic marker. The pictures were of erect penises and breasts and vaginas, not much more sophisticated than stick figures. They looked as if they were done by a child's hand.

Two chains with metal rings hung from a basement support beam. One garage door was nailed shut. A hundred feet from the house was a little Dutch barn, a storage shed. Inside, there was an easy chair and a floor ashtray filled with cigarettes. Around it, a collection of stuffed animals.

"I thought, something was going on here," Edie told me. "This was some kind of special place."

And then they found another odd thing: large bundles of greeting cards from the Sexton children, proclaiming their love to their mom and dad.

One area inside stood out, in that it didn't seem to conform to the rest of the house. The master bedroom looked as if it had been well-appointed. It showed no sign of some of the cruder carpentry and repairs the home-owner had obviously done after the fires. There was a cove for a built-in TV. It had its own bathroom, the ceramic tile work professionally lain with sparkling white grout. There was a new sink, a new toilet, and a large new shower stall designed for the handicapped.

By then, they'd found the wheelchair in the basement and the hospital bed, which had gone unsold at the first auction sale. Bob Johnson found it curious. Eddie Sexton had never talked of any disabled children. And he'd certainly had no trouble walking around his lot.

The Johnsons decided they'd gut the house. Remove the flooring. Take the entire interior down to the studs and put up new drywall. New moldings. It seemed the only way to bring the place back.

They took down the tarnished metal cross and sent the amputated Christ off in one of eight large Dumpster loads. Eventually, they learned the statue had once belonged to Eddie Sexton's mother. He'd brought it home after her funeral. No one knew whether it had its hands then or not.

When I first interviewed the Johnsons one night in 1995, social workers, police agencies, and prosecutors in Ohio and Florida had probed many aspects of life in the Cape Cod. Some investigations were still going on.

Ironically, in researching the Sexton case, the newly renovated 8149 Caroline Street Northwest was one of the only times I felt entirely comfortable. The house was warm and clean and cozy. The Johnsons were gracious and hospitable.

And they had nothing to hide.

It seemed that every one of the many times I drove from

my home in Michigan to this part of Ohio, the sun never shined. For nearly three years I visited filthy homes, cramped prison interview rooms, and the chaotic offices of reluctant authorities. They were, perhaps, fitting settings to document rape and torture and murder, but trying conditions nonetheless.

When I first began, even in my darkest imaginings, I never guessed the extent of the brutal darkness that once filled the house. The first hint came when I listened to the account of a former baby-sitter.

It was a story about days of sunless skies and rain.

When the Sexton children were grade-schoolers, she said, they would bolt into the front yard during thunderstorms. They would huddle like a flock, their small faces looking upward, the lightning flashing in their eyes.

Finally, she asked them why they kept doing this.

"They were saying 'Jesus is coming,'" she said. "They were hoping He was coming to take them away. . . ."

Take them from 8149 Caroline Street.

They would get only the hapless statue. Real saviors were hard to find.

i

When I'm With You

1

Terry Turify first noticed the girl in the well-waxed halls of the high school. Her only company was an armful of books. She always looked as if she needed a good night's sleep. One day in study hall, Terry walked over and introduced herself. She felt sorry for her, always sitting there alone.

The girl said her name was Stella. "Stella Sexton," she said.

Stella was wearing a blousy print dress. It looked like it had time-traveled from the 1970s. Terry thought, go home and wash your hair. Don't let it hang there in dark, oily strands. Get rid of the dandruff on your shoulders. Don't you know you could be very pretty? Not that Terry was a clotheshorse. God knows since Terry and her twin sister Traci had transferred to Jackson High School, they'd discovered plenty of those in the halls.

Terry and Stella Sexton had *that* in common. They were both outsiders, Terry a transfer student from the Cleveland area, Stella on the outside simply because of the way she looked. No one in the school seemed to have the remotest interest in the girl.

Terry tried to connect, trying harmless questions about their classes, their school, their studies. Stella gave one word answers, mostly "yes" or "no."

After a few minutes, Stella gave up a complete sentence. She said she'd been born and raised in the Canton area, but she was also part Native American.

"Really?" Terry said, always fascinated with Indian culture. "What kind?"

Stella named a tribe. It was such an odd name, something Terry had never heard before, she later wouldn't be able to recall the designation.

"Do you know how to speak Indian?" Terry asked.

Stella opened her notebook and spelled out Terry's name in this tribe's language. Her father had taught her the language, Stella said. He was involved with Indian tribes. He restored old furniture for Indian organizations. That's how he made his living, she said.

Stella handed her the notebook paper. "Keep it," she said.

The next day, Stella brought her another sheet of odd-looking markings. She said it was the entire Indian alphabet.

"We speak the language at home," Stella said.

"Hey, maybe I could come over to your house some time," Terry said. "I'm really into this stuff."

Stella's eyes narrowed. "No," she said. "Absolutely not."

"What do you mean, absolutely?"

"I can't do that. My dad would not approve."

"Why?"

"He'd be real mad if he even knew I was telling you."

Terry figured, some people are sensitive about sharing their cultures. But in time, she would learn Stella's father was sensitive about a lot of things.

Throughout their junior year, Terry tried inviting her to do things.

"Hey, Stella, want to catch a movie?"

"No," Stella said.

"We could go to Canton Center Mall."

"No."

"How about Belden Village?"

"No."

She thought, maybe Stella didn't have any money.

"All right then," Terry said. "How about you just come over to my place?"

"No," Stella said. She couldn't do anything, she said. Her father would not approve.

Summer vacation came. They didn't talk again until early in their senior year. Terry saw her sitting alone at a big round table near the door in the high school cafeteria. Stella was wearing a blue and white sailor shirt. Her eyes beamed, her dark circles not so apparent as the year before.

Terry saw her tummy. Stella Sexton looked pregnant.

When Terry asked, Stella said the baby was due in October. She announced it proudly.

Terry thought, now her ostracization at Jackson High School would be complete. Stella seemed oblivious to the ramifications.

"I mean, she had that glow," Terry would later say.

Terry pulled up a chair, asking, "Gosh, Stella, who's the father?"

"He's in the Navy," she said.

"Where?"

"Overseas."

"Are you getting married?"

"I think so."

Terry looked into her eyes. "My God, Stella, what do your parents think?"

"They don't care," Stella said matter of factly.

"They *don't care*? My parents would kill me."

"As long as I'm happy," Stella said, "they don't care."

Terry thought, *Don't care?* Last year her parents wouldn't even let the girl out of the house.

2

It wasn't until after she saw the blockbuster movie, Traci decided he was a lot like Forrest Gump. The slim, handsome boy was standing in the corner, his books cradled under his right arm, looking as if he was waiting for something, or someone.

First period, government, Mr. Paul's class. Every morning, Traci Turify killed 20 minutes with her twin sister Terry, both of them in the building early, waiting for school to start.

She asked Terry, "What is *he* doing?"

Terry, leaning over, whispered, "You're sitting in his desk."

"Am I sitting in your seat?"

He nodded.

"Well," she said. "That's just too damn bad."

He said nothing, and didn't move a muscle, as if he was entirely prepared to wait her out.

She popped up, saying, "Just kidding."

He walked over slowly, setting down his textbooks, and looked at Terry.

Terry said, "Joel and I are buds."

Joel M. Good. That was his name, he said when they got to the formal introduction. They called him Joey at home. But in school, people called him Joel, or just Joe. Right off, she sensed he was different, not full of bravado or the nervous energy common to other senior boys.

Tracy wanted to know more. He was a transfer student, he said. He came from another suburb called Perry, between Massilon and Canton.

Traci said that she and her twin sister Terry were transfer students, too.

He said he came to Jackson as a junior, lived with his aunt and uncle now. He said he used to live with his grandparents in Perry.

"What about your mom and dad?"

They were both dead, he said. They'd died when he was 13, his father from a heart attack, his mother from diabetes.

"Where you from?" he asked.

"We're from Cleveland—the real world," Terry said.

In fact, they were from a working-class suburb of Cleveland called Parma. It was only 50 miles due north on I-77. But the way the Turifys saw it, Parma was an entire world way. They were still having a hard time of it, even as seniors. Terry absolutely hated Jackson High School and most of the students. Traci had managed to make some friends.

Jackson just wasn't normal, they would tell people who bothered to ask. Normal schools don't call their school auditoriums a "center for the performing arts." Normal teenagers don't drive to class in BMWs and new Jeep Wranglers. Normal teenage girls don't wear Liz Claiborne blazers, and normal boys don't strut down the halls in pink golf shirts and yellow Izod sweaters. Tracy had never been in a school before where the class bell signaled a stampede of Ralph Lauren horsemen down the halls.

"In Parma, a prime car is held together with duct tape," Terry would say. "A pink shirt? That would be the same as committing suicide in our old school."

Jackson High School, the pride of Jackson Township, a suburb north of Canton, Ohio. Students from the west side came from homes that pushed a half million. They had clothes and money and worries about how many photos and club references they could stack in the yearbook index. Their senior class called the yearbook: "What Goes Around Comes Around."

"And they *let you know it,*" Terry would say. "If you don't have it, they let you know you do not belong. They look right through you in the halls."

Joel Good was more like them, one of the invisible people. Traci Turify knew that right off, sitting in their corner before government class.

As the 1988-89 school year unfolded she found more to like about the boy. He eventually took a job as a dishwasher at Don Poncho's and enrolled in a class in the building trades. He rode a Schwinn 10-speed everywhere. He biked around his sub after school, visiting with neighborhood friends. Parents liked him. They were always inviting Joel Good to stay for dinner. He'd eventually buy a brown, rust-pitted Datsun hatchback for $400, feeding it gas a couple bucks at a time. It was always breaking down. But rather than complain, he'd just get back on the bike again.

Joel hung out mainly with underclassmen, kids from his neighborhood. They went bowling a lot up at Colonial Lanes. Or Joel took them to a couple old drive-in movie theaters south of Canton. He avoided endless discussions about the world-class prep football being played in the Canton-Massilon corridor and the hottest new videos on MTV. He was satisfied with the hapless Cleveland Browns and liked bands popular in the 1970s, Lynyrd Skynyrd and Peter Frampton. A neighborhood friend took him to his first concert, Cheap Trick. They stood in the front row. Joel complained he couldn't hear for two days.

At first, he didn't make a big deal about girls and dating. He never made cat calls at them, hanging his head out of a speeding car in the school lot like Traci had seen others do. The closest Joel Good ever came to a date was a movie outing with a group of underclassmen. He hung around that night with another transfer student, a girl who was 75 pounds overweight.

"He made me feel like a person," the girl later said.

"A sweet guy."

"Very caring."

"The nicest guy I ever met."

They described him that way, the few who took the time to know him. As for those who ignored him, Joel Good didn't appear to care. He took each encounter as it came, seemingly unaware the preppies looked through him and that the burnouts thought he was a square.

And he was funny, Traci often thought. The routines they found comic were not about others, but about mundane foibles of Joel Good's own life. A story about his car breaking down could put them in stitches.

He hobbled in one day.

"So there I was stuck on the freeway."

"So what did you do?" somebody asked.

"I kicked it. That's how I broke my toe."

It wasn't the punch line. It was the delivery. Straight-faced, and usually in a monotone.

Just like Forrest Gump.

Traci learned they had much in common. Joel Good would turn 19 in January. He'd been held back a year in grade school and placed in the slower classes most of his school years.

"God," Traci said. "You too?"

Traci had trouble with numbers. "A form of dyslexia," she explained. "Like a phone number. I'll get one of the two digits all mixed up."

Math was difficult for Traci. For Joel, school was a struggle across the board. In his old high school he studied in a special curriculum. In Jackson, they appeared to have tossed him in with the mix, expecting him to fend for himself. His grades fell from B's and C's to D's and F's after he transferred. His aunt hired a personal tutor, who worked with him twice a week. Traci depended on Terry, who did her homework and coached her on tests. She passed her twin's tips on to Joel.

"Make up little skits in your head," Traci told him. "It's a good way to remember."

Joel eventually raised his grades to C's.

Other students rarely insulted his lack of intelligence. Joel Good wouldn't argue, and he certainly couldn't be goaded into a fight. People gave up quickly on trying to push his buttons, especially when their insults were met with that Forrest Gump stare.

Even Traci's sister Terry, the consummate cynic, noticed it. "He believes in people," she said. "He always thinks good of people, no matter what they do."

Like when Traci took his desk. That became their morning routine, their little ritual through the fall and winter. Traci in his seat, talking to Terry. Saying a nasty line, then giving it back to him when he showed up.

Then Traci landed a baby-sitting job in Joel Good's neighborhood. He began dropping by to see her after school, pedalling over on his bike. They talked about homework and the Cleveland Browns and life after high school.

One day she asked, "What are you going to do after graduation?"

"I'd like to have a family," he said. "I'd like to have a wife and kids."

"That's a good goal," she said.

Terry pulled her aside at school one day. "Traci," she said. "I think Joel wants to ask you out."

He asked her a few days later, in front of his aunt's house, standing in the driveway, looking at his feet.

She didn't want to hurt his feelings. But she'd been going with a boy named Eric for six months. Eric had already asked her to the prom, she said.

"You're still my friend, Joel," she said. "Is there anybody else you want to ask? Maybe I can help."

He answered the next day. "I sort of like that girl you guys sometimes hang around with."

"What girl?" Traci asked.

"Stella," Joel said. "She seems nice."

3

The day she first heard the girl's name, Teresa Boron panicked. Joel Good had sprung the question on her at 10:30 that morning, a Saturday, when mall parking was a major challenge in and of itself.

"What do you wear to a prom?" he asked.

She always called him Joey.

"Joey, you're going?" Teresa asked back. Her eyes filled with disbelief.

He nodded.

Teresa asked, "You're going with Traci?"

Weeks ago, she'd suggested her nephew ask the neighborhood girl who often stopped by their house after school. He'd finally gotten up the nerve, only to be rejected. Teresa thought, Traci must have changed her mind. Now Joey had waited until *the day of the dance* to break the news.

"Traci has a boyfriend," Joey said. "I'm going with a girl."

"What girl?"

"Her name is Stella."

"And who is Stella?"

"She's a girl at school. Traci kind of set it up."

Stella, Teresa thought. That was an unusual name.

Her nephew had shown little interest in dating. He had moppy brown hair and innocent eyes that might have charmed a half dozen girls, if he'd only had the confidence to make the moves. He was shy and academically slow. Not retarded, but his IQ was borderline. She'd hired a tutor to help him, but she could only guess what he was up against in the high school's social scene.

Joel Michael Good, Jr. was four weeks from graduation. Unlike most of the students at Jackson, he did not have a stack of college acceptance letters to consider. But in her house, Teresa Boron figured, he had a shot at making a life for himself. She was the co-owner and bookkeeper of her husband's machine shop. They made guide rollers for mills in the rust belt. She handled the payroll and the accounts payable and receivable between raising four kids of her own under the age of 10. She never thought twice about taking in Joey. As a child, he called her "Aunt Tee Tee." Sometimes he still did. He'd lived with her sister Velva, then her parents. Joey's younger brother Danny was still living with his grandparents in south Canton. When Joey said he wanted to move in with her, Teresa figured she was fulfilling an old promise.

Her sister Linda had called her to her sickbed six years ago, blind, her organs failing. "I have to make sure my kids are going to be okay," Linda said.

That day Teresa promised, "I'll always be there for them."

She wished her sister could be there now. A first date, to the senior prom no less. How proud his mother would be.

"You wear a tux to a prom," Teresa said.

Joey did not have a tux, or reservations at a restaurant. He'd given no thought to flowers, color coordination, or any of the other details most students spent weeks planning.

Teresa glanced at her watch and reached for the Yellow Pages. "My God, Joey," she asked. "What color is Stella's dress?"

"I don't know," Joey said.

He didn't have Stella's phone number, either, and only vague directions to her house.

4

Eight hours later, they sped down Wales Avenue toward Massilon, Joey in the backseat, Teresa's friend in the front, along for the ride.

They would find this Stella's house, pick her up and take the young prom couple to a restaurant called the Leprechaun. They would let the two seniors dine by themselves on the other side of the restaurant, while Teresa and her friend sipped a couple of drinks. Then, they'd drop them off at the McKinley Room in the Canton Civic Center, site of the 1989 prom. They were calling the dance "When I'm With You," inspired by a song by the band called Sheriff.

Teresa scanned the houses, her eyes straining from behind the wheel of her Chevy van. It was twilight, the sky a dark off-white from a murky overcast. Dusk had turned the lawns and homes and leafless trees into ill-defined dark shapes.

They were looking for a pond.

"She said it was the house on Wales next to the pond," Joey kept saying.

So far, they'd gotten lucky, Teresa figured. Her nephew was dressed in a brilliant white tuxedo, complimented by white shoes and a powder blue tie and cummerbund. They'd found a rental shop that did one-day alterations. There was a table waiting for the couple at the Leprechaun. At the flower shop, Joey had picked out a rose corsage.

"You can never go wrong with a red rose," Teresa said.

When they found the pond, Joey went up to the house on the north side of the water, but returned after a few moments. When he got back into the backseat, Teresa spun around, wondering.

"Wrong house," Joey said. He pointed south. "The people said there's a girl named Stella who lives over there."

Teresa wheeled the van back around on Wales, then up Caroline, finding the driveway. The house was almost imposing, sitting there on top of the hill at dusk. She watched her nephew walk slowly up the sidewalk, carrying the clear plastic case with the rose corsage in front of him, doing it carefully, as if it were a liquid that might spill.

When he returned minutes later, the girl Stella was with

him. Teresa Boron got out of the van and walked toward them, a camera in her hand. She could see the parents hovering near the front doorway on the deck. They didn't come out to introduce themselves. Teresa didn't approach. She figured this was no time to chat. After all, this was Joey's night.

Besides, Stella Sexton had captured Teresa's eyes.

My God, she thought, this girl is very pretty. Her dark brown hair was pinned up on her head. She was wearing a full-length formal, not one of the tight body dresses or skimpy satins popular with teenage girls today. The outer shell was white lace, her bare shoulders covered with a transparent lace shawl. The color was powder blue and white, the same shades as Joey's tux. Stella had pinned a white carnation on Joey's lapel. But Joey was still holding the red rose corsage in front of him, the flower still in its plastic case.

In the back of the van, the two of them said nothing. They remained silent for miles. The two shyest students in Jackson High School have somehow found each other, Teresa thought. A perfect match.

Teresa broke the silence, asking about their plans. Stella said her father and brother would be picking them up from the prom. She spoke in a hardly audible voice.

"I have to be home early," she whispered.

Teresa thought, on prom night?

That would not be the only deviation in prom protocol. As Teresa dropped them off at the Civic Center, Stella still hadn't put on the red corsage. Later, Teresa learned the flower never left its plastic case. Stella Sexton had emerged from the house on Caroline Street wearing a blue-and-white wrist corsage.

She would not replace it with the rose.

"It's a gift from my father," she said.

5

They watched them in an awkward slow dance. A couple of times, Joel tried to hold her hand, but Stella would touch him only for a few moments, then slide her fingers away. They sat at Terry and Traci's table. When Joel slipped away for a cigarette, Traci followed him outside.

He sucked hard on the smoke. Traci Turify had never seen him so frustrated.

"Man," he said. "She hardly says anything."

Traci was feeling like little miss matchmaker. She'd personally gone to Stella Sexton and told her that Joel Good wanted to ask her out. Only after she said she'd probably go did Joel decide to invite her as his date.

"Maybe she's nervous," Traci said.

"Nervous?"

"Well, she's not well-liked at school. You know that."

They'd talked about her pregnancy. Neither Traci or Terry had been able to get a straight answer from Stella about the father of her baby, whether he was ever coming back.

"Maybe that's it," Traci said. "This boyfriend in the service."

"I don't know," Joel said.

Joel wanted to ask her to a class trip the next day to Cedar Point, a world-class amusement park west of Cleveland.

"But, man, she sure is shy," he said.

Coming from him, Traci thought, that had to be about as shy as shy gets.

They went back inside.

Well before midnight, Traci came back from the dance floor and realized Joel and Stella were gone.

A couple days later in school, Traci asked him, "So, how did it go?"

Joel looked disappointed. "I took her home and that was it."

"You didn't go to Cedar Point?" she asked.

He shook his head.

Joel Good never mentioned Stella Sexton again until their graduation ceremony. Stella had just walked past Traci with her diploma. She said hi, but Stella just kept walking, not even bothering to look at her or wave.

When she saw Joel, she asked, "Hey, what's the deal with Stella?"

"I don't know," he said. "She doesn't call or anything."

"That was short-lived."

"Yeah, I guess," he said.

It was the last conversation they would ever have.

6

It was summer the next time Teresa Boron saw the girl. Joey had decided to try to ask Stella Sexton out again. Teresa suggested he invite her to a family cookout. Teresa drove over to the house on Caroline Street to pick her up. Stella Sexton came walking out of the door with a baby in her arms.

"Is that your sister?" Teresa asked in the car.

"No," she said. "It's my baby."

Her name was Dawn, she said.

Teresa didn't probe. It was the girl's business. She thought, kids sometimes made mistakes.

Later, Joey told her about the father in the Navy. "The guy walked out on her," he said. "He claimed it wasn't his."

When Teresa looked at the baby, something seemed profound about the girl's looks. What an uncanny resemblance to her mother, she thought.

At the cookout, Teresa tried engaging Stella in conversation. She spoke in a hardly audible voice.

"Getting any information out of her was like pulling teeth," Teresa later recalled.

Teresa eventually put a few facts together. Like Joey, Stella had been held back one year in school, but it wasn't because of her grades. She had a high B average in high school. She'd repeated the first grade after she'd been hurt in a cooking accident in the family home. She was hospitalized for two months, her arms and chest burned by hot grease. She'd studied culinary arts in high school, but dropped out of the co-op cooking program when she had the child. She'd worked at Pizza Hut and Frank's Family Restaurant in Massilon.

"What does your father do?" she asked.

"He has his own painting business," she said.

Estella May Sexton. That was her full name, exactly the same as her mother's. Stella was the oldest girl in a family of 12 children. There were seven boys and five girls, ranging in age from 6 to 23. Her parents had given her a nickname.

"At home, everyone calls me Pixie," she said.

Pixie Sexton said she had to be home by no later than eight. It was summer, daylight savings time. It wouldn't even be dark.

"That's awfully early," Teresa said.

"My father wants me home by eight," Pixie said.

For the next date, Joey got his rusted Datsun working and drove over to see her. Then he began visiting her a couple of nights a week.

"What do you guys do at Pixie's?" Teresa asked.

"We sit around and talk," Joey said. "We watch TV. The baby really likes me."

He began bringing Pixie to their house on weekends, sometimes Pixie's brother William in tow. They called him Willie. He was a dark-haired, gangly boy Joey's age. He was as quiet as his sister. The three of them would sit in Teresa's family room and watch TV. They had to be the quietest teenagers in Stark County, Teresa thought.

The first time Teresa Boron heard the rumor, it came from a boy in the neighborhood who mowed their grass. He'd gone to school with the Sexton children. He claimed the family belonged to some kind of cult.

"Cult?" Teresa asked. "What kind of cult?"

"Some kind of strange rituals," he said. "And the Sexton boys used to come to school looking like they'd been beat up and stuff."

She pressed him for details, but he had none. She tried to dismiss it, but as the weeks went by, it lay there in the back of her mind.

Joey said one night, "I really like Pixie."

She thought, *like* wasn't the word. He confirmed that when he added that he'd like to marry Pixie Sexton one day.

She said, "You don't know her. I mean, you don't even know who her child's father is?"

Joey repeated the story about the father being in the Navy. Later she would get a more developed version, Pixie saying now that the baby's father had died.

Teresa Boron began to worry. The cult story kept coming to the front of her mind.

It wasn't just these mysterious Sexton kids, it was Joey. She couldn't count on her nephew to discern fact from fiction. His slowness hampered him in the simplest of things. The first time he tried to get his driver's license, a frightened state examiner aborted his road test, made him park the car on the street, and walked back to the state office. Teresa discovered he needed glasses, but it still took him three more tries to get his permit. She had to remind Joey to take a shower. She still had to coax him to brush his teeth. Not because he wanted to be dirty, he just forgot simple necessities like that.

"My nephew wasn't ready for marriage," Teresa Boron would later say. "My nephew wasn't ready for life."

Teresa believed she had two extreme options. She could ignore what appeared to be happening to Joey with Pixie.

Or she could get him declared incompetent by the court. She'd be damned if she'd do that. That was not "taking care" of her sister's son.

Teresa tried to find middle ground. "You need to live your own life for a while," she said. "Then, later, you can think about marriage and a family."

But he continued seeing her, spending more evenings at the house on Caroline Street.

"He became head over heels with this girl," she later recalled. "And there is just no reasoning with a teenager in love."

Then one day in September, Joey announced that he wanted to move to Montana.

"Montana?" she asked. "With who?"

"Pixie. And Mr. and Mrs. Sexton. The whole family is going to move out west."

He explained that the Sextons were buying a big ranch there. It was located on top of a mountain, a millionaire's mansion with hundreds of acres. There were guest quarters and a guard house. Mr. Sexton had shown him a video of the spread.

"They want me to work in the guard station," Joey said.

That evening, Teresa Boron drove to the house on Caroline, Joey tagging along. The man who introduced himself as Pixie's father met her at the front door. Ed Sexton was a tall, thin man with a pronounced widow's peak.

She told Ed Sexton she needed to talk about Joey.

Ed Sexton smiled, inviting her to sit on the deck. His wife Estella emerged, but Sexton turned to her and said, "Go inside and get some iced tea."

It was an order. The wife silently complied.

As she settled into her chair, Teresa noticed a couple of girls and a young boy, ages maybe 8 to 12, quietly come outside. Soon eight or nine Sexton children came out, taking positions, all of them absolutely silent. They stood looking at her with their chins lowered, their dark eyes peering up at her, as if she were some new, strange species they'd never seen before.

When Estella handed her the tea and returned inside, Joey took Dawn for a walk down by the pond, Pixie and several other of the children following. Ed Sexton looked as relaxed and cordial as a southern gentleman sipping a mint julep on a plantation porch.

"You know, Joey is just terrific with little Dawn," Sexton drawled.

Sexton began asking the questions. He wanted to know the fate of Joey's mother and dad.

She gave him the brief version. His father died unexpectedly of a sudden heart attack three years before his mother, she said. Neither lived past the age of 35.

"Did the parents have insurance?" he asked. "I mean, to take care of the boy?"

She thought, *That's a nosey question,* but answered anyway. "They didn't have a lot of insurance. He gets Social Security."

"Do you invest the money?" Sexton asked.

He got $450 a month, she thought. They gave him money for allowance and expenses. They put the balance in CDs and a savings account. But she didn't tell Sexton that. She skirted the question. It's none of your business, she thought.

Already, Teresa Boron didn't like this man.

"Joey says you want him to move to Montana with you," she began. "And I don't think that's good."

She pled his case. He had a younger brother who needed him. He needed to get established in a good job. If they wanted to be together, perhaps Pixie could remain behind while they dated.

"After his brother Danny graduates from school, maybe then they could go out and join you," she said.

She thought, at the very least she could buy time, until her nephew's infatuation passed.

She told Sexton, Joey needed to be able to support himself before he could support a wife and a child.

"Well, Pixie did make a mistake," Sexton said of the baby. "But I still love her."

Sexton said he had it all worked out. He talked about the scenario as if it were a done deal. They were buying a place called the Skytop Ranch, he said. It was on 1,200 acres, on a mountaintop just south of Helena, Montana. Later, she'd learn he'd found the place through an advertisement in *The Robb Report,* a magazine for millionaires.

Sexton had a brochure. It read: "More than a home, Skytop Ranch, Montana is a lifestyle . . . Expansive views of Montana's beloved big sky are rivaled only by the mountain peaks, pine forests and wildflowers that are visible from every window of this three-story mansion. Here, the nearest neighbors are deer and elk, coyote and cougar. Here, the distractions are subtle—the rustle of the wind, the laughter of a trout stream, the soft morning whistle of a mountain bluebird."

The brochure showed a sun-drenched family room with a huge circular leather couch and a telescope aimed at the nearest mountain peak. In the formal living room, a black grand piano stood across from a large fireplace, its walls adorned with modern art. There were many rooms, "cozy niches for reading, playing and being," the brochure said. Skytop had sophisticated fire and security systems. It had a helicopter hangar and a red, two-man chopper.

Sexton also said he had a video of the property. He offered to send the tape home with Joey someday. Joey would be working for him, handling security, he said.

As if Joey knows anything about security, she thought. Teresa Boron eyed the weathered deck and Ed Sexton's worn blue jeans. She couldn't help but notice the simple clothes the kids were wearing. She thought, where was this guy going to get the money for a mountaintop mansion? She thought this even before she learned the asking price for Skytop. The owner wanted $1.9 million for the ranch.

Sexton brought the subject up. He said he was making a multi-million-dollar deal with the Wendy's and Burger King franchises to do a nationwide promotion.

"Promotion of what?" she asked.

"The Futuretrons," Sexton said.

She asked him to repeat the word.

"Futuretrons," he said. "You see, my daughter and I are Futuretrons."

Teresa said she didn't understand.

Ed Sexton held out his left hand, showing her his palm. He pointed to what looked like normal lines in the skin. He said his second youngest daughter, Lana, had the same lines.

"If some of these Satanic cults knew she had this mark, they'd hunt her down," he said. "If they knew of her, or her whereabouts, she'd be in grave danger."

Teresa wondered, what kind of danger?

"They'd want to sacrifice her. The mark on her hand makes her so powerful, she could destroy them. The power can wipe 'em out. I mean, wipe 'em out."

The girl Lana looked hardly 10 years old, but Ed Sexton was serious.

"Okay," Teresa said, humoring him.

He talked about markings on his other children. He said his 6-year-old Kimberly had the mark of a Christmas tree on her leg. When his wife was pregnant with Kimberly, he said, the family tree fell down and the baby jumped in her tummy. When the child was born, it bore the mark of the tree.

"Really," Teresa said. But she was thinking, Joey isn't going anywhere with these people. God, it was true. The Sextons were into cults.

Pixie and Joey returned to the deck.

"Pixie, why don't you stay here instead of going to Montana?" Teresa asked.

"My dad says it's best I go," she said quietly.

"Joey will eventually be getting an apartment. You guys can still see each other."

"My dad says it's best if we were out there," Pixie said.

Dad plays a big part in this girl's life, Teresa thought.

She looked back at Sexton. He was staring at her now. His eyes had a penetrating, dark quality. Now he's trying to intimidate me, she thought. She'd dealt with men like that before. She'd had a lot of practice in the steel business.

Teresa stared right back. "Well, it's not going to happen," she said firmly. "Joey is not going to Montana. His main obligation right now is to take care of his brother. It is not to follow you guys out west."

She remained cordial saying goodbye. But couldn't wait to get off that deck.

A few weeks later, Joey came home from work depressed.

"It's off," he said.

Teresa wondered, the trip to Montana?

"Me and Pixie," he said.

She didn't want to see him anymore.

Teresa Boron thought, *Thank God.*

7

Joel found a job at a local nut and bolt manufacturer. Teresa Boron helped him find his own apartment on Sixth Street, a one bedroom with a kitchen, living room, and bath. Her older sister Velva also pitched in for the move. Teresa gave him an old couch. Velva bought him new towels. They both equipped him with dishes and kitchen utensils.

Velva could practically see his apartment from her two bedroom home on Park Avenue.

"You're moving him close to me because you know I'm close enough to watch him," Velva said.

The whole family worried about him, not only Teresa and Velva, but their parents Lewis and Gladys and their brother Sam. They'd all had a hand in raising him. They all wanted to see him find independence, but they were concerned about his trusting nature.

"You would have to know Joey to understand," Velva would later say. "He was a good, gentle person. But he was also very naive."

Velva was as close to Joey as Teresa. She, too, thought of him as a son. Joey and his brother Danny had spent weekends with Velva when his mother was dying. When Linda passed, her will gave Velva custody of her sons. They stayed with her and her husband for two years on their 40-acre farm in Mineral City, 20 minutes south of Canton. Then, when Velva's marriage failed, the boys moved in with their parents. Joey had finished high school at Teresa's while Velva got her life back on track.

Velva did watch Joey. She was working the day shift putting together baby strollers and car seats at Century Products. But she found time to drop by to see him, bringing food or items he might need for the apartment. He didn't have a telephone. So every time she heard an ambulance, she'd find herself going outside to look down the street, making sure it hadn't stopped at his apartment complex.

Velva couldn't help but admire his tenacity. He nursed his Datsun to the bolt factory. On days it wouldn't start, he'd mount his bike, thinking nothing of pedalling five miles to work. The company was using him everywhere in the plant, boxing, sorting, and shipping. Soon he was running a production machine. He'd qualified for health care benefits and was earning vacation time. With his paychecks, he bought his own stereo, then a TV and VCR.

Then, after New Years 1991, Pixie Sexton showed up again in Joel Good's life.

Velva had just come home from work. She found them all sitting on her living room couch. Not only Joey and Pixie, but two children: a 3-year-old hanging onto her knee, the other an infant, cradled in a baby seat. The older girl was Dawn. The second child was called Shasta. Pixie had given birth in November, 1990. That was more than a year after Joel and Pixie had broken up.

They were dating again, Joey said.

"I came right out with it and asked her," Velva later recalled. "Do you know who the daddies are? Are they the same daddies or different daddies?"

"I don't know."

"Joey, do you know what you're doing?" Velva asked.

She looked at Pixie. "I can accept one mistake, but not two."

Pixie Sexton stared straight ahead with her dark, sleepy eyes.

Velva called Teresa and put Joey on the phone. He told Teresa he was seeing Pixie again. He said he'd run into Willy Sexton at Canton Center Mall. The family hadn't moved to Montana, he said.

"Willie said things are all worked out," Joey said. "He said Pixie wants to see me and stuff."

Joey said he'd driven over to the house on Caroline Street and asked Pixie to go for a ride. He wanted her to see his new apartment, but Ed Sexton stopped them.

"He said I couldn't take her to my apartment," Joey said. "He jumped all over me about it."

Teresa wondered why. She wanted to hear it from him, though Velva had already told her.

"Pixie had another baby," he said, shyly.

"Is it yours?" she asked.

"No, it's that guy from the Navy."

The old boyfriend had returned, had a one night stand with Pixie, then disappeared again.

"I thought he was dead," Teresa said.

"I don't know," he said. "That's what they told me."

Make a mistake once, Teresa thought. Every kid was entitled to that. But twice, that's a pattern.

'Joey, you really need to find somebody else that doesn't have kids," she said. "Somebody you can have kids with."

"But I love Pixie," Joey said.

His luck appeared to turn with Pixie Sexton's first appearance. Both aunts noticed he was always short of money. He decided to let the sister of a former classmate move in to share his apartment expenses. He came home from work one day to find his stereo missing. Then his TV and VCR disappeared. He asked the girl to leave, but she refused. One night, he got up from his bed to go to the bathroom and found a man walking naked down his hallway.

"Get back in your bedroom," the stranger said, "or you're a dead man."

A few days later, Joey showed up at Velva's door. "I haven't been able to do things right," he said. "Can I come home, Aunt Velva?"

She hugged him, saying, "Why sure."

They moved him into Velva's upstairs bedroom and began seeing more of Pixie Sexton firsthand. Joey would go to Pixie's house after work and bring her back to Velva's, often without her kids. When they arrived or left, Velva couldn't help but notice the way Pixie always stood behind her nephew, peeking at her over his shoulder, as if she was trying to hide. She remained a girl of few words. The two of them would sit on her couch, Velva trying to pry a conversation from Joey, Pixie in silence, her eyes on the living room TV.

Velva told a friend one night, "God, she acts like I'm going to hurt her or something. The girl is very weird."

The family was weird, Velva thought, though she'd never met the parents. Joey always had to have her back by ten.

"You're how old?" Velva asked her one night.

"Twenty-one," she said.

The girl seemed oblivious to the point she was making.

It just didn't make sense, Velva thought. She'd had two children out of wedlock, but she couldn't even stay out until midnight as a legal adult.

Joey's brother Danny moved in with Velva. She felt good about having the two brothers reunited, but it soon became clear that even his own brother wasn't going to diminish Joey's infatuation with Pixie Sexton. He began spending less time at home, leaving every night after work to go see Stella at the Sexton's house. The hours became later. One night, Velva came home after midnight to find an infant's car seat in her living room.

The next morning she yelled up to his room. "You don't have Pixie up there with you, do you?"

No, he explained, his car had broken down on the freeway the night before. He'd walked home.

"Why do you have that car seat?" she asked.

"I didn't want anybody to steal it."

Velva thought, the girl is taking over his life. She wondered, what if she tries to get pregnant again? Velva's 32-year-old son Jack decided to have a man-to-man talk with Joey, advising him about sex and the precautions he had to take.

A couple of days later, Velva overheard Joey talking to his brother Danny. Joey wanted his brother to go with him to the drugstore. He said he needed condoms, but was too embarrassed to buy them for himself.

Later, she questioned Danny. Yes, he'd bought them for him. He said Joey had plans to take Pixie to a motel that night.

She told Teresa, "I wonder what this Stella wants with Joey. I mean, he's not a boy who's ever shown much interest in sex. And she's had already had two children. I just can't figure what the connection is."

Soon Joey stopped coming home at night, sometimes for a couple days at a time. Teresa and Velva tried to put their heads together. Their only option was to try to give him gentle advice. Yelling at Joey would only alienate him.

Once Velva had given him hell for leaving fast food containers around his bedroom. He'd gone outside and sat on the backyard swing, sulking like a hurt child.

It was on Christmas Eve, 1991, that Velva began to notice how his appearance was changing. He spent the holiday with Velva and her family. Pixie wasn't with him that night. Velva gave him socks and underwear and flannel shirts. He'd always been clean cut, but now his hair was over his ears and he was sporting a scraggly beard.

"Your razor break?" Velva asked him.

"Pixie likes it on me," Joey said.

Then he disappeared for several weeks. After the first few days, Velva and Teresa took turns calling the Sextons. Sometimes the parents answered the telephone, sometimes one of the older children. It was always the same response.

"No, he's not over here."

Had they seen Joey?

"Yeah, he was here with Pixie."

They left messages for him, but he never returned the calls.

The family began checking the places they knew he frequented. The whole family joined the search. They took turns dropping in at Canton Center Mall, walking from store to store, hoping to find him shopping or just hanging out. Teresa visited the house on Caroline, but the Sextons said she'd just missed him. One day, their father Lewis thought he saw him drive by in a car. He followed the car for several miles until it pulled into a driveway, but it turned out to be a look-alike.

Then, in January, 1992, Joey called Danny.

"Pixie's pregnant," Joey told Danny.

He said was going to marry her. He claimed he'd used the condoms, but there must have been some kind of accident.

A few days later, Joey showed up at Velva's with Pixie. He wanted all the phone numbers and addresses of relatives. They were planning a wedding, he said, in February, just a few weeks away. They planned to marry on Valentine's Day, 1992.

Velva went to the basement to get some clothes out of the dryer and collect her thoughts. Joey followed her. Velva began crying, searching for a way to talk some sense into him.

"Aunt Velva, don't you think my mom would want to be a grandma?" he asked.

She grabbed his hand. "Yes, but she'd also want you to be careful."

"Careful of what?"

"You don't know this family." She'd heard the cult rumors from her sister Teresa.

"But I love Pixie."

"I love you, and believe me, I want you to be happy. But I also want you to think things out."

As February approached, Teresa, Velva and the rest of the family certainly did their share of thinking. They did it out loud in telephone conversations and family visits. They began comparing observations, particularly of Pixie's children. Except for a couple of primitive words, everyone agreed, the girl Dawn wasn't talking, at *age 3*. She showed no interest in toys. Mostly, she just huddled next to her mother, staring blankly, a bottle always in her hand.

"There's something wrong with those kids," Sam said the first time he saw them.

"They're too backward," Joey's grandfather said.

Teresa recognized something in Shasta that she'd seen in Dawn, something she'd seen that day on Ed and Estella Sexton's deck.

"There's something wrong with that entire family," she said. "That child has got that same Sexton stare."

ii

Dad's Way

1

After five years on the job, Stark County child protection worker Wayne Welsh had come to recognize the smell. It permeated homes. It emanated from children he interviewed, filling his office in the Stark County Department of Human Services, lingering long after they were gone.

Some thought the odor was the smell of poverty. Welsh disagreed. Many people who didn't have money did not have that odor in their homes. No, the smell was more distinctive, and the cause not necessarily economic. The smell meant parents weren't washing sheets and towels. It meant clothes and underwear had clung too long to little bodies. It meant children were not getting regular baths, or being instructed in basic hygiene.

This had little to do with money.

"It's the stench of neglect," Wayne Welsh said.

Neglect was one of the three criteria that allowed the DHS to act. That was Ohio law. A neglected child was a child abandoned by his parents. Or, he lacked proper parental care, such as going without proper food, education, moral guidance, or health care.

A second criteria was abuse. An abused child was a victim of what the Ohio code called "sexual activity" and/or physical attack. The law did draw certain exceptions, allowing parents to use corporal punishment, unless it threatened the child's "health or welfare."

The third was dependency. A dependant child was homeless or destitute, and not necessarily through the fault of his parents, guardian, or custodian. Dependency also applied if a child was in danger of being abused or neglected by the parents themselves. Because the latter condition dealt with something that had yet to happen, that kind of dependency could be the most difficult to prove.

Wayne Welsh left those judgements to the legal department, where lawyers argued the definitions of the statute's terms and decided if they had enough evidence to file a state custody case. Usually, the best evidence was the child's word. If a child disclosed a situation covered under the statute, they could remove the child from the home, then prevail in a shelter care hearing in the Stark County Probate Court. In any month, Welsh had 15 to 20 child protection investigations underway. His caseload ranged from 150 to 200 a year.

When he was assigned on the morning of February 11, 1992 to investigate a counselor's referral at Jackson High School, Wayne Welsh began thinking about disclosure. The agency had been accumulating a file on the Sexton family of Caroline Street since 1979. But across 11 years and a dozen referrals, reports, and investigations about strange behavior in the Sexton family, not a single Sexton child had disclosed.

Now, Welsh had been told, Machelle Sexton was waiting for him at Jackson High School. Machelle's guidance counselor, Ruth Killion, reported Machelle, a senior there, was "willing to talk about problems at home." Welsh knew that when it came to the Sexton children, that could mean anything. It certainly didn't guarantee that she would disclose.

The Sexton case file had been an exercise in frustration for Welsh. He'd first become involved because of another high school referral three years ago. It began a series of probes involving Sexton teenage girls and boys. On February 1, 1989, a student reported to a school official that Machelle's older sister Sherri had told her that her father had beaten her with a belt. Sherri reportedly had marks all over her legs. The next day, Sherri did not show up at school.

Sherri Sexton's counselor was particularly acquainted with the family's dynamics. It was a job Welsh knew well. Before joining human services, he'd counseled 7th through 12th graders in schools in east Canton. Welsh knew confidentiality reigned in the field. It fostered rapport and trust. He also knew that if a situation blew up, if a case generated sensational headlines, a counselor could not step forward and publicly discuss details of a case. That was left to administrators, who typically shared little more than general policy. He worked under similar restrictions in DHS, unless a situation became public in open court.

In Welsh's 1989 investigation, the Jackson High School counselor did not believe Sherri Sexton was in imminent danger. Sexton children were frequently absent, "and the parents always provide excuses," the counselor said. The counselor predicted the other Sexton children would not talk about discipline in their home. They were under orders to share any problems they had with their oldest sister, Stella, also known as Pixie. In fact, they were forbidden from discussing any aspect of home life with anyone, the counselor said.

However, agency records showed a few small cracks in this wall of silence had opened from time to time. In October of 1988, a counselor reported concerns about different stories Pixie Sexton was giving relating to her pregnancy, but the agency couldn't investigate because she was a legal adult. A month later, a teacher reported that 7-year-old Lana Sexton said her father teased her, tickled her and touched her "titties." A DHS worker investigating determined there were "no indications of abusive behavior," adding "teasing and tickling" do not constitute abuse. Six weeks later, the same teacher reported that every time Lana played with a Barbie doll, she pulled off its top, pointed to the chest and said, "Look at those titties." When a counselor tried to interview Lana, however, she refused to talk.

A similar pattern extended back to 1979. In three other referrals, an anonymous relative, a hospital professional, and township police had contacted Human Services. The referees concerned dirty children, cruel punishments, and family fights. Workers talked to Sexton children privately, but they maintained everything was fine. Surprise visits to the home in 1979 and 1983 revealed not filth and squalor, but a clean and well-organized household. One worker noted that Ed and Estella Sexton appeared to be concerned parents struggling to raise a large family. In a 1983 investigation, one worker even noted that she had complimented Ed Sexton on his parental skills.

In the 1989 referral concerning Sherri Sexton's beating, Wayne Welsh started with Pixie. He pulled the oldest daughter out of class. She maintained there were no problems at home with her sister Sherri, or any other sibling. Welsh told her he understood she'd had a baby. He asked where the father was.

"He's in Mexico," she said.

Welsh interviewed Sherri Sexton in 1989. She was a full-figured 16-year-old with dark features and penetrating eyes. He went gently, trying to find common ground by talking about his cats and dogs, what kind of pets she might have. He tried talking about schoolwork.

"I couldn't make any kind of connection," he would later recall.

Eventually, he asked to see the back of her legs. She lifted her skirt. Her thighs had several horizontal red marks.

"Sherri," he asked gently, "who beat you?"

"No one," she said.

He tried the question several ways.

"I told her my job was to protect kids, to make sure kids were safe," he later said. "If there was something scary happening at home, we can protect her. But she refused to disclose a thing."

That same day, he received new information from the counselor. Another Sexton child, Willie, a junior, was reportedly a fire starter. Twice he'd set the family home on fire. Welsh interviewed several teachers, staffers, and other students, but came up with nothing the legal department could use in court.

He met with Sherri Sexton again a couple of days later. He wondered if there had been any repercussions at home from his interviews.

Not one, she said.

Two years later, during May of 1991, it was Machelle Sexton who brought Wayne Welsh back to Jackson. She looked different than the other Sexton teens Welsh had interviewed before. Unlike her siblings' stark, dark coloring, she had blond hair and eyes that sparkled blue.

Machelle had been quite talkative with Ruth Killion. The counselor appeared to have a very good rapport with the girl. Before Welsh arrived, Machelle told Killion that her parents had shunned her. She said she got home from school, cleaned, cooked, and got her younger siblings ready for bed, then had to be asleep by 9 p.m. Her brothers and sisters were told not to talk to her, her father accusing her of trying to "poison their minds." She told the counselor she wasn't allowed to leave the house, or even use the phone. She was threatening to kill herself.

Killion reported to Welsh what he suspected two years earlier. After the report from Sherri in 1989, Machelle said, the father had instructed the kids to travel in groups.

Every morning, Ed Sexton gave them all a quarter. They were to find a pay phone and report to him if a sibling talked to classmates or school staffers. If a sibling spotted a contact and didn't call, he or she would be punished as well. Despite this, the counselor predicted Machelle might talk to Welsh.

His interview with Machelle was more frustrating than the one two years earlier with her old sister Sherri. She confirmed what she'd already told her counselor, but wouldn't disclose what the family had to hide.

Welsh asked her if he thought the family's home life was appropriate.

"There's only one way to do anything," she said. "There's only one way to think."

"And what way is that, Machelle?" he asked.

"Dad's way," she said.

The father appeared to be the common denominator in all her fears and concerns. Machelle said her father had told all the children that if they talked to officials they would be taken away and he would be thrown in jail. They would be helpless without his care.

Welsh explained that the goal of the agency was to keep families together, but that some parents did need help, such as counseling.

"He would not go to jail unless he did something pretty bad," Welsh said.

"I just can't," she said.

After that 1991 interview, Welsh decided he was seeing a pattern, but not one common in dysfunctional families he'd investigated in the past. He recognized it from a professional seminar he'd attended months earlier in Akron—a symposium on cults.

A DHS report later summarized this evaluation of the Sexton situation: "Worker (Welsh) describes the family dynamics as a cult with Dad as the undisputed leader . . . Worker noted that he had very strong suspicions of dark secrets being held within this family."

Welsh later explained, "Whenever you've got somebody who's controlling everybody else by that much fear, and encouraging other members of this group to turn on each other, it shows that the leader is very frightened about something getting out. The leader is guarding something that is terrible."

Exactly what, as he drove to the school on this cold afternoon in February, 1992, he could only guess.

2

She was sitting in a counselor's office, wearing a black and white sweater, jeans, and a pair of white tennis shoes.

"I'm pregnant," Machelle Sexton said. "And they're trying to kill the baby."

Wayne Welsh wanted to know more.

It was her boyfriend's baby, she said. The day before, her younger brother James, nearly 16, saw her kissing her boyfriend and told her dad. Her father backhanded her under the right eye, she claimed. She showed him a scratch left by his ring.

"Then he tried to kick me in the stomach," she said. "James did."

Her sister Sherri forced herself between them, she reported, screaming, "Get out, you child killer."

Welsh wondered why Sherri would call James that.

"Sherri was pregnant a year ago, too," Machelle said. "Dad didn't want her to deliver the baby." Machelle said James kicked Sherri in the stomach. She miscarried the next day.

It didn't take much effort to count. If Sherri was indeed pregnant, that meant at least four babies conceived by Sexton daughters out of wedlock in the past four years, in a house where dating was rarely allowed.

When she finished, Welsh found himself in a familiar situation. Machelle Sexton was a long way from meeting the statutory guidelines of neglect, dependency, or abuse. More importantly, Machelle was well into her 18th year. She was now a legal adult, beyond the jurisdiction of child protection by the DHS.

"But I can't go home now," she said.

Legally, he couldn't help her. But that didn't mean he couldn't do her a favor, from one adult to another. Maybe if Machelle Sexton did leave home, he thought, she would begin talking about the other minor children, something that fell within the definition of the child protection laws.

Welsh offered to drive Machelle Sexton to the Canton YWCA. They had a program for young women in crisis, he explained. She could stay there until the organization located a family willing to give her shelter.

That afternoon, school officials contacted the house on Caroline Street to inform Machelle's parents. She'd left with a worker for the Department of Human Services, Ed Sexton was told.

She would not be coming home from school.

3

That afternoon, Machelle Sexton and Wayne Welsh showed up at the Jackson Township Police Department, Welsh suggesting on the ride over to the YWCA that she make a police report of her father's assault.

"But I don't want to get anyone in trouble," she said.

Welsh told her she didn't have to press charges, but it was in her best interest to document the assault.

Sgt. Barry Lyons, a road patrol supervisor and 10-year veteran, met them in the small lobby. He escorted the teenager to the department conference room where he could question her about the basic details he needed to make a report.

It was not the first time a Jackson officer would write the Sexton name and address on department paperwork.

Department contacts with the family dated back to when a handful of township cops worked out of a Stark County Sheriff's substation in the mid-1970s. Now the department was housed in a modern one-story office building on Fulton Road. Nearly 30 police and a dozen auxiliary officers covered Jackson's 36 square miles. The department had grown with the population.

In the 1980s, residential and commercial development earned Jackson the title of the second fastest growing suburb in America. It stood at 28,000 residents now, with another 125,000 visitors and employees populating the crowded Belden Village mall and commercial district each day. Belden generated reams of paperwork from retail-related petty crime. Some of the reports on the Sexton family appeared equally inconsequential. But among the older Jackson cops, there were few veterans who didn't have a story about the family who lived in the house on Caroline Street.

Nearly 30 incidents and reports were in department files, many of them generated in the 1980s as the older Sexton boys hit their teenage years. The two oldest, Patrick and Eddie, Jr., had been investigated for alleged neighborhood theft and threatening or striking siblings or classmates. Ed Sexton had filed runaway reports on Patrick, Eddie Jr., and the third oldest, William, all of them returning home shortly after they left.

The Sexton family often appeared to be on the receiving end of trouble. In 1982 and 1987 there had been major fires at the house on Caroline, the latter causing $32,000 in damages. Ed Sexton reported numerous burglaries and vandalism of his house. Somebody stole a Coleman dome tent from the front yard in 1990. Somebody dumped a chemical into his pond in 1991.

In July of 1991, Sexton filed a report that his house had been broken into while he was on vacation. He detailed more than $20,000 in stolen items. He presented a three-page itemized list to police and his insurance company, serial numbers, cost and place of purchase noted. Among the listed items were VCRs, stereos, dozens of video tapes, and a $2,700 entertainment center. He also listed four large brass eagles valued up to $300 and a "Certificate of Recognition" from the U.S. Congress for Vietnam service. He placed no value on that item, noting "can't replace."

Ed Sexton seemed well-versed in the law. Police suspected Sexton's theft reports, and his fires, were fabrications for insurance money. But they lacked evidence to bring a fraud case. Recalled one veteran, "The man was a pro. He had an answer for every question, an explanation for every inconsistency. And he knew every aspect of the legal system as well."

There were other police calls. In early 1991, Sexton reported a nephew staying with the family was kidnapped from his home by the nephew's brothers at gunpoint. A brief investigation revealed the 45-year-old nephew was retarded. Ed Sexton had applied to become his guardian and receive the nephew's Social Security benefit. The nephew reported he had no desire to be at the house on Caroline. He claimed his uncle beat him. His brothers had rescued him from the house, he said.

The incident that most Jackson cops talked about was one Sgt. Barry Lyons worked on himself. He was in the detective bureau then. He lived in the Sextons' general neighborhood.

The case involved a retired neighbor named Walter Dundee, his wife, and their retarded daughter, Kathleen. Early on, the family seemed to get along well with the Sextons. Until she died of cancer, Dundee's wife often dropped in on Estella Mae Sexton to visit and sip coffee. Then, what appeared at first to be a disagreement erupted into a feud. Sgt. Lyons and another Jackson detective, a 25-year veteran named Larry Aventino, soon were making regular visits to Caroline Street. At its peak, Aventino was seeing Walter Dundee nearly every day.

A bit of neighborly advice from Ed Sexton preceded the

conflict, Aventino recalled Dundee saying. It all started when Sexton told Dundee that his retarded daughter was eligible for Social Security disability. Sexton suggested Dundee contact his lawyer, and his advice proved to be absolutely sound. Not only did Kathleen Dundee begin receiving regular SSI checks, the government gave her a handsome retroactive settlement for all the years she didn't collect.

Then, as Dundee's own health began to fail, Sexton had another suggestion. He told Dundee, why not let him be his legal guardian. He could get him the best benefits and find top rate doctors to treat his stomach cancer. Sexton offered to handle all his financial affairs.

"That became the whole crux of the thing from day one," Aventino later recalled. "He set himself up to take care of the Dundee family, and when Walter Dundee refused, he began to terrorize them."

Some of the incidents were documented in police files from 1990. But Aventino and Lyons recalled that a good many more were not, as Dundee became fearful and reluctant to make official complaints. Sexton boys climbed the back fence and beat on Dundee's doors, the police said. Dundee suspected them of breaking windows and vandalizing a prized tomato garden he'd nurtured for years. He suspected them of stealing tools out of his garage, then trying to light it on fire. Sexton also struck back with police. Once he filed a complaint, claiming Dundee had hit his son Charles with a car.

"He became terrified to even leave his house," Aventino would later recall. "They'd break a window, then next time break two windows because he'd called the police. They'd pull out one tomato plant. He'd call the police. The next time they'd take the whole garden out. And it was clear old man Sexton was orchestrating it. Sexton would knock on the window, making sure Dundee saw him running the show."

When Aventino inspected some of the early damage, he

also saw Sexton peering out of his back windows. He was holding a black Bible to his chest. When he came out, he showed Aventino a minister's card.

Aventino explained his business there.

"I don't want trouble," Sexton said. "I'm a man of God."

"I'd like to talk to your kids," Aventino said.

"Not without an attorney present," Sexton responded.

"Then maybe you ought to get one."

"Oh, no," Sexton said. "But I will say a prayer for the man."

Later, Aventino entered the Sexton house after one of the family's burglary reports. Everything was filthy. The carpeting looked as if it had never been cleaned. Upstairs, the cop saw dirty sheets with what appeared to be unwashed menstrual bloodstains. He saw crusty towels that looked as if they'd hung on bathroom racks for months.

Aventino later recalled that he made phone calls to the county health department and child protection services.

"They complained they were short on money and manpower," he said. "And nothing got done."

Sexton, according to Dundee's frequent conversations with Aventino, continued to use the carrot and the stick, even as it became clear the cancer would take his life. "It was simple," Aventino recalled. "If he let Sexton become his guardian, all of his neighbor problems would stop."

Lyons also remembered the first time he was in the house. He found Ed Sexton sitting at the kitchen table, slumped in a wheelchair, but talking about taking a trip to Florida. He showed Lyons a line on his hand. He and one of his children were the only two people on earth with the mark, he said. This oddity had earned him a multi-million-dollar promotional deal with Burger King, Sexton continued. He was going to Florida to visit the franchise's national headquarters in Miami, he said.

"I figured, this guy is wacked," Lyons would later recall. In the spring of 1990, Lyons had police business in the neighborhood again. One day at a local coffee shop, Aventino heard from neighborhood paperboys that Sexton's oldest son Patrick, then 22, was making moves on the retarded Kathleen Dundee. Soon came another complaint from her father. Walter Dundee said the day after he deposited $13,000 in his daughter's account, Patrick Sexton went with his daughter to the bank. She withdrew $2,000. Now the money was missing.

Lyons investigated, first talking to Kathleen. She was a portly, short woman with cat-eye glasses. She had the intelligence of a third grader and the gullibility and innocence that went with that age. Kathleen said she'd given the money to Patrick Sexton because he did favors for her, such as taking her to her doctor visits. Patrick promised to take her to Florida, she said.

Lyons called the bank, furious with the bank manager at first. The manager said Kathleen Dundee was authorized to withdraw money. His hands were tied, no matter what kind of suspicious people she might be with.

Lyons didn't find Patrick Sexton at home. He'd gone to Florida to stay with an uncle. Lyons called him there. Patrick said he felt sorry for Kathleen. She would buy him gifts sometimes because he was nice to her. But he hadn't taken the $2,000, he claimed. He did admit he'd asked her to go to Florida for a visit.

"You ever come back to Ohio I'm going to hunt you down," Lyons told him. "I will have a warrant here and I will arrest you on the spot."

The Stark County prosecutor's office disagreed. Because of Kathleen Dundee's mental state—she couldn't say exactly how much money she gave Patrick Sexton—and her authority to withdraw money at the bank, the assistant prosecutor said it would be impossible to try the case. The warrant was denied.

Now, two years later, Sgt. Barry Lyons had another Sexton to interview, but this was the first time he'd had any dealings with a Sexton girl.

Machelle Sexton told him how she'd been struck by her father. She told Lyons the same circumstance she'd revealed to Wayne Welsh. She listed her counselor, Ruth Killion, as a potential witness.

Lyons filled out four pages, a standard form.

"So, do you want to press charges?" the sergeant asked.

"No, I don't want to do that," Machelle Sexton said.

4

The next morning, Wayne Welsh picked up Machelle Sexton at the YWCA in downtown Canton. Accompanied by Sgt. Barry Lyons, all three went to the house on Caroline Street. Machelle needed to pick up her clothes.

Lyons went inside first to talk to Ed Sexton, then motioned Welsh and Machelle to come inside. Ed Sexton was waiting in the living room. It was Welsh's first face-to-face encounter with the man.

Welsh glanced around the living room. The home appeared relatively clean and orderly, certainly nothing like the hellholes Welsh had seen through the years. More than two dozen portraits of Sexton children lined the shelves in the living room.

Sexton looked well-groomed, the goatee around his chin smartly trimmed. He said that there must be some kind of misunderstanding. He appeared to be an exceptionally gentle man, his voice soft, his southern drawl refined, not harsh and twangy like many of the southerners who'd migrated from West Virginia, Kentucky, and Tennessee over the years.

Ed Sexton turned to Machelle, saying in a calm voice, "Now, Machelle, now tell the truth. Did I hit you?"

"You don't have to answer that, Machelle," Welsh said.

And she didn't have to tell him where she was going or where she was staying, either, he'd tell her later.

Wayne Welsh had already detected that smell.

5

As Valentine's Day approached, the announced date of Joey and Pixie's wedding, only Danny, Joel Good's younger brother, displayed any excitement. Joel had promised Danny he would be his best man. Every day, Danny waited for his brother to call with the details: the exact place and time, where the reception would be held. The rest of the family waited for the invitations they were promised, but nothing came in the mail.

Velva, or Teresa, or their parents hardly saw Joel in late January and early February, but they assumed the wedding was still scheduled. Velva's daughter Jeannie had gone with Joey to Canton Center Mall to help him pick out a wedding ring. They picked out a simple, inexpensive gold band.

During one rare visit, Joey said he and Pixie were looking at an apartment in the same building he used to live in, near Velva's.

"You sure you want to do this?" Velva said.

"I love her," Joey said.

Velva and Teresa learned that they weren't the only ones advising Joey against the marriage. He said his fellow workers were trying to talk him out of it, too. They pointed out to him the last thing he needed at his age was an instant family. Then Joey was laid off and certainly was in no position to marry, Velva and Teresa reasoned.

Valentine's Day came and went with no word. Danny sat around all day, still waiting for a call.

Joey showed up alone at Teresa's a few days later. They sat at the kitchen table. She could tell something was on his mind.

He announced they were married.

"When?" Teresa asked.

A couple of days before Valentine's Day, he said. The ceremony was held at the house of Ed Sexton's sister,

Nellie. Ed Sexton, with his ordained minister card, had officiated the ceremony himself.

"Why didn't you tell anybody?" Teresa asked. "Why didn't you wait until Valentine's Day?"

"That's the way they wanted it," Joey said. "They just said it was best if we did it that way."

"Who's they?"

"Mr. Sexton."

"Why, Joey?" she asked.

"What would you have thought of me if I didn't? She was pregnant."

"That doesn't make a difference," Teresa said. "I mean, she's already had two without a husband."

"Those kids call me dad," he said.

He said he'd moved in with Pixie and the Sexton family.

It wasn't the only bad news.

Joey said a few days after the ceremony Pixie had miscarried. Teresa had her doubts about the pregnancy, but they didn't concern Pixie's ability to carry full term.

She asked Joey if Pixie had seen a doctor.

"No," he said.

Had she gone to the hospital?

He shook his head.

"There's things women have to take care of after a miscarriage," Teresa said. "Joey, she wasn't pregnant, believe me."

He looked at her innocently.

My God, Teresa decided, maybe this Pixie was more clever than she thought.

A few weeks later, Teresa Boron received a call from her ex-sister-in-law. She worked in birth records at the Massilon Health Department. Joey had come into the office with Pixie and filed a certificate of paternity, she told Teresa. He was claiming to be the father of Dawn.

That was impossible, Teresa thought. Dawn was born five months before he even dated Pixie.

Her sister-in-law explained the office procedure. The

paternity papers would go the capital, then the original birth certificate—with no known father—would be destroyed. It would be replaced with one listing Joel M. Good as the father. There would be no record the original had even been amended.

"I tried to talk him out of it," the former relative told Teresa. "I told him, do you realize what you're doing?"

But Joey insisted, with Pixie standing there at his side. He planned on amending the younger daughter Shasta's certificate in another jurisdiction as well.

It wasn't until years later that someone would put all the dates together. Ed Sexton may have had good reason to marry off his daughter before Valentine's Day. And Pixie Sexton may have had very good reason to find a father for her children, at least for the official paperwork.

The Sextons had been busy the morning of February 12, 1992. The wedding had taken place only hours after the Jackson Police and the Department of Human Services had accompanied Machelle Sexton to get her clothes.

iii

The Girl at the Dike

1

Anne Greene first heard about the girl named Machelle during her oldest daughter's wedding reception on Valentine's Day, at a restaurant called Created For You.

The executive director of the Pregnancy Support Center of Stark County walked over and said, "We just placed a girl in shepherding today, but decided not to call you." The director grinned. "We figured that even *you* would be too busy today."

Anne Greene headed the non-profit organization's shepherding program and had been on the center's board for three years. The center gave women free pregnancy tests and counseling. The shepherding program placed troubled clients in stable homes. Anne Greene found nurturing families for young women kicked out by parents or boyfriends. Some were hardly more than girls.

The center was Christian and pro-life, and Anne made no apologies. Four full-time staffers and 100 volunteers didn't fire-bomb abortion clinics or shoot abortionists.

They were too busy counseling clients, finding host families, and sharing the Gospel way of life. Nor was Anne a dowdy, humorless Bible thumper with a beehive. With her wavy Irish red hair cascading to her shoulders and sparkling green eyes, the 41-year-old mother of four looked hardly thirty. Her humor was blunt, often sarcastic. Her laugh was loud and infectious. She'd found faith through her father, a retired Baptist minister. Support for her volunteer work came from her husband, a sales manager for a Canton container manufacturer.

"A ministry of evangelism, love, non-judgemental attitude, acceptance, desire to nurture and help," she would say of her mission. "A desire to show the face of Christ to those who have never seen him, and the cleansing and the peace of God. And yeah, Jesus hung out with the riffraff. That's absolutely scriptural, too."

A week later, Anne met Machelle Sexton for the first time at a greenhouse in Hartville. The center had found Machelle work there after she told counselors she liked working with plants. Machelle also had been placed in a shepherding home in Stark County. But she was running into trouble with the shepherding program's house rules. She'd violated a couple of curfews and not kept the host family informed of her whereabouts.

Anne decided to talk to her in the backseat of the director's Cadillac as they gave her a ride back to her shepherding home.

"She was very small at the time, underweight," Greene would later say. "But when I think of Shelly, I think of her eyes. She had really catching blue eyes, but eyes that also were afraid. She wouldn't look at you when she talked. Yet, there still seemed to be an eagerness to be wanted. She was kind of walking a grey line of 'I don't trust you, but I want you.'"

Anne was the program's dorm mother. It wasn't the first time she'd been called in to explain the rules. She leaned close to Machelle and arranged the hair behind her neck.

"You know the rules are for a reason," she said, rubbing her shoulder. "People who care about you need to know where you are. It's all about accountability. Not punishment. It's something we all need in our life."

Machelle turned, nodding.

Those eyes, Anne thought. There's something more here than a young single girl expecting a child.

Eleven days later, Anne received surprising news. The clinic's pregnancy test showed that Machelle Sexton was not pregnant. She had no explanation as to why she thought she was expecting. When a counselor asked her who the father was, she fell into a dark silence.

Machelle's shepherding family also was reporting strange behavior. She slept in a cozy, carpeted bedroom in the host family's basement, but there she was besieged with nightmares. A couple of nights they found her sleeping under the bed. Another night they found her huddled in a dark closet, her eyes filled with fear.

Technically, Anne knew Machelle Sexton was no longer eligible for the shepherding program. But obviously the girl was in crisis. The directors decided to provide services until Machelle could get her problems sorted out.

Anne decided to do a little digging. She'd never been reluctant to evoke her official-sounding title to get police, prosecutors, and social workers on the phone. She called up Ruth Killion, Machelle's guidance counselor at Jackson High School.

"What can you tell me about this girl?" she asked.

Killion gave a long narrative about all the Sexton teenagers. Two other girls had tried to hide their pregnancies in school, she said. She told Anne about the hitting incident that had prompted Machelle to come to her in the first place. The father ruled the family like the gestapo, Killion said.

"The parents pick them up and drop them off every day."

"They don't take a bus?" Anne asked.

"The parents drop them off every morning. They pick them up every afternoon at the front door of the school."

Killion told her about the quarters they were given to turn each other in.

"What happens if they don't call?" Anne asked.

"They say they get whupped," Killion said.

Not whipped. *Whupped.* Anne wrote it down. It was the first of hundreds of notes she would make on Machelle Sexton. She made entries in her journal or grabbed anything handy, sometimes writing on napkins, paper towels, or brown shopping bags.

On February 29, Anne was called to Machelle's shepherding home again. Machelle was still breaking curfews. The family was getting frustrated. Now a new problem had come up. A neighbor was complaining that her daughter disappeared with Machelle for several hours one night.

"I think I need to spend some time alone with her," Anne told the family.

Anne found Machelle sitting on the edge of the bed. Her blond hair was unkempt, her shoulders hunched. *And those eyes.* They looked as if they held a thousand secrets.

Anne sat next to her, putting her arms around her, drawing her cheek to her breast. She decided, now was not the time to talk about the rules.

"Machelle, you need to tell me what has happened to you," Anne said.

She felt her body tremble.

"We know you're not pregnant," she continued. "But Machelle, why do you think you are?"

Machelle began to cry softly.

Anne thought, this girl doesn't even know me. I'm just a stranger. I'll never get through.

When the girl finally spoke, her body was shaking, her voice hardly audible.

"My dad raped me," she said.

2

They talked over the next 10 days. Anne gave Machelle her home phone number. She'd never done that with a client before. The rape should be reported to authorities, Anne finally said, suggesting it would help Machelle put the trauma behind her.

"No, I try," Machelle said. "But I can't forget."

One day, she also asked Anne, "I don't understand why I bled."

That's what happened with virgins, Anne said.

"It was all my fault," Machelle said. "If I'd just been stronger."

Machelle began dropping hints of other abusive behavior in the household. Her father beat the children. He beat her mother. There were other secrets. Her younger sisters were in danger.

Anne suggested again she talk to police, for the protection of her brothers and sisters.

"No," Machelle said. "There are secrets that should never be told to *anyone.*"

Her father had spies and sources everywhere, Machelle said. He had friends in the police department. In fact, Ed Sexton was a booster member of the state lodge for the Fraternal Order of Police. The Sextons had FOP cards for their wallets and bumper stickers for the cars.

If she told, her father would find out, track her down and kill her, Machelle said. He'd been promising that for years. He'd lift an index finger like a cocked gun and say, "A good snitch is a dead snitch."

Machelle said, "I'm afraid."

Anne made the first overture to the police herself. Her new son-in-law was a Stark County sheriff's deputy. He had contacts in the Jackson Township Police Department. A phone call led to the desk of Jackson detective sergeant named Glenn Goe.

"This girl is opening up to me," she told the detective. "She says this is the first time she's told anyone. She was raped by her father. And beaten. But I think there's even more going on in that house."

"Can you get her to come in?" Goe asked.

It took another 10 days of talking, 10 days filled with other problems. Machelle's shepherding family was getting phone calls—someone calling, not saying anything, just breathing. The host family, already frustrated with Machelle's curfew problems, wanted Machelle Sexton removed.

Anne checked the teenager into a Canton safe house for battered women, its location secret, its security insured by a host of resident rules.

Machelle finally agreed to talk to the police, but only if she did not have to go the police station.

"Dad always said if I went there they would lock me up there and take his side," she said.

3

Detective Glenn Goe suggested the compromise. They could meet at the D.A.R.E. office in Shortridge Villa. The office was small and unofficial looking, used by police for a drug prevention program for teens.

"That might work," Anne Greene said.

Considering Machelle Sexton's apprehension, Goe in some ways was the perfect choice for the interview. At 31, he had boyish good looks, a fondness for sweaters and a frequent, easy-going smile. He'd been with the department for 11 years, making sergeant after only four years on the road. Goe already was somewhat familiar with the Sextons. He'd made a run to the house on Caroline years ago to secure property after a suspicious fire.

Goe had been a detective for a year, handling typical suburban crimes. Now and then a criminal assault would come through. But mostly, Jackson detectives dealt with property crimes: B&Es, petty theft, vandalism. Goe had only handled a handful of sexual assaults.

"We'd actually be a very quiet community if it were not for an interstate going through the township, an industrial park, and a good-sized mall," Goe would later say. "As a detective here, the upside is you get to handle everything. The drawback is you're not sharp on any one thing because you're not specializing like big city departments do."

On March 19, a couple hours after sunset, Goe met Anne Greene and Machelle Sexton at the D.A.R.E. office. Machelle Sexton sat down at a small desk, Anne Greene at her side. Goe had a pen and legal pad. He wanted to hear what the teenager had to say before he committed anything to tape.

They began slowly. But within minutes, even Anne Greene appeared lost. Machelle Sexton was generating so many names and nicknames within the Sexton family, it was impossible to keep track of all the principals in the teenager's story.

Goe asked Machelle to break the family down, name by name. Ages would be helpful, too, he said.

Her father Ed Sexton was 49, Machelle said. Some people called him Eddie, others Eddie Lee. The children all called him Dad. Her mother was named Estella May, or Estella Sr. She was 44. They called her Mom. Most people called her May.

They moved on to the siblings. She was one of twelve children: Patrick, 24; Eddie Jr., 23; Stella, 22; William, 21; Sherri, 19; Charles, 16; James, 15; Matthew, 14; Christopher, 13; Lana, 12; and Kimberly, 7. Machelle said she was in the middle, the sixth oldest, 18 months older than Charles and 14 months younger than Sherri.

There were more family members. Stella had two daughters, Dawn and Shasta. Stella had just gotten married. Her husband Joel Good was living in the house. Sherri also had a baby, an 8-month-old son named Christopher.

Goe counted 17 people. "All these people live in the house?" he asked.

No, she said, just 15.

Machelle explained the layout. Her parents had a master bedroom on the first floor, off limits to all but one of the kids. Young Kimberly slept with her parents. There were three more bedrooms upstairs. Machelle used to share the largest bedroom with Pixie, Sherri, and Lana, but Pixie moved to a smaller room with her two babies, and eventually Joel. When Sherri had her baby, she relocated to the den, sleeping on the couch. Charles, James, Matthew and Christopher slept in another bedroom down the hall.

The two oldest brothers left home at 18, she said. Patrick and Eddie Jr. were married. Patrick was a half brother, really, born before her parents married. Both brothers lived in Canton now. "Eddie Bug," she said, still came around a lot.

They all had nicknames. Eddie Jr. was Eddie Bug. Patrick was Bozo. Stella was Pixie. William was Willie Bug. Sherri was Bunny. Charles was Skipper. James was Bird. Christopher was Sugar Tooth. Lana was Angel. And Kimberly was Ground Hog, or just Hog. Her father had come up with them. He'd named Pixie's daughter Dawn "Cockroach," or just "Roach," because she was short. Machelle Sexton said she was Candy, until she began to rebel in her teens. Now her father called her "Diarrhea Mouth." She figured it was because she talked too much and asked too many questions.

An idiot clown. A fairy. Animals and insects and God's messenger sent from on high. Goe looked at Anne Greene, then back at Machelle.

"Your sister's children," Goe said. "Where are their fathers?"

"Everyone knows they're my dad's kids," she said.

"How do you know that?" Goe asked.

"We just do."

She said it like somebody relaying a mundane fact of life, as if she were naming the make of a car someone drove.

The interview continued. She rarely responded in more than one or two sentences at a time.

Goe asked her about her father's assault.

It was in December, she said. Her father told her he wanted to take her for a ride to discuss her future. She was a B and C student. Maybe she could go to college, he said.

"It was a big deal," Machelle said.

College is a pretty big deal, Goe agreed.

No, the ride was a big deal, Machelle said. Other than attending school, she was not allowed out of the house on Caroline Street. For as long as she could remember, a ride with her dad to the gas station or local convenience store was a big deal. It was a big deal to get out of the house. It was a big deal to ride in the family's 6-year-old brown and yellow Chevy van. It was a really big deal if Dad would buy her a candy bar.

Dad drove the family van to the Wales Square, a quarter mile from her house. He didn't park in front of the market there, she said. He drove to an isolated lot behind the store. It was evening, a dark winter night.

"I told him, I thought we were going to talk about my future," she said.

"And what did he say?" Goe asked.

"He told me to shut up."

Machelle said then her father slapped her, then forced her into the back of the van. She was wearing a jean skirt and a blouse. He ripped off her panties. He pinned her arms so hard, she said, his handprints showed up as bruises the following day.

She was reluctant to talk about the details. It took Goe several tries.

"Did he penetrate you?" he asked.

"Yes," she said.

"Did he threaten you?"

She reported her father saying: "Say *anything* to *anybody* and I'll kill you. It would be very easy. Girls disappear every day."

"Did you believe you were in danger?" Goe asked.

"He knows people who would do it for him," she said. And, she added, her older brother Eddie Jr. hung out with some tough people as well.

Goe wanted to know more about the family. With a family that size, he asked, just where did the household income come from?

"He's on some kind of disability," Machelle said.

He supposedly had a back injury, she explained, but she'd always been suspicious of it. Dad had a part-time house painting business with her uncle, Otis Sexton. They painted in the summer. She believed her father also received help from charities for multiple sclerosis and muscular dystrophy.

"He gets in his wheelchair whenever those people come to the house," she said. "Then after they leave he gets up and he's fine."

When the interview was over, Anne Greene said she'd also placed a couple of calls to the Department of Human Services.

"I've got a call in to Wayne Welsh," she said.

4

Anne kept asking her husband Gerry, "Did Glenn Goe call?" It became a daily question, as was her husband's answer: "No."

Two weeks passed. Welsh apparently hadn't returned her calls. It seemed as if nothing was getting accomplished. She thought, Lord, what more do they need? Why don't they march right over there and arrest Ed Sexton? Children were in danger.

Anne not only continued visiting Machelle, she began bringing her home for visits. Machelle appeared as excited as the kids at the holiday dinner in Dickens' *A Christmas Carol.* She touched dishware and accessories in the kitchen. She tried out furniture. She gazed at portraits of the Greene family on the mantel, then met the children and Gerry.

She appeared more awestruck by the way they all joked and hugged and talked than the material possessions.

"I realized this was the first time this girl had seen a normal family with genuine love," Anne later would recall.

She was tempted to have Machelle move in with them. But when she began discussing it with other family members, her son-in-law, the sheriff's deputy, told her it wasn't prudent to get so close. Anne spoke to a longtime Jackson officer, a name her son-in-law gave her.

"Look, you don't want to get involved with the Sextons," the cop said. "That family has been nothing but trouble out here for years."

Anne thought, is that what Christ would do? Not get involved? In this Christian family, that's not what we do. She wanted to invite Machelle to move in with them, but she couldn't do that if it would put her own children at risk.

Machelle Sexton began to disclose even more. She said the real reason she'd gone to her counselor and left home had little to do with her father hitting her. That morning, she said, she'd watched her father kiss her sisters Kimberly and Lana on the lips, saying goodbye before school.

"I didn't want to see the same thing happen to them that had happened to me," she said.

It became clear to Anne very little was normal in the Sexton household. Machelle often revealed anomalies in the middle of otherwise banal conversations, seemingly unaware of their impact. They seemed routine to Machelle, but sometimes made Anne's heart pound.

Conversations that went something like:

"That's a nice dress, Anne."

"I got it at Belden Village."

"I've never been there."

"You've never been to the mall?"

"I've never been shopping. My mother bought my clothes. I told you, I never went anywhere."

The only time she was out of the house for any extended period was in the summer when her father took them on short camping trips.

Or:

"So, Machelle, what were your neighbors like?"

"You don't talk to neighbors. You get whupped for that."

The *whuppin's* seemed to have a ritualistic quality, Anne learned. The children were required to go to her parents' bedroom, remove their pants, and expose their naked bottoms. Her father would hit their thighs or buttocks. Her mother was usually there, watching.

"Sometimes you got to pick out your own stick in the yard," she said.

The thick ones left bruises, she said, while the thin ones stung. She didn't want bruises. Bruises kept you home from school.

"I loved school," she said. "School meant I wasn't at home."

"When did the whuppin's stop?"

"They didn't."

"How often?"

"Every day, more or less. Me, especially. I was the rebel of the family."

Or:

"Machelle, what did you want to be when you grew up?"

"Normal."

She apparently spent her teenage years researching exactly what *normal* entailed. It came slowly by reading and watching and listening, Machelle said. She read about "normal" people in romance paperbacks and novels in high school literature class. Restricted to the house, she took advantage of her only luxury at home, a 52-inch Mitsubishi TV. She could watch TV in the living room after school and after dinner if her chores were done. Normal families functioned in TV sitcoms like *Full House*. Normal adults had fun in shows like *Cheers*. She regularly watched a program on Channel 4 called *After School Specials*. The show covered school and family life, relationships, friendships, sex and conflict. What behavior was appropriate, and what behavior was not.

"A lot of people say TV is no good for kids," Machelle would later say. "But the way I figure, television probably saved my life."

Anne wondered, didn't other students suspect something was very wrong in her life?

"I learned to fake it," she said.

She studied her classmates, she explained. She listened to what they said about friends and parents. She listened to them talk about the activities they did after school. She tracked the movies they saw and learned the names of stores inside Belden Village, what hits were selling in record stores. Then, in school chatter, she mimicked them, as if she'd done that, been there.

The only dances Machelle attended were the ones held by her father. On Friday nights, he would gather all the boys and girls in the living room, turn on a rock station, and order them to dance, sometimes for hours.

"He'd sit in his chair, just smoking a cigarette and watch," she said. Or, he'd move the girls around, putting them up front where he would dictate the way they moved their torsos and their hips.

There seemed to be two sets of rules. Some of the girls were restricted constantly, others allowed to have restaurant jobs. Boys had more leeway. They got to go places with their father and leave the house alone. Some participated in school sports. Willie, though out of high school, spent much of his time at his father's side.

When Anne asked about her mother's role in the home, Machelle would say her father was the one in charge of the house. She was not defensive about her mother. She was evasive. The kids appeared to do all the housework. To Anne, May Sexton seemed to be little more than a shadow in the house.

In the two months before she left home, Machelle said, her father changed one stringent rule. It started when he suspected she was pregnant. It was as if he had ESP, she said. She'd never told him she'd missed her period. But when no one else was looking, he would thrust his hips forward and waddle by her, folding his hands in front of him as they were resting on a bulging belly. Then he would plop down in his chair, light a cigarette, and laugh. One day he came right out with it. He patted her tummy and said, "I know what's growing inside."

Then he told her she could find herself a boyfriend, Machelle continued. She'd never been allowed to date before. When she was 13, he'd turned away a boy who brought her a present for her birthday. A couple years ago, another boy who dropped by to study was told to leave at gunpoint, she claimed.

She invited a boy over who'd shown some interest in her in literature class. He was short and skinny and wore glasses. His name was Jeff.

"The perfect nerd," she said.

Jeff was allowed to come over and study, or watch TV in the living room. Her father watched them closely. Soon, she said, Dad was spending more time with Jeff than with her.

He could turn on the charm, she said. He told folksy tales about the mountains and coal mines of West Virginia. He spun stories about deer hunting. He'd stand under the Airborne flag he'd hung in his den and describe battles he'd fought in Vietnam. He could talk for hours about the little church he ran in Canton years ago. Honor and honesty and the importance of family. This was all that mattered, Dad would say. He showed Jeff how to use tools and explained the trade secrets of house painting. He took him along to the hardware store and the gas station and the used car lot. He made him feel like part of the family, she said.

Just as he'd done with Joel Good, she said.

One night in December, Jeff sat down with her in the living room and pulled out a ring. It looked like a quarter carat diamond. She wondered where he got it.

"Your dad gave it to me," he said. Jeff wanted her to marry him.

Yes, Machelle told him.

"I thought it was my ticket out," she told Anne Greene. After she left home, she never saw the boy again.

One night in late March, Anne received a call from the women's shelter. Machelle Sexton had signed out earlier that day, but hadn't signed back in by curfew. It was well past 10 p.m.

Anne thought of Ed Sexton's threats. "We've got to find her," she told her husband Gerry.

They sped from North Canton toward downtown, then cruised up and down Market Avenue, looking. When they didn't spot her on the street, Anne insisted Gerry stop at the curb. She explored bars and bowling alleys and gas station bathrooms. They drove down alleys. She looked in Dumpsters and dark rear doorways.

The search went on for two hours.

They were on Market when Anne saw her.

"Stop, honey," she yelled.

Machelle Sexton was shivering inside a flimsy coat and hole-ridden stretch pants. She was walking, one cheek turned into the blowing snow.

Anne leaped out before the van stopped, running across four lanes of traffic.

Inside the van, Anne asked why she'd left the shelter.

"I hate it there," she said.

They took her home that night and let her spend a couple of days with them. After she returned to the shelter, she didn't stay long. Soon the shelter evicted her for revealing the location of the safe house to a boy she'd met.

Machelle moved in with an older woman she'd met at the shelter. It would begin a series of stays at a half dozen locations over the next few months, with relatives and battered women she'd befriended at the safe house.

Machelle Sexton, the rebel of the Sexton family, had a problem with authority figures, Anne decided. And was it any wonder? Ironically, it had liberated her from the house on Caroline Street.

Now she seemed incapable of shutting it off.

In early April, Anne received another alarming call concerning Machelle Sexton. This time it was from a triage nurse at Timken Mercy Medical Center. Machelle was in the hospital's psychiatric ward. She'd been admitted the night before. Machelle had asked the nurse to call.

Anne and Gerry sped to the hospital. They rang the security buzzer to the psychiatric ward, but were admitted only after the staff checked their names on the visiting list.

They found Machelle lying in a hospital bed, and very talkative. Her stomach had been pumped the night before. She'd taken a couple of handfuls of painkillers, at the house where she was staying.

The rape. Her fears. The talk with police. The continuing nightmares.

"I just couldn't take it anymore," she said.

Now, in some ways, she seemed enamored with the attention she was receiving.

"Pixie and Joel were in to visit," Machelle said. "Pixie told me she'd testify against Dad. Joel said the more he learned the more sick he was about it all."

She'd also been in contact with her older brother, Eddie Jr., she said. He'd called her on the phone, she said.

"He told me if I talked about what went on at home, he'd shut me up," she said.

Machelle said, "Oh Anne, I only want to live with you."

Anne couldn't believe Machelle was so oblivious to the potential danger she'd put herself in by revealing to family members where she was.

Move in?

Now, that was just out of the question, Anne thought.

5

It wasn't the first hospital call he'd ever received or the first troubled voice he'd heard asking for help. For nearly 20 years Otis Lee Sexton had ministered, first to his small flock in Canton, then across nearly 10 years of revivals, on the road six days a week in Ohio, Kentucky, Tennessee, then back to Canton to preach Sunday in his church.

Now his niece Machelle was on the phone, calling from Timken Mercy. She was being discharged from the hospital, she said. She'd left home. Now she had no place to stay.

Otis Sexton hadn't spoken with his younger brother Eddie Lee since they'd argued on his porch last summer. He hadn't seen Machelle, or spoke with any of his brother's children, since that day. But it didn't surprise him that one of Eddie's children was calling him now from a psychiatric ward.

Otis waited until evening visiting hours, then made the 15-minute drive in his '84 Buick Skylark to Timken Mercy, picking up his older sister Nellie on the way.

They talked in the visitors' room. Machelle looked as if she wanted to tell him something. Already, Otis had a good guess as to what it was.

"Honey, listen," he said quietly. "Nothing you say is going to put me back on my heels."

Machelle told him about the rape.

"Honey," he said. "I've got to be honest with you. I've been suspecting it for years."

Machelle pulled a gnarled business card out of her pocket. He saw the name Wayne Welsh, the Department of Human Services.

"Uncle Otie," she said. "I think you should call this man."

The next morning, Otis Sexton reached the social worker.

"What did she tell you?" Welsh asked.

Otis relayed the story about the rape.

"Mr. Sexton," he said. "You've just made my day."

6

On April 2, the Department of Human Services received an anonymous telephone tip, someone identifying themselves as a female relative of the Sexton family. The woman said that Sherri Sexton had been sexually abused by her father. The tipster feared the younger children were next.

It was 14 days after Machelle Sexton had disclosed to Jackson police about possible incest in the family. Why the agency waited until the anonymous tip to investigate again would remain unclear in records released later. But the call had prompted officials to put Wayne Welsh back on the case. On April 3, he interviewed young Lana and Kimberly Sexton at school. It was the same old Sexton story. Both denied there were any problems at home. But the day held one more interview.

Machelle Sexton was waiting for him at her uncle Otis Sexton's house.

The interior of Otis Sexton's home bore little resemblance to the house on Caroline. It was a well-kept two-story in an aging neighborhood on Canton's east side. Family pictures of Otis Sexton's six grown daughters, three son-in-laws, 14 grandchildren and other relatives covered the walls, television and bookshelves. There were proclamations from the city and state legislature for his community volunteer work. Otis Sexton organized Little League teams and poured hours into maintaining and improving a neighborhood ball field where a young Thurmond Munson once played. At 52, Otis Sexton was two years older than his brother. They both had receding hairlines and high cheekbones. But unlike the wiry Eddie, Otis was built more like a retired linebacker for the NFL teams he followed on his small console TV.

"He seemed like a really decent individual," Welsh later would recall.

Welsh and Machelle talked alone. She went a little further than the account she'd given Detective Glenn Goe. Her father tried to molest her when she was 12, she said, "but he couldn't get it in." She detailed the rape in the van. Then she told Welsh her sisters Pixie and Sherri had been having sex with their father since they were 12. She revealed that she and her younger brother Matt saw her father having sex with Sherri in the family van.

Welsh wondered about punishment in the home.

"You get the belt until you're 16," she said. "Then you graduate to the fist."

For the next two weeks, Welsh tried to find more information. If Ed Sexton molested his older daughters and routinely beat his children, that put the minor kids in the home at risk, grounds for a dependency case. He talked with Glenn Goe, then to Otis Sexton again.

Welsh tried talking with more Sexton children at school, but he could only arrange interviews with James and Charles. Like the others, they said nothing was amiss at home.

There was a certain passive quality about the children's denials. They responded with one-word answers and stared, emotionless. In time, DHS workers would coin a phrase about the look.

They called it "The Sexton Stare."

7

The offices of the legal department for the Stark County Department of Human Services were located in the Renkert Building, an aging 11-story office building.

The imposing red-brick structure was classic downtown Canton. Save for a new Hilton and a few other buildings, most of downtown looked as if it hadn't changed since World War II. Just north on Market Avenue was an adult bookstore with a vintage, neon Playboy bunny head in the window. A boarded-up boxing gym was due east on Tuscarawas. Law firms filled small buildings near the county courthouse. Other storefronts stood vacant. The name Timken showed up on schools and foundations and medical agencies. Some locals believed if the Timken bearing company ever pulled out of greater Canton, the entire town would close up shop.

Judee L. Genetin, the director of legal services, worked halfway up the Renkert Building in a cramped office with a window. She was not listed in the lobby directory. Transcripts and case files covered her small desk. A small, round conference table held more paperwork, a bowl of candy and often carry-out food. Judee Genetin was an attorney, but her job rarely afforded the luxury of a legal power lunch, even if there was a suitable restaurant nearby.

Genetin was the gatekeeper, the attorney who ultimately decided which child protection cases warranted decisive legal action, such as removing children from homes and placing them in foster care. Among abusive and neglectful parents, Genetin and her staff of a half dozen attorneys had enemies. That's why she did not advertise her location. That's why the doors of the office were often kept locked.

On the morning of April 16, staff attorney Dave Rudebock showed up in Genetin's office. He was working on the wording for a dependency complaint and pick-up order, based on Wayne Welsh's investigation. If signed by a judge, the papers would allow DHS to pick up all the minor Sexton children. That would be followed by an emergency shelter care hearing to determine whether there was probable cause to put the children in custody of the DHS.

"This is a weak one," Rudebock said.

Genetin agreed. The complaint was based entirely on Machelle Sexton's allegations. But Genetin had also talked to Welsh. The social worker believed that once the children were removed, they'd begin talking.

"He thinks we'll be able to prove all this stuff," she said.

Genetin had learned much since joining the DHS five years before. A former public defender and divorce attorney, the 38-year-old woman was the social services division's first lawyer, originally serving as a liaison between social workers and prosecuting attorneys who used to handle cases of abuse and neglect. By 1990, she was running her own staff of attorneys who now prosecuted the cases. It was a daunting workload. In 1992, the social services division would generate nearly 4,000 cases in Stark County. Most would involve physical abuse and neglect. Less than 20 percent involved sexual abuse.

Genetin had heard about the Sextons before.

"I had one social worker describe the family as a birthday cake that looked good on the outside, but on the inside it was all rotten," she would later recall. "They would say, 'My gut tells me something is wrong.' Now what am I supposed to do with that? As an attorney, I need evidence. I can't put somebody on the stand to testify about their gut.

"But after working here awhile, I learned to listen to that. I learned that it's more than their gut. It's their observations, it's all these little things that click for them with interactions and body language. And what they are saying is that if you really delve into this, you can get the information out of them."

However, Genetin also knew that in 30 days her staff would have to show up with evidence in court, or a judge would give the children back to the parents.

To her way of thinking, that made the Sexton case "a very risky complaint." It was risky because if there was indeed something going on in that house and DHS gave the children back, they would be the ones who would suffer, not the DHS staff. At the very least, no Sexton child would ever come forward again.

Judy Genetin decided to trust Wayne Welsh's instincts.

"Let's get it before a judge," she said.

8

That afternoon, armed with a pick-up order signed by a Stark County Family Court judge, Wayne Welsh, other social workers, and Jackson Township police showed up at the Jackson schools. They picked up Kimberly, 7, Lana, 12, and Matthew, 14.

Welsh later recalled, "What we said to the kids was something along the lines that your parents have some problems that they need to work on at this point and we believe for now you need to be in a home where you're going to be safe. Then, hopefully we'll be able to get these problems resolved so you'll be able to go back home at some time with your parents—if that's what you want."

They went without protest.

Christopher, 13, wasn't at his middle school, and James, 16, wasn't at Jackson High. At Jackson, Welsh found Charles, the 17-year-old called "Skipper." When Welsh approached him, he became belligerent. He was a sinewy teen with intense eyes. He'd competed in the lower weight classes on the school wrestling team.

"I'm not going with you," he snapped. "And you can't make me go."

It took Welsh a few minutes to talk him into the car.

After they left, Estella May Sexton arrived at the high school, looking for her son, but was told by school officials that they'd been picked up by the Department of Human Services.

She raced home and told her husband.

Not long after, at 4:30 p.m., police and social workers arrived at the house on Caroline Street to execute the rest of the pick-up order. Inside, police found Christopher and James. As they came out of the house with the two teenagers in the car, the parents followed them out to the driveway.

Ed Sexton calmly told everyone he'd done nothing wrong. "This is all a big misunderstanding," he said in a soft West Virginian drawl.

Estella May Sexton's eyes were full of fire. She gestured wildly. "He doesn't molest anybody," she shouted. "He doesn't hurt none of these kids."

Officials took all the children to the home of Otis Sexton. He'd said his daughters would help him care for his nieces and nephews until a shelter care hearing scheduled for the following day.

"The agency always tries to place kids with an appropriate relative when we can because the kids are less discombobulated," Welsh later explained. "It's less traumatic that way."

It was Holy Thursday, the day before Good Friday, 1992. Sixty-six days had passed since Machelle Sexton had walked into Ruth Killion's office at Jackson High School and complained about her father. Forty-six days had passed since she'd disclosed to Anne Greene about the rape and 28 since she'd revealed the assault to Jackson police.

"I'm so very proud of you," Anne Greene told Machelle. "You're the only one of 12 who was finally strong enough to try to break the chain of abuse."

But the Sexton saga was just beginning.

Later, Anne Greene would come up with a more appropriate metaphor for the teenager with the mysterious blue eyes.

"She was the girl with her finger in the dike," she said. "Little did anyone know that when she removed it, all hell was going to break loose."

iv
The Test

1

Nearly three years after her children were removed, Estella May Sexton sat at a small table, sipping on a cup of machine coffee and explaining how she met the young West Virginian who called himself Eddie. People said she had an exotic beauty when they met in 1967. Now bolts of grey streaked her raven hair and her dark eyes drooped with lack of affect.

"It's unbelievable, really," she said. "Real unbelievable what eventually happened. My dad was a thirty-three-year career soldier. I was strictly raised on military bases from a good family. Fort Knox. Fort Meade. Fort Devons. Fort Hayes. In Albuquerque, he was stationed at White Sands. Nothing went on in my family. Arguing. Fighting and that.

"I was born in Willing, West Virginia, while my father was in the service. My mom's from Ohio, my dad from Willing, right across the border. My dad was almost one hundred percent Wyandotte. My mom was Cherokee and French. When he first went in the service he was a Ranger.

He was in the Second World War and Korea and Vietnam. He retired a master sergeant. There were ten kids in all. I'm the fifth oldest. It was hard hauling a big family around to those bases and towns, but he did it.

"Growing up was a normal childhood. Nothing like my marriage. My parents weren't harsh disciplinarians. Punishment was getting restricted from the telephone and school things. I think my mom smacked me in the face twice, but I honestly deserved it. Girls just didn't talk bad and she heard me call one of my brothers a name. They always called me the rebel in the family.

"I began dating at age fifteen or sixteen. You could go to movies with other couples. And I liked going to school dances. I went to high school in Toledo and finished in Farmington, Ohio. I was a cheerleader. I belonged to the Future Nurses of America.

"In Farmington, my father had left the Army and became a sheriff. But the service called him back in 1967 to be an advisor in Vietnam. I was working at a nursing home and became really close to patients. But it would hurt me when they would pass away, and I got out of that. Then I thought I was going to make a lot of money being a cosmetologist. I started doing people's hair out of my mother's home.

"Marriage never entered my mind until we moved to Farmington. Back then, it was a big thing to be a go-go dancer, and I was also interested in that. I loved to dance. Still do. My parents let me go to dances every weekend. That's where I met Pat's dad, Bill, the father of my oldest. There was a small town down the road where they had a big barn that had rock and roll. As teenagers, we all went there on the weekend. I went to a few dances with him and he enlisted in the service. But we dated a lot before he left, and I got pregnant. Then he went to Vietnam. But we never married. That's the last I heard of him. I don't know if he's still alive or got killed.

"Pat was born in 1967. I was twenty. I went to Canton

to stay with my oldest sister. From Farmington, you had to travel to far down into West Virginia to get work, or go north. So I came up to Canton and got a job working at Grant's, a five-and-dime. I was saving money so I could go to a cosmetology school which was right across the street.

"My brother-in-law, Dwayne, introduced me to Eddie. Eddie's brother Otis had a church at the time. They asked me to go to church with them. They said Otis had a nice looking younger brother so I went to church with them. I was raised a Lutheran. I was really shocked, me being in that kind of church. It was store-front with only thirty people. His version of the Bible. He stomped and yelled a lot.

"I sat next to Eddie. Afterwards, a couple days later, we were invited to a weenie roast at Otis's house. I had Patrick with me. He was nine months old at the time. At the picnic, that's where I really met Eddie.

"We just start talking. He was working for Goodwill as a truck driver. He also did painting on glass. He was painting an advertisement or something for Otis's church. He asked me, was I married? I told him, no, I've never been married. And he said he wasn't married, which I later found out was a lie. He asked me if I was dating. I told him I still had feelings for Bill.

"A couple months later I went back to West Virginia with my mom. And he came all the way down to West Virginia to see me. We went out to eat while he was down there. He was real mannerly. He was real polite with my mom. And I came back to Ohio and stayed with my sister.

"We began dating. Most of the time we'd go out to the bar and listen to his brother-in-law play. His brother-in-law had a country and western band. Eddie drove a burgundy Firebird. His mother bought it for him. And he was real good to his mom. Anything she wanted, he would get for her. And he was the same way with my mom.

"We went out three or four times before he even kissed me. And I thought, maybe he was gay, you know, but I didn't ask. Afterwards I told him, I was having my doubts. I thought, you go out with a boy, the least they're gonna do is kiss you. But he was just real polite. And he was real nice looking. He had a lot of hair then. It was dark, curly. He was clean-shaven and he was well-built.

"I had no idea he'd just gotten out of the penitentiary at the time."

2

The Family Court hearing room was not built for protocol, but efficiency. Hardly the size of the average living room, it contained only tables, chairs, and a raised platform for a presiding referee. These were closed-door, juvenile proceedings, meant to protect children's identities. The records of the proceeding were sealed to the public. Not that it mattered. On April 17, one day after the Sexton children were removed from their home, local reporters were oblivious to the emergency shelter care hearing and the entire Sexton case.

Edward Lee Sexton would later recall his version of what happened at the hearing in a videotape he made for higher authorities. He said he protested his children being removed by the DHS. Sexton told the court referee he was upset his children had been placed with his older brother Otis. He claimed his daughter Machelle and Otis had trumped up the charges.

Sexton said, "And that one social worker, Mr. Welsh, he gets up . . . and really vilified me and my wife. And we were sitting there the referee says all right, you've ground up enough meat—you've ground up enough hamburger . . . So then my wife and myself asked our attorney if we could have the children taken from Otis's home, because Otis, he's got a mental condition and he's always doing this kind of stuff. He's always interfering in everybody's life."

The court ordered the minor children placed in temporary foster care while the DHS continued its investigation. A couple of weeks later, Ed Sexton would return with an attorney named Patrick Menicos and secure a court order preventing his brother Otis or any family member from having contact with his children while the case was pending.

Otis Sexton told social workers he never wanted custody of the children. Any suggestion of a conspiracy, he said, was entirely in his younger brother's mind. Eddie was always doing that, he said, taking his own faults and trying to attribute them to him. Later, in fact, Machelle would reveal that her father had told her that Otis liked to have sex with his girls.

Some of the resentments went back many years.

They were the two youngest boys, Eddie Lee the seventh son in a family of 10 children, Otis the sixth. Their late father was a coal miner and a Baptist preacher in Logan County, the same eastern West Virginia coal territory that spawned the battle between the Hatfields and the McCoys. The Sextons later moved to Sheridan, Ohio, 60 miles up the Big Tuck Fork and Ohio rivers, then to Ironton, Ohio. When their father died of a sudden heart attack at 52, Otis was 12 and Eddie Lee nearly 10.

Otis Sexton later recalled those hard years.

"We had a normal home," he said. "The boys had a room. The girls had a room. None of these people raping each other. My dad would bring the whole church home on Sunday. They all sat in the yard and talked the Bible.

"But let me tell you, we were poorer than a church mouse. We had to raise our food . . . hunt. Heat? We didn't have money to buy coal. We had to walk about three miles across old Route 52, down in Ironton above Ashland, Kentucky. We'd take turns going over there and picking up lumps of coal that fell off the trains. Poor took on new meaning. It wasn't like the people who get welfare these days."

Eddie Lee never had to pick coal, Otis said. Their mother Lana spoiled him. "Man, he was a momma's boy all the way." While the rest of the boys did chores, Otis remembered her coddling Eddie, reading him stories in a rocker next to a pot-belly stove.

"Or, let's take Dave, my older brother. When we were growing up we had to share our toys. At Christmastime, there were two beebee guns bought. Eddie was given his own gun. Dave and I had to share ours. We'd go to the store, my sister Maggie and me with my mom. We'd ask, can we get a candy bar? She'd buy two. We'd bring the candy home. Eddie would get the whole bar. I'd have to split mine with Maggie."

After their father died, Otis took a job setting pins in a bowling alley for six cents a line. In his teens he worked construction and later became a painter's apprentice. He gave all his earnings to his mother, he said.

"I used to get blisters on my hands. I had to wrap towels around them so I could use a shovel. I'd save fifty cents for myself to go to the theater and get a pop. Eddie Lee worked about a month at best. Then he quit."

Otis enlisted in the Navy. Eddie, at 14, landed in an Ohio reform school for a year after he broke into a store in Ironton and took some watches. Eddie eventually enlisted in the Army, but was discharged for bad conduct within six months as far as Otis knew. Ten days before his 21st birthday, police arrested Eddie Lee Sexton for robbing a gas station near Williamson, West Virginia. He served five years in the state penitentiary in Moundsville.

Still, as Otis recalled it, Eddie remained the apple of his mother's eye. Otis believed she sent him some $6,000 during his prison stay. Meanwhile, Otis was struggling in Canton, starting a family and his ministry.

"At that time, we didn't know where our next meal was coming from. But Eddie, yeah, he had it all. In prison, he gambled and set up a store. When he got out of prison, I'm driving this banged-up old Buick. It looked like death takes a holiday. But within seven days of Eddie getting out, mom bought him a brand new Pontiac—within one week!''

By 26, Otis was preaching. In 1966, he founded a small church on Navarre Road. Then he created his road ministry, called Burning Bush Revivals.

"When I converted our church to the Church of God of Prophecy, that's a worldwide organization. I was scrutinized, let me tell you, by the bishops of the church. You had to have Bible knowledge and some sociology. I became a bishop myself.''

In 1971, Eddie, out of prison and married to May, decided he was going to preach. According to Otis, he took an easier route. He opened a tiny storefront church in Canton, taking Otis's old name, the Calvary Church of God.

Recalled Otis, "Anybody can go out there and get a five-dollar license and go preaching as an independent. As a matter of fact, I offered to help Eddie where I could. But then I went over there to one of his services and when I heard what was going down, I said, that's it.''

Otis recalled his brother distorting scripture. Eddie preached that God had thrown a third of the angels out of heaven with Lucifer and they had "gone to earth and married among men." He told his congregation that this and other scriptural references made men as gods. Otis said he walked out. The church lasted only six months. Few were there to listen anyway.

"The only people in the congregation were Eddie's family and a couple of friends,'' Otis said.

As Otis recalled it, over the years they floated in and out of each other's lives. They held garage and yard sales together. He suggested to Eddie that he start a painting business so he could put his teenage boys to work. Otis showed Patrick, Eddie Jr., and Willie how to hold brushes, glaze windows, and do detailed trim work. Eddie put a business phone for S&S Painting in his den. The little company got jobs for a couple of summers.

Otis would drop by the house on Caroline a couple of mornings each week. They'd sit at the kitchen table, drinking coffee and smoking cigarettes, shooting the breeze.

Yes, during those years he got along with Eddie, Otis would admit, but yet he didn't.

Especially when the girls started having babies.

"There's two sides to Eddie," he would say.

3

The afternoon of the shelter hearing, Wayne Welsh interviewed the Sexton children again. They hadn't even been out of their parents' care 24 hours, and already they were talking.

Charles, or Skipper, the tough wrestler, began crying. He pushed the tears back into his sandy hair and winged ears, then admitted both parents beat him frequently. He said his father once made him and his brother Matt stand naked in the living room in front of the entire family as they held encyclopedias in their outstretched hands. He was punished for eating without permission or leaving a ball in a neighbor's yard. He said his mother had choked and scratched him only a few months ago after she accused him of fondling his 12-year-old sister Lana. But he also added that his mother wasn't spared his father's wrath. He sometimes beat her, and once held a shotgun to her head.

Matt, another sandy blond, had more stoic features than his older brother, but the same penetrating Sexton eyes. He confirmed the encyclopedia story and the frequent beatings. He told Welsh that once Machelle told him she'd gone downstairs and seen her father and Pixie having sex on the couch.

James, 16, spoke slowly. With his brown hair cut short by home shears, his eyes focused inward, he looked like a young prison camp survivor. Later, the agency determined he was marginally autistic. James said everyone was beaten—frequently. His father usually used a belt, leaving bruises and cuts. He "whupped" Lana on her bare butt. He smacked or struck the older children in the face. Pixie, James said, also struck her children with a belt. He quoted what would turn out to be one of several Sexton mantras: "Until sixteen you get the belt. After that, you get the fist."

"How often did you get the belt?" Welsh asked.

"About every two weeks," James said.

Punishment and promises. James said his father alternated between the two. He promised them Disney World and college educations and a mountaintop ranch. The promises came with a condition. They had to spy on their brothers and sisters—and they couldn't talk to anyone from the DHS.

James confirmed Charles's story about being choked.

"There's lots of sex in the family," he said.

Welsh tried to extract details.

"The lovin' belly," James said. He and Kimberly would have to sniff each other's belly and armpits, then their legs and feet.

"He wants me to be a dog," James said.

He wouldn't explain any more than that.

James said he never wanted to see his parents again, but was afraid now that he was talking.

"If Dad knew, he would kill me," James said. "He's said he would shoot me with a gun."

Lana had sophisticated features for a girl of 12. Her hair was dark and long, her cheekbones high and her eyebrows dark and arched. She confirmed the beatings revealed by her brothers and added a few more of her own. When her brother Christopher failed a class, she said, her father beat him so hard with a belt he bled. Her father beat Willie for trying to run away from home. Willie has scars on his nose and forehead, she said. Recently, she said, her father beat Skipper so bad with a stick his back bled.

Two other children had been taken into DHS custody.

Christopher was a stocky 13-year-old with a flattop. At only 7, Kimberly had doll-like puffy cheeks and flowing brown hair.

Neither were talking.

"The worst that ever happens is we get grounded," Christopher would later say.

Four days later, DHS officials transferred the Sexton investigation to its ongoing unit, a group of social workers who would monitor the children in their foster homes and begin to prepare a case for court. After almost a dozen investigations across 13 years, an entry was made in the Sexton case file for the first time:

"Abuse and emotional maltreatment both substantiated."

DHS attorney Judee Genetin later said that the Sexton children were also making their own evaluation, conducting their own test, this one on the DHS.

"If they can, a child starts testing the system," she said. "They're thinking: Is the system going to protect me? Or are the threats my father made true? So the kids try out the system with a few disclosures, then wait to see what happens. But then, if the father's threats start coming true, they will only shut down again."

4

Four days after the children were removed, Machelle Sexton returned to the Jackson Township Police Department for another interview with Detective Glenn Goe. This time she wasn't afraid to visit the police department. She was accompanied by her uncle, Otis Sexton, who also wanted to talk with police.

Despite Anne Greene's insistence, Goe didn't feel he was in the position to ask for an arrest warrant for Ed Sexton.

"We had no physical exam," Goe later recalled. "No

corroborating evidence. It was her word against her father's. And that was about it.''

He'd also been struck by Machelle's odd behavior in their first interview: Her fragmented accounts. Her inability to recall dates and times. Her absence of emotion. She'd given him no indication she'd be able to testify, and even if she did, he wasn't sure she would be believable in court.

"Frankly, I wasn't convinced Machelle was telling the truth," he added. "It wasn't so much the allegation, because her details were consistent. Her behavior was just real odd. Was that behavior because she was abused, or because she was fabricating? I just wasn't sure.''

Wayne Welsh arrived at the department. He would sit in on the interview. Both men needed more details: Possible witnesses. Names of relatives. Hospital or police reports they could link to abuse. And this time, Goe wanted to get Machelle's account on tape.

Otis Sexton waited outside while Goe and Welsh took her into an interview room. It was a Monday afternoon.

They went over the family structure again, the nicknames. Machelle Sexton spoke in a quiet voice, but this time she was using more complete sentences and seemed to be responding thoughtfully to the questions the detective asked.

Goe began asking about Pixie. Goe wanted to know how Machelle knew her children Dawn and Shasta were her father's. How did she know Stella and Ed Sexton had sex?

Machelle said before Dawn was born, she and her sister Sherri and her brother Matt began confiding in each other, wondering if her father and Pixie were involved sexually. One night they hatched a plan. Pixie, or Stella, was sleeping downstairs in the living room that night. Machelle pretended to sleepwalk down the stairs. When she shuffled into the living room, she saw her father naked with her sister.

"What were they doing?" Goe asked.

"They were doing what husband and wife do," Machelle said.

She reported what she saw to Sherri and Matt, but later she also suspected Sherri of having sex with her dad. One time Sherri and her father took a drive in the van. When they came back, her father's zipper was halfway down and his shirt was hanging out of his pants.

"Didn't you ask Sherri?" Goe asked.

"No," Machelle said.

"Why not?"

"We never talked about each other. We'd only talk about our sister Stella."

"Did you ever talk to Stella about what happened?"

"No."

"Why?"

"Because she was Daddy's girl. She'd tell him everything we said."

Machelle was convinced Dawn and Shasta were her father's because Pixie did not date until after she had the children. Then her father encouraged her to date Joel Good.

Goe wondered how Pixie and Joel supported themselves.

Pixie was on welfare, she said.

"She has to turn the money over to my dad," Machelle said. "She thought he was saving it, but he was spending it. When they'd ask him for money, he made up an excuse."

Goe wanted to know why she suspected Sherri's son Christopher was her father's.

"She's never had a boyfriend in her life," Machelle said.

Sherri also was pregnant once before, she said, but she miscarried.

"Any other instances when your father had intercourse with a sibling?" Goe asked.

"No, but I know he's got other kids. He's got other kids out there."

Goe asked her to elaborate.

She named a relative on her mother's side of the family.

She'd had a little girl by her father, she said. Goe noted the name.

The detective moved on to the physical abuse. "I know there is a difference between abuse and discipline," Goe said. "Is there a time you felt like you or your brothers and sisters were abused?"

"It depends how old you are," Machelle said matter-of-factly.

"What do you mean by that?"

"If you're sixteen you get the fist. If you're under sixteen, you get the belt or the switch."

"Did you ever get it?" Goe asked.

"Oh yeah, I got it. Getting bad grades in school. When I was sixteen, I got the fist because I talked to a black person."

Goe pressed for details.

Her father sometimes used his trouser belt, often wielding the buckle end, she said. He also used a "kidney belt," an eight-inch-wide belt used by truckers and weight-lifters for support. All the kids were beaten totally naked, she said, usually in her parents' bedroom. The number of times they were hit depended on how they reacted.

"How much you move is how much you get," she said, saying it as if it were sacred law.

One time, she said, her father produced a paddle drilled with holes and beat them simply to determine who could take the most punishment.

"He said it was an Army thing," she said.

Routinely, he'd line them up and beat them one after another, bending each over the living room couch.

"Did that happen a lot?" Goe asked.

"Yeah."

"Every day?"

"No, every week. Usually on weekends. Not on weekdays because of school."

They needed time to heal, she said.

After punishment, they often had to stay upstairs.

Machelle said the last birthday she'd been allowed to celebrate was at 13. Her father always had a reason to deny her a little party. The last five years, she said, he'd beaten her the night before.

Sometimes their mother administered the naked whippings. "To me, she got a thrill out of hitting my brothers," Machelle said. "Because when she started, she couldn't stop."

During the bedroom beatings, she said, other siblings would huddle outside the door and listen, counting the lashes. One time, they counted Skipper getting 49. That was the night he'd been accused of fondling Lana, Dad's Angel. Mother also attacked him, she said, choking him, leaving his neck swollen and marked.

Goe asked, did she witness this?

"I don't know, because I wasn't in the bedroom," Machelle said. "But I could hear her. My mother was making cat calls and everything. . . ." She ran out of words trying to describe her mother's guttural sounds.

After the beating, she said, Skipper was locked in a closet until the next day.

"When he let him out, my dad said, 'It hurt me more than it hurt you to do that to you, Skipper. But you know how it stands if anybody touches one of the girls.'"

Goe asked, "Was that something that happened? Were kids locked in the closet for a period of time?"

"Just that one night."

"Has that ever happened to you?"

"Yeah. I bought some cards. Me and Sherri went to the store with my mom and we bought some cards. My mom didn't see us get them. We came home. Started playing. Got caught."

"You were locked in the closet?"

"Yeah. He put roach spray in there."

"In the closet?"

She said her father sprayed it under the door. She passed

out. Her mother took her out, but then her father found out.

"He beat my mom and put me back in," she said.

Goe wondered if she'd ever been hospitalized for injuries.

No, she said, adding later that none of the children had.

Her father received all the medical attention, she said. He took powerful painkillers such as Darvocet and Percodan for his back. She was suspicious of his back problems. He climbed ladders painting. She added that he put Eddie Jr., Patrick, Willie, and Pixie to work in his painting business, too.

"Where does he work, out of the house?" Goe asked. "Where's his office?"

"He calls it under the table," Machelle said.

"So is he disabled?"

"My dad can move faster than I can," she said.

Machelle said her father also told everyone he had muscular dystrophy. She'd heard him say he had terminal cancer.

"These charity people came out and looked," she recalled. "They remodeled the house for my dad," she said. Foundations gave him a hospital bed, a wheelchair, and completely refurbished the master bathroom with new fixtures.

"Is he on disability?"

"My mom says he is."

Machelle explained how her father became more vigilant after DHS investigated the marks on Sherri's legs three years ago. He made all the children keep diaries. They had to list all their activities and contacts in school. She said her father paid them for telling on each other.

"I wasn't a snitch," she said. "I knew a lot, but I never told."

Goe wanted to go over Machelle's rape in the van again. She began by recounting the argument they had before he assaulted her.

"My dad asked, did you see anything in the basement?" she began. "Then he started getting madder and madder."

Goe made a note. He hadn't heard anything about the basement before. He'd follow up later. For now, he wanted to establish the statutory elements of first degree rape.

She stuttered through the details. Yes, he'd penetrated her with his penis. Yes, she'd asked him to stop. Yes, it was against her will.

Afterwards, she added that he'd taken her to a gas station and told her, "Clean yourself up." When they got home, she ran upstairs. Her father complained to her mother that she'd started her period.

Goe wondered if she'd had any previous sexual contact with her father. She told him when she was twelve he took her for a ride in the car, her first with her father. She was excited.

"We got halfway there and he said, 'Have you ever had a secret? Can you keep a secret?' I said, yes. 'Do you know about sex?' I said, no. 'Do you want me to teach you?' I said, I don't know."

They stopped by the house on Caroline to pick up the mail. At the time, they were living elsewhere while the house was being repaired after a fire. He took her inside.

"He tried," she said. "But I was too small."

Machelle grew silent. They took a five-minute break.

When Goe turned the tape back on, he switched the subject to house fires. Machelle remembered a fire when she was 12. They were being set by a "cousin." As they left the house, the cousin tossed a cigarette into the house through a window.

"His name?"

"I don't know his name," she said. "His wife's name was Rose. I remember that."

"There was another fire after that?" Goe asked.

"There were a lot of fires. I don't remember how many there were."

She was short on details, but she remembered what her father said after the fire when she was 12.

"Dad told us to keep our mouths shut," she said.

"But you weren't supposed to tell the firemen?"

She nodded.

Goe backtracked to the pregnancies. He wondered about Machelle's mother. Was she aware of what was going on?

She answered, "Me and Sherri were talking about my sister having the kids with my dad, and I said, what does Mom think? And Sherri said Mom knows what's going on but she's too scared to say anything."

"Why?"

"Because my dad's a big guy. I don't know, all of us are scared of my dad."

She told Goe how her father put a shotgun to her mother's head. One time, when he was beating their mother, he threw her against the sink, then the children came to her aid.

"I bit his leg and Sherri got his arm and broke his arm, trying to get him off my mom," she said. "Then, after that, I got in trouble, because they got back together. Me and Sherri did. So we got beat for even getting involved. I got in trouble for helping my mom. And then when we got in trouble, she didn't stand up for us."

"Do you know why she puts up with it?"

"I don't know," Machelle said.

Goe moved back to Machelle's rape.

"You mentioned he was talking about something you'd seen in the basement," Goe said. "What was that about?"

She said she was walking up the basement steps after getting some laundry soap. She could see into the basement garage from a small window at the steps.

"My dad and Eddie was down there. I dropped the bottle thing. And ran upstairs."

"What did you see?"

"I don't know specifically if it was alive or if it was dead.

But I thought I'd seen something in the back of the car. That was it. That's all it was all about.''

"What is it you think you saw? Did you have an idea?"

"Yeah, I had a pretty good idea. But I'm not going to say."

"You thought you saw a body?" Goe asked.

She nodded.

"What kind?"

"Human."

"Who was there beside your dad?"

"Eddie."

She nodded.

"Your brother?"

"Did your dad explain anything as to what you saw?"

"He said it was none of my business."

In their talk in the van, she said, her father said if she said anything, she wouldn't go to college. Then he raped her, apparently to punctuate the threat.

As they talked more, it became clear that in the world of the Sexton children, a simple telephone was forbidden fruit. They all wanted to phone friends, Machelle said, but to do so had to outwit their dad. There was a phone in his bedroom and one in the hall. Repeatedly through the day, her father would hit the redial button, to see if they'd made any calls. They found a way to fool him. They'd call a friend, then afterwards call the weather or the time. He finally stopped them by buying a Radio Shack device that taped calls any time an extension picked up. He kept the recorder in his bedroom closet.

"Oh, he was smart," Machelle said, her eyes wide with awe.

Wayne Welsh asked a question. "When was it you decided you didn't want to live like this anymore?"

"When I was fifteen and realized this wasn't normal," Machelle said. "I started going to high school and saw what everybody else was doing and it didn't click."

She said she'd run away after her 18th birthday and

stayed with a friend from school for a few days. But her dad found her and brought her home.

"Since you left the house have you had any contact with your mom or dad?" Goe asked.

"No," she said. "But I had respect. I sent a birthday card to my mom. I sent my brothers birthday cards."

She said she called her father once, curious for family news. "I started freaking out and couldn't handle it," she said.

She'd contacted Eddie Jr. "I started telling Eddie what was really going on in the house. I didn't know he was passing it to my dad. After I found that, well, they're after me now."

"How do you know he was passing it on?" Goe asked.

"I started getting phone calls in the hospital from him, saying, 'You're no longer my sister. So therefore I have no respect for you. I'm going to finish you off.' And my sister Sherri told me she no longer wanted to be my sister because all the kids would be taken from my dad and it was all my fault. She said I opened my mouth and said things I shouldn't have said."

Welsh told her some of the other kids were starting to disclose. "Why wouldn't they have said anything before this?" Welsh asked.

" 'Cause they're scared," Machelle said. "My dad's a big guy."

Both Goe and Welsh wanted to know if girls in the house were treated differently than boys.

"Sexually?" Machelle asked.

"Sexually or otherwise," Goe said.

"My dad had a little thing with the boys, but—"

"What was that?"

"Poodentang." She laughed.

"Okay," Goe said, then probing with silence.

"My dad would be like, you know: 'I get some butt tonight.' Or do this: 'I'll be up tonight getting some butt.' I don't know if he was joking or what."

She said one night last summer he took the boys into the bathroom and measured their penises.

"Why did your dad do that?" Goe asked.

"I don't know."

Then she named all their sizes, as if she'd memorized them all. Skipper was one of the shortest.

"Skipper said, 'Well, mine wasn't hard'," she said. "My dad said, 'Do you want to try it when you're hard?' Skipper said, 'No, I don't have to prove anything.'"

The boys were also allowed to date, Machelle said.

"Why?" Goe asked.

"Because my dad said the girls would get pregnant. And the guys can get the girls pregnant."

As the interview moved into its third hour, Machelle Sexton appeared to be lightening up. She began smiling, giggling at some of the stories.

She covered ground familiar to Jackson police. Responding to a general question about neighbors, Machelle said her father had ordered her oldest brother Patrick to befriend their retarded neighbor Kathleen Dundee.

"Somehow he got her to get money out of the bank and stuff," Machelle said.

Goe asked, "On his own, or did your dad tell him to do that?"

"My dad did. And my dad showed him how." She said she was there when her father explained it to him in the dining room.

"Dad gave him a ring to give her," she said. "I thought it was mean."

She knew all about the Dundee feud. She said one day her father took Skipper outside and beat his arm against the side of the house, then called the police, claiming the neighbor had hit Skipper with a car. The children had to join in on the harassment, she said.

"If my dad hates someone," she explained. "We have to hate them, too."

Goe tried to dig deeper. "Are there more secrets?" he asked.

"Yes," she said. The smile left her face. "There's been sexual things that happened to me that I haven't even told you."

"Is there a reason why?"

"Yeah, because it's hard to talk about it."

Wayne Welsh asked Goe, "Can I ask a couple questions?"

"Sure," the detective said.

"What was your nickname, Machelle?"

"I don't like to say my nickname," Machelle said, her eyes staring straight ahead.

Welsh let silence work for the answer.

"It's Deep Throat," she finally said.

"Who calls you that?"

"My dad."

He wondered about the origins of the nickname.

Machelle said she'd learned to swallow a hot dog whole when she was 16. Her father seemed proud of it. He made her demonstrate to relatives like Uncle Otis.

Goe wanted to know if father and Otis got along.

"They don't get along anymore," she said. They'd had a fight over a stolen ring late last year, she said.

She also said her uncle rescued her once when his daughters were baby-sitting, a time she'd been tied up in her bedroom.

Wayne Welsh had heard from one of the other children that Machelle and one of her brothers had witnessed Sexton and Sherri having sex in the van. Supposedly, they were playing in the vehicle when Ed Sexton and Sherri came out. Machelle and her brother hid under a cover behind the backseat.

"We just heard things," Machelle said.

"What kind of things?" Goe asked.

"Doing their thing."

"Having intercourse?" Goe asked.

Yes, she said. She thought the year was 1987.

"Did you hear your dad talking?" Welsh asked.

"He asked her, did she want kids? And Sherri said, not right now. Because she was in school. My dad said, how about later on in life? Sherri said she didn't care."

"Why would your dad ask that?" Goe asked.

"Did she want any?" Machelle asked back.

"Yeah," Goe said.

"I don't know," Machelle said. She giggled nervously. "Ask him."

Goe went back one more time to the rape. He asked, "If at some point in time it would be possible to file criminal charges on your father for that, you would want that done?"

Machelle thought for a few seconds then said, "You mean to get up in front of a judge and tell a judge what happened?"

The detective nodded.

"I mean, yes, I would want to do that. But at this point I can't say every detail what happened as to what my dad did to me because I'll probably start cracking up. Not laughing, but emotionally, I don't know what would happen. I'd like to get to the point where I'm strong enough to handle it. The only reason I'm here and want to stay here is my brothers and sisters are out of the house."

Both Goe and Welsh wondered if in the future she'd talk to someone—maybe a counselor, one-on-one—about other secrets in the house.

"I'd like to have one person," she said. "Every time I find one person to begin talking about it they say, I can't handle this, and run away."

"You'll never have that with us," said Welsh.

5

After they talked with Machelle, they brought Otis Sexton into the room, talking to him alone, the tape recorder on again. Goe had talked with Otis Sexton informally before.

"You said at one point in time you thought there was some type of abuse or problems in the family, some things that struck you?" Goe asked.

"I didn't think," Otis said bluntly. "I knew."

He said 10 or 15 years ago, his daughters had called him while they were baby-sitting at Ed Sexton's former home on Cathy Drive in Canton.

"One of my daughters went over to baby-sit and called and told me the kids were tied up," he explained. "I told them to immediately untie them. I went over to pick my daughter up and I talked to Eddie."

In fact, he recalled the kids being tied up on at least three occasions during his daughters' baby-sitting jobs.

"I can't remember which ones, but I know it was little Eddie Lee and Willie. The last time I told Eddie, I've had it."

Otis said he told his older sister Stella, now deceased. "I guess the next day, Stella turned him in."

Apparently, it was the 1979 anonymous tip in the DHS case file.

Otis Sexton said he also suspected incest. He was working on a painting job with his brother. "Eddie and Sherri I saw kissing on several occasions," he recalled. "She was fifteen or sixteen at the time."

"Did you approach him about it?"

"I told him it didn't look right."

He said when Sherri became pregnant, his brother claimed the child belonged to a boy she was working with at a restaurant in Massilon. They'd supposedly had sex in the restaurant freezer.

"But the thing they forgot," Otis said, "Sherri hadn't worked at that restaurant for about fifteen months."

Otis digressed into the incident in Jackson police files, the time their retarded cousin was "kidnaped" from Eddie Lee's house. He said his brother was beating the boy regularly and cashing his Social Security checks. Otis said he went to the house to try and straighten out the situation, the cousin complaining he was being held hostage.

"This was the same day Eddie told me that our father had abused my sisters," Otis said. He added that he'd checked with his sisters on this, and they denied it.

Eddie, he said, flew into a rage against the cousin.

"I was ready to hit Eddie over the head with a chair before he stopped," he said.

Otis Sexton said sometimes the Sexton boys, Willie usually, would call and complain about their father's behavior.

"Willie was the main one who came to me and talked. Eddie Lee is aligned with his dad now. I don't understand why."

Otis gave a brief description of his brother's criminal past. Otis had a theory. Prison had corrupted his brother sexually.

"That's when I think all this started," he said.

At the end of the interview, Goe asked, "You've heard some of the things Machelle has said. Do you think she's telling the truth?"

"Yes, she is. This is not a put-on. I told her, 'Machelle, don't exaggerate.' And this fear that she has is real. And I know for a fact that if her dad knows where she's at, he's going to come and get her. But he won't come to my house, because he knows what I'll do to him."

All the kids were scared, he said, adding, "It's like Willie said when he called me the other day. 'If my dad knew I was talking to you, he'd kill me.' "

He said Willie had called him over the ring incident mentioned by Machelle. Willie had stolen Otis's diamond-studded 25th anniversary ring, but later confessed and offered to pay him back. He gave $300 to his dad to give to Otis.

"But his dad spent it, and tried to put me off. That's why my brother and I split. It was over this ring."

Goe was intrigued by the baby-sitting story. Before Otis left, he wrote down the names and addresses of Otis's daughters. He wanted to check the stories at the source.

Two days later, Wayne Welsh called Goe. He said in interviewing the children again, some said their father had never been in prison. He was a licensed minister, they said. Uncle Otis was the convict, their father told them.

Goe ran criminal record checks on both men. Ed Sexton had a sheet, a five-year term at Moundsville State Prison, then parole. Otis Sexton's record was clean.

Over the next two weeks, Goe interviewed all three of Otis Sexton's daughters, all married and living in Canton and nearby towns. One after another they came to the PD and told disturbing, detailed stories.

Theresa Samblet, now 29, remembered arriving at the house to baby-sit at 16. She found 3-year-old Machelle lashed to the bed, her wrist tied to one post, her ankle to the post at her feet. Machelle's hand was purple. She was lying in her own waste. She said she called her father because she couldn't get the shoelaces untied.

Eddie Jr., Skipper, Machelle, and sometimes Sherri were tied up most often, she said. Never Pixie. "She seemed to be her dad's favorite," Samblet said.

"A lot of times the kids would be locked in the bedrooms," Samblet recalled. "Not every one of them. Just certain ones. Sometimes I'd use the knife to get the doors open. Sometimes I couldn't get them open, so my dad would have to come over."

They'd find the children naked in a pitch-dark bedroom removed of furniture. The baby-sitters would find urine and stools on the floor.

"There was no electricity," Samblet said.

"Was there an explanation for that?" Goe asked.

"The father said the kids peed in the light sockets and he had to disconnect the wires so nobody got shocked," she said.

Samblet remembered a particular night she found James in a room, then just a toddler. He was in a playpen in a bare, dark room. A blanket was over the window.

"When I took him into the light, he went nuts. Like the light was killing his eyes. He was a mess. He had dried up stool all over him. God knows how long he was in there."

James was "slow" now, she said. "In my opinion that's the reason. The way he was treated growing up."

Goe asked another sister, Faith McDaniels, now 25, what the parents said before they left.

McDaniels said, "The father would say, 'The kids are upstairs. They're bad. Don't worry about them.'"

When the sisters liberated the children, at first they moved around the room cowering, like skittish, abused dogs.

"As soon as the parents pulled out of the driveway, I went to get the kids out of the rooms," Samblet explained. "And the ones that were out said I was going to get in trouble, or the kids were going to get in trouble. They'd getting a whuppin' because they got out of the bedrooms."

"Were they ever a problem to baby-sit?" Goe asked.

"No, they were angels," McDaniels said.

McDaniels told the story of how the children would run into the front yard in the rain, waiting for Jesus to come.

All three former baby-sitters relayed their suspicions of incest. None of the Sexton girls had boyfriends. Willie even took Sherri to the senior prom, they said.

Lana and James had stayed with Theresa Samblet the night they were taken from the Sexton home. The two of them kept asking her, "You promise I don't have to go home." Lana spent the night playing in Samblet's daughter's room, enthralled with dolls and toys. The two kids talked with her that night.

She recalled, "They kept asking, 'Don't you ever hit your kid?''

When she appeared to be hungry, Samblet gave Lana a beef stick.

"You promise I don't have to go back that house," Lana asked again.

Samblet promised. Then Lana told her that her father used to buy long beef sticks and use them to hit her in the head.

When the DHS removed the kids to take them to foster homes the next day, per the court order, James and Lana cried, she said.

"It was heartbreaking," Samblet said.

"Did you believe them?" Goe asked.

Theresa Samblet seemed shocked the detective had even asked the question. "Oh yeah," she said. "Especially after what I've seen."

6

Later, Detective Glenn Goe decided there was one more way to put Machelle Sexton's story to the test. On the morning of May 5, Goe and a detective named Tom Taylor drove Machelle to Richfield, south of Cleveland, to the Bureau of Criminal Identification and Investigation, a forensic unit run by the state attorney general.

Machelle Sexton had agreed to take a polygraph.

Goe asked Taylor to stay with her in the lobby while he went upstairs to talk to the examiner about the case. As they were waiting, Machelle suddenly became impatient and stomped out the door. Taylor caught her on the highway outside. It took him several minutes to convince her to come back inside.

Two hours later, she emerged from the lie detector test. Her eyes were bright, her mood upbeat.

Examiner James Krakora had tested her on her father's promise to talk about her future, the rape in the van, and his threat to kill her if she told. Krakora reported no indications of deception, writing in a later report: "It is to be considered, therefore, that this person told the substantial truth during the tests."

Afterwards, they drove back to Canton. The detectives offered to buy Machelle lunch. They stopped at an Italian restaurant.

After the waitress handed Machelle a menu, she asked, "What do you do?" She was looking at the menu as if it were in Arabic.

"I've never been in a restaurant before," she said.

V

Freedom and Fear

1

Pixie was pregnant again.

"You're kidding," Teresa said, smiling, but thoroughly shocked.

The baby was due next January, Joel and Pixie said.

They were at the Faith Bible Church in North Canton. It was after Sunday service. For several months Joey and Pixie had been attending. They'd been baptized together there in a ceremony for newlywed couples. It had given Teresa some hope.

Now this. She couldn't believe they'd done such a foolish thing. Neither had jobs. She thought, another baby? That meant three kids.

Joey said they were looking for an apartment in Bolivar, a small town about 15 miles south of Canton.

Teresa asked, how were they going to pay for an apartment?

They were on welfare, Pixie said. He was receiving unemployment.

Teresa tried to look on the bright side. Joey was getting away from the Sexton family. And Teresa's brother lived in Bolivar. At least Joey would be close to family there.

A few days later, Teresa's sister-in-law, Sue Barrick, said the couple had stopped by to chat during their apartment search. She reported their conversation:

"We've got to get out of Stark County," Joey said.

"Get out?" Sue asked. "Why?"

"You wouldn't believe the things they're accusing her dad of up there."

When Sue tried to find out more, Joey became evasive. Later Teresa coaxed a fragment of information out of him. Pixie's sister Machelle, he said, had made accusations against their father. She'd accused him of punishing his kids too hard.

"They're all lies," Joey said. "It's just tearing the family apart."

When family members pushed for details, Pixie offered explanations. Machelle had always been a troublemaker, Pixie said. She'd run away before. The only reason she'd made the accusation was that she was still in high school and needed an excuse to move out of the house.

The whole family began to notice the change. Before Pixie had been the silent partner. Now Joey seemed to be the one with no words. Pixie would sit on the couch, chatting about the kids or their latest plans. Joey's mind was somewhere else.

"It got so that Stella was saying everything," his aunt Velva would recall. "It was as if Joey wasn't allowed to answer. And if you asked him a question directly, he'd just look at her."

And then there were the kids. The whole family had theories, Teresa, Sam, Velva, their parents. Now nearly 4, Dawn still was sucking on a bottle and not talking. Dawn couldn't identify colors. Dawn couldn't count. Both girls lacked any sort of natural animation, as if they were cartoon figures who only moved their mouths.

"It's as if they're not real people or something," grand-mother Gladys Barrick said one day.

"It's like they're afraid," her husband said.

One day, Sam Barrick came right out with it. He'd seen family photographs of the Sextons.

"I don't want to say this," he said. "But you know, those look like her father's kids."

2

Estella May Sexton took another sip of coffee and began to recall the years she came to fear the man his relatives called Eddie Lee.

"We were together about two or three years, and then everything started changing. It started with me talking to another man. I guess he got jealous . . . but really I didn't have any commitments from him, and he shouldn't have gotten jealous. This other guy asked me if I wanted to go out. I told him Eddie's coming over. He said, what if he doesn't? I said all right. Then they both came over at the same time.

"After the guy left, we were standing on the porch and he smacked me and called me a couple of names. He called me a slut. I swung back at him. But he ducked and it went through my brother-in-law's window. I still have the scar on my wrist here. It was bleeding real bad. I said, 'I'm not going out with you anymore.' The next day he apologized. He was calling me 'baby.' He acted like he really cared, and he just didn't want me to go out with anyone else.

"Well, I lived with him before I got married. Because *he* was married, but I didn't know it. I wanted to get married and he finally told me. His wife lived in Delbarton, West Virginia. He hadn't been with her for years. He had to get this divorce, and it was going to take him a while to get it. But he kept putting it off. I had Eddie Jr. before we got married. I quit working at Grant's and I couldn't go to beauty school. He said, if we're going to stay together, the man does the work, supports the family. The woman doesn't do it.

"He was working at Canton Drop Forge. He kept everything in the house we needed. We'd go out on the weekends and he treated the kids—the two boys—real well. If I needed anything, he'd get it. We got along real well.

"Then we had this argument on a Wednesday. He'd started drinking on the job and smoking pot and coming home real drunk. I told him he was a grown man. I wasn't brought up like that and I didn't like it around the kids. During the argument, he smacked me around pretty bad. The same night he apologized. We got into an argument on a Wednesday, then got married on that Saturday. Otis performed the ceremony in Eddie's mom's living room. I had a black eye when I got married . . . I thought I was in love.

"He began to say, I'm supposed to spend my time with him. If I wanted to see anybody, it had to be with him. I couldn't go anywhere by myself, and he didn't like my dad. See, my dad sensed something about him. And Dad's the one who finally told me that he found out Eddie had been in prison. And when I confronted Eddie about it, he really hit the ceiling.

"And that's the first real bad beating, and I wanted to get away from him. He put soap in a sock, saying they did that all the time in Moundsville Prison. That's where he told me he was from. He really beat me with that sock. And I was out of it for a while. And I got a few back at him, too. I threw a vaporizer at him and knocked him down. Then I took off. Well, I got as far as the porch . . . I think he knocked me out.

"After he went to work, I called my sister, Irene. I went to her house. For a week, maybe. I don't think it was that long, because he found out where I was. He told me if I didn't come back, he was going to kill her and her children.

And he'd always add, 'Your mom and dad, too.' 'Cause he knew how close we were. I didn't want anybody hurt because of me, so I went back.

"After I confronted him about prison, he changed—as different as night and day. He started going somewhere shooting craps. He would lose all his pay. We ended up going on welfare when they went on strike. Then he put on this act like he got hurt at work . . . but there's nothing wrong with him.

"Every time I said something, it was wrong, or I said it at the wrong time. I was afraid to say anything. He wouldn't let me have a phone put in. He wouldn't let me get my driver's license. He also said, 'You don't see your family no more.'

"We stayed away from them for ten years."

3

As a new season came to central Ohio with budding oaks and the scent of lilac, Ed and May Sexton did a little spring cleaning for the Department of Human Services.

Not long after the pick-up order, social workers told Pixie and Sherri Sexton that it would be advisable for them to move out of the house on Caroline, otherwise the agency would have no choice but to remove their children from the home. Joel and Pixie moved to Bolivar. Sherri Sexton and her 1-year-old son Christopher's departure was more abrupt. One spring day a car showed up on Caroline. It was driven by a nephew, the son of Sexton's older brother Dave. Dave Sexton lived 1,000 miles south, north of Tampa.

Sexton stuffed a couple of bags with clothes and escorted her to the car. She needed to "start a new life," Eddie Sexton had told his brother.

Sherri would recall a different reason: "He didn't want a blood test taken of me and my son."

The Sexton case was now being assigned to what the DHS

called its Ongoing Unit. A social worker would oversee the family, eventually arranging supervised visits between children and parents at a supervised center called Harmony House. The worker would arrange counseling and therapy if they were called for. Like other cases, the goal was to work out the family's problems. Work toward reunification. "The DHS does not want to be in the business of breaking families apart," Judee Genetin would say.

Assigned was a worker named Bonita Hilson, a DHS veteran with a respected work record. From the beginning, Ed Sexton, the father who once beat a daughter for simply speaking to an African-American teen, would not be happy.

Bonita Hilson was black.

On the legal front, the DHS and the Sextons became emeshed in a series of motions, show cause hearings, and judicial orders in Family Court. While the Sexton's attorney had succeeded in getting a no-contact order against Otis Sexton, the DHS also had one in place for the Sexton parents, except for authorized visits at Harmony House.

The paper chase started on May 21, when Estella May Sexton filed an affidavit and a motion in Family Court. She wanted all child welfare and custody matters regarding her children be transferred from county and state courts to the Allegheny Nation Tribal Council. She was an American Indian, she claimed. By federal law, she was entitled to have all child welfare matters concerning her family handled by Indian child welfare officials.

The court scheduled a hearing on the matter for late June, then took it under advisement and rescheduled the matter for July.

In some ways, the tribal motion was the least of the DHS's problems. Kimberly, Lana, Christopher, Matthew, Charles, and James all were in foster homes. But soon the DHS suspected the Sexton parents of making unauthorized contact with some of the kids. A teacher, a custodian, and a cook saw them outside Faircrest Middle School in Canton, where Christopher was enrolled. Christopher's foster parents also believed that the Sextons had followed them home one day.

DHS attorneys filed a complaint to the court. The Sextons filed their own motion. They wanted interim visitation with their children. The court scheduled another hearing for July.

One night in late June, Otis Sexton received a call from James at his foster home in Andover, Ohio, a small town near the Pennsylvania border, 90 miles from Canton. James, Matt and Charles were staying in the same foster home.

"Uncle Otie, my father is coming to get us at midnight," James said. "He's coming to pick all of us up."

Otis called the DHS. Authorities sped to the home. They removed the boys and interviewed James. Dad visited frequently, James said. The boys planned walks so they could meet him. He said his father promised to buy them cars if they recanted their stories of abuse.

Skipper had revealed the location, workers learned. They removed Charles Sexton from the foster home and placed him in the Canton Children's Residential Center, a juvenile detention facility. DHS attorneys filed a second no-contact order complaint against Ed Sexton, the same day the Indian matter came up for hearing.

When asked for proof of her heritage by the court, Estella May Sexton produced a tribal card she'd acquired a couple weeks after the children were removed. It was from the Allegheny Nation Indian Community Center, located in a deteriorating Victorian in east Canton. One study had shown the Allegheny group to be a mix of white, black, and Native American blood with unclear origins. The Canton tribe had never been recognized by either the State of Ohio or the Federal Bureau of Indian Affairs.

On that basis, Family Court Judge Julie Edwards rejected the motion on July 6. But informally she turned over the investigation of the Sexton's heritage to the North American Indian Cultural Center, an organization licensed by the state to handle Indian welfare cases. The federal law required the court make every effort to determine whether a family fell under the act.

Two days later, DHS staffers, the Sextons, and attorneys appeared again before the court on the original no-contact complaint. The court decided the parents had shown up in the school parking lot, but DHS had failed to prove beyond a reasonable doubt that it was intentional and in contempt of the court.

DHS attorneys were running out of time. The original complaint filed three months ago was expiring. But that same month, Lana, Dad's 12-year-old Angel, began disclosing for the first time to her foster family that her father frequently beat her. DHS attorneys put together a new complaint covering four of the children's charges. But two children, Christopher and Kimberly, had yet to disclose any abuse. They were maintaining that everything in the house on Caroline Street was fine.

The court set new hearing dates.

DHS attorney Judee Genetin knew it was easy enough to get the children removed from the home, but obtaining long-term custody of the children by DHS was a far more demanding standard. By statute, Family Court also made every effort to preserve families. Their tools included counseling, home monitoring, and self-help groups. DHS staff would have to prove a pervasive pattern of sexual and physical abuse with the minor children. So far, only Machelle had claimed sexual abuse.

Genetin later recalled, "When we finally moved by removing the children in April, we were very concerned. We felt very strongly at that point that the abuse was happening. But we weren't able to stop them from showing up at the schools. We had a hearing on the contempt and were told we didn't prove it, even though we had witnesses who saw them at the school, on the grounds. We felt that these people were dangerous, that the dad was dangerous, but we were also watching the case slowly slip away."

The Sexton children also were watching.

"Unfortunately," Genetin said, "it would soon become obvious to these kids that we could not do what we said we could do."

4

Many months later, Charles Sexton would explain what happened during his first summer away from home. Little did DHS officials know that Skipper had made contact with his parents only days after he was removed the house on Caroline. In April, he said, after he was placed in a temporary placement home, he and Matt went skating at the Playland Skatery north of Canton.

The day he was removed from the home, he said, he'd promised to let his mother know his whereabouts. "I don't know. If my mom wasn't there, I wouldn't have said anything. I just love her with all my heart. I just needed to let her know wherever I am.

"So, we called from the Skatery and told them where we was. My parents picked us up and took us back to the house. It was weird. I never seen my dad act that way. It would have been nice if he was like that when we were growing up. He asked me if I wanted a cigarette. Before I wasn't allowed to smoke. I took it in a second. We ate pizza. Pat and Eddie Jr. was there. My father said, where I go, let him know where I am. So, the jackass I was, I did it."

Skipper called his parents from Andover.

He recalled, "We were living with a single guy. He'd let us go out, meet chicks. Do about everything. Go camping. Hunting. Real good time. I had a girlfriend. A good job. My mom and dad used to come up to Andover and give us money and cigarettes. My mom always gave me money. But my dad, that was the first time."

Two weeks after DHS transferred him to juvenile detention for disclosing the foster home's location, he ran away. On July 13, DHS notified police he was missing. He was last seen wearing blue jeans, a tank top, black high-top tennis shoes, and a Marlboro baseball cap, worn backwards.

The escape, Skipper said, was arranged at a supervised visitation with his father. "The case worker, she walked away, and me and my old man set it up real fast. I told him where I was. He was like, well, are you across from the school? He said go back there in the woods and I'll be back there by the church. So I went back there and no one was back there. I thought, I'm going to get locked down for this. And I went to this guy's phone. Made up a bullshit story like my brother had left me out there. Used his phone. Told my mom and then my dad and Eddie Jr. came up and got me."

They drove him to Indiana, dropping him off at an aunt and uncle's home near Jeffersonville, 20 miles from the Kentucky line.

5

Anne Greene logged hours on the phone with Otis Sexton and his wife Jackie, and miles and more miles on her car.

Otis spun one story after another about his younger brother's family. He told her about Ed Sexton's criminal record, his house fires, his suspicious disability, and the flow of government money into the house. May was on welfare because her husband supposedly couldn't work. And not only did Pixie and Sherri receive welfare for their children, Sexton's sons generated income. James and William both had been judged disabled by the Social Security Administration. They each received some $400 a month in Supplemental Security Income. One later estimate put the family's tax-free income at more than $50,000 during peak years.

Willie was his father's constant companion, Otis said.

He stuttered and could hardly read or write. He'd graduated from Jackson High as a special ed student. He was a good mechanic, but couldn't do other simple things. If he was thirsty, he might easily pay you $50 for a can of pop. Willie painted and did landscaping work for a couple of years, but living at home at 21, was still under his father's thumb. Eddie barked orders at him incessantly. Machelle also said her father beat Willie frequently, though he was 5-foot-10, pushing 180, his biceps swollen from landscaping work. The description reminded Anne of Lenny in the Steinbeck classic, *Of Mice and Men*.

Ed Sexton also had plenty of outside muscle, Otis said. He dismissed claims that Eddie had made that he knew people in the mafia. But he did believe in the existence of a henchman, a former cellmate he called "The Ice Man." Anne had heard Machelle talk about the man, how her father would threaten to call him to kill people. Otis said Eddie once offered to contract the thug to kill the wife of his brother Dave.

Anne Greene thought, what kind of people am I dealing with here?

It didn't surprise her when she learned Otis was keeping a close eye on Machelle. Machelle complained to Anne that he kept her restricted to the house. Otis told Anne he was worried for her safety. Ed Sexton wasn't above snuffing one of his own, he said.

One night Anne got a call from Otis. Upset with his house rules, Machelle had left his home. She'd moved in with a girl she'd met in a women's shelter, now living in Brewster, a small town south of Massilon.

Then Machelle called Anne. "I had the feeling something was going on that she wouldn't tell me," Anne would recall later. "I had the feeling she was going to be involved in drugs, or turning tricks."

Anne and Gerry sped to Brewster. They called Machelle from a local store. She agreed to meet them there, and came walking up the street a few minutes later. She was wearing tight black shorts and a tank top. She looked like she hadn't had a bath in days.

"You've got to come home," Anne pleaded. "You're going to screw up your life here."

Machelle said, "But I like it here."

A couple of days later, when Anne could no longer reach her by phone, she and Gerry returned to Brewster. This time local police accompanied them. They arrived at two in the morning, figuring that was the best hour to catch Machelle at home. Police knocked on the door, then told Machelle, "There's people here who want to take you home."

The roommate came outside, screaming, "Don't go with them. They don't love you."

Now Machelle wanted to go.

Anne and Otis Sexton shared responsibility for Machelle. But Anne also was concerned about her own family's security. Otis would drive Machelle to a McDonald's in Canton. Anne would pick her up there. She stayed with the Greenes on weekends. They'd chat, paint nails, go to church on Sunday. Anne arranged for Machelle to see a psychotherapist who specialized in abused children. As it turned out, the psychologist, Robin Tener, would also be used by the Family Court to evaluate other Sexton kids.

But Anne Greene couldn't shake the feeling that the Sexton family would one day find her. Otis called her one day, saying he'd seen the Ice Man's car in a store parking lot. Soon, Anne was getting hang-up calls at her home. She began noticing dilapidated cars cruising past her house. She'd heard Machelle's family had several cars. Someone would tell her: A '78 black Grand Prix. An old, two-tone yellow Chevy van. A mid-'80s Ford Custom. But she didn't know cars. And Machelle had said the family had connections with a chop shop and stolen vehicles.

Anne didn't know if she was just paranoid, or if there was a real threat.

By early spring, the new goal was to make sure Machelle

graduated from high school. She'd been in four different schools since she'd left home. Now she was completing her studies with McKinley High School in Canton. Anne had met with an assistant principal, explaining Ed Sexton's threats. McKinley allowed her to finish her classes through a correspondence course.

Machelle began calling Anne "Mom," and Gerry "Dad." And Machelle wanted to be called by a new name. No longer Machelle, but Shelly. A new name for a new life, she said.

Shelly sent Anne a Mother's Day card with a poem inside:

> The days ending.
> The night is near.
> I live for freedom.
> I run from fear.
> I have some love,
> Some love to give away.
> Will you be the one to take it from me?
> And hope for me that someday I will be free.

On May 9, the night before Mother's Day, Anne received another call from Timken Mercy Medical Center. Machelle had been brought there by Canton police, she said. Machelle had given the nurse Anne's number and name.

Anne and Gerry found her behind curtains in the emergency room, detained on a bed with leather restraints. Machelle was livid.

"Take off these straps," she screamed.

Anne began stroking her hair, calming her.

She'd run away from Otis's house, she said. He didn't allow her to use the phone or visit friends, she complained. She couldn't go outside, even sit on the porch. He made her do housework. He'd had her apply for general assistance welfare, then cashed her checks. Otis Sexton seemed to have evoked too many reminders of Shelly's life in the house on Caroline Street. She'd been brought into the hospital after Canton police had stopped to question her on the street, and she'd gone into a rage.

Anne talked to an internist. But in minutes, Shelly was calling for her again.

"Over there," she whispered urgently. "That man, over there."

Sitting on a chair in the emergency room was a friend of her father's, she said. Anne walked over to the reception desk and questioned a nurse. The man had shown up just after the Greenes arrived, claiming he'd hurt his leg.

Anne thought, my Lord, we're being followed.

She hustled into a nurse's office and called the Canton police. Soon she was speaking to a detective.

"Maybe you should just leave town for a little while," he said.

She went back to Shelly's bed and explained. Maybe it was best they not see each other for a little while. She'd keep in touch with Shelly by telephone.

"You can make them let me go," Shelly said. "You're my mom. You can make them let me go home."

No, they had to keep her the night for observation. Anne looked at the clock. It was past midnight.

"Happy Mother's Day," her husband said.

Two days later, they left town for two weeks and stayed at her mother's in Alabama. Her husband wrote a letter to detective Glenn Goe, informing him what happened. Anne kept in touch with Shelly by phone.

They returned to Canton in time for Shelly's graduation ceremony. The break seemed to bolster Anne Greene's courage.

Plus, she missed Shelly.

"You've got to understand, I loved this girl," she would later recall.

Anne took Shelly to Belden Village Mall to buy her a graduation dress. As they approached an escalator, Machelle froze momentarily. She stared at the moving stainless stairway in awe, then had to ride it up and down several times.

"That's when it really hit me," Anne would later say. "It would be like me seeing the Eiffel Tower for the first time. She'd never seen an escalator before."

They found her a light blue dress. At home, Anne gave her a necklace of her own. Machelle's eyes brightened like she'd been given the Hope Diamond, though it was only imitation pearl.

A few days later, Machelle Lynn Sexton graduated with 300 other McKinley seniors, but not without some effort. Prior to the ceremony, Otis Sexton called school officials. He was worried about auditorium security. At first they suggested she not attend the ceremony, then agreed to work out a plan.

As graduates marched out of the auditorium, Machelle darted out of the line, removing her cap and gown. Two security guards hustled her out the back door, where Otis waited in an idling car.

Anne and Gerry met up with her again at a small reception at one of Otis's daughters. There were only a couple of cousins there. No big party like those in Jackson High School, where parents pitched backyard tents so proud graduates could snag cards with cash and party into the night with their friends.

There was only a cake inscribed, "Congratulations Machelle."

They took pictures, several with Machelle clinging to Anne's husband Gerry as if he were the proud parent.

Shelly had written him recently: "I always dreamed about having a father like you . . ."

Anne Greene thought, this all is so very sad.

6

The day in late July had been planned this way: Otis Sexton would take Machelle to her late morning appointment with the psychologist, then drop by the North American Indian Culture Center for another meeting. A counselor there named Melton Fletcher had called him. He wanted to interview both he and his niece about May Sexton's Indian heritage claim.

Machelle was upset when she left the appointment with Robin Tener. She wanted her to write down some of her emotions, Shelly later would recall.

"I didn't want to dredge it all up again," she said. "I was sick of it. I wanted to forget it. And that's all Uncle Otie ever talked about."

As they drove to the Indian center in Akron, Otis Sexton knew what he'd tell the Indian official. He did not believe May had Indian blood, and certainly not Eddie, as he sometimes claimed. Otis knew about his side of the family. The Sextons were English. His mother Lana Toler was from West Virginia. His father William Dewey Sexton was born in Pike County, Kentucky. His grandmother's maiden name was Reynolds. Both sides were old southern families.

Otis had also heard Eddie and May talk about her side of the family. Just a year ago Eddie was bragging that he and May had found May's real mother. Years ago, when May's father was stationed in Texas, the family had a Mexican housekeeper. May said her father had an affair with the housekeeper and that she was really the housekeeper's daughter. Her father and legal mother had adopted her when she was born.

"Eddie and May claimed she was coming up to visit them in Ohio," Otis would later recall. "But as far as I know she never came."

When Otis and Shelly arrived at the cultural center, Mel Fletcher wasn't there. Otis talked for 20 minutes with Clark Hosik, the center's director.

Then Mel Fletcher arrived. He took Otis and Shelly into his office, leaving the door open.

"He told us straight out," Otis later recalled. "He said, 'My objective is to get this family back together.'"

Otis thought, Eddie and May must have spoon-fed this guy a real bill of goods.

Otis heard someone shuffling outside. He turned around and saw May Sexton and her son Patrick sitting in the hall outside. Otis jumped to his feet. We've been set up, he thought. Later he found out from Patrick that Fletcher had just been to May's house. He accused Fletcher of taking sides.

"You realize you're in violation of a court order?" he shouted.

Technically, Fletcher was not. But Family Court Judge Julie Edwards later confirmed she had not assigned the staff at the center to assume any sort of counseling role. It was only to research heritage. Counseling was in the hands of the DHS.

Otis stormed down to director Hosik's office to complain.

Later, Machelle was crying as they drove away. Otis still was furious. He was yelling about Fletcher. Then he yelled about May, when he found out she'd talked to Shelly in the hall. Machelle Sexton thought he was yelling at her.

"It was as if the parents were saying, we can find you Shelly when we want to," Otis later would say. "They were sending her a message."

That night, another message apparently was sent.

Otis and Jackie were in their bed, Shelly in her upstairs bedroom, when suddenly glass began shattering on the back staircase. The barrage of rocks came through two back windows just below Shelly's bedroom. Otis ran to the window, but saw no one. The family basset hound, normally a noisy watchdog, hadn't even barked.

"That's got to be someone we know," said Otis.

The next morning at breakfast, he announced, "That's it. We've got to do something."

He began writing out a leaflet by hand, later taking it up to a local copying machine. He planned on heading to the Family Court building in downtown Canton. Shelly didn't want to go, but offered to make the picket signs.

She printed: "Arrest Child Abusers" on white poster board.

It was Tuesday, July 21. Otis called up his sister Nellie. Jackie joined them as well. Soon all three were walking in a small circle outside the Citizens Building, Otis shoving the leaflets in people's hands. It gave a brief description of the Sexton case and concluded:

"What has the law done? NOTHING."

And, "Join me to help stop abuse."

Dave Knox, a reporter for the Akron *Beacon Journal,* happened to be walking by the courthouse. He saw the little demonstration and stopped by to listen to Otis Sexton's story.

Knox faced a considerable reporting obstacle. Family Court proceedings were sealed by the court. His newspaper did not print the names of minors in such cases. Knox called Jackson police and DHS officials for comment. Detective Glenn Goe said his investigation had been turned over to DHS officials because minors were involved. But he had an angle with the Indian claim.

His story appeared two days later, headlined: INDIAN HERITAGE CLAIM VEXES STARK COURT. It reported the heritage claim by a "Jackson Township" couple facing child abuse charges, but did not include the Sexton name.

By the time the story appeared, Otis and Shelly's relationship was deteriorating quickly. She resented having guards hustle her out of her graduation. That was not *normal,* she groused. She didn't like the idea she had to do dishes. She'd called Jackie a "bitch" a couple of times in recent weeks.

Jackie Sexton was hurt by the words. When she first moved in, Machelle didn't know basic feminine hygiene. She taught her niece how to keep herself clean, how to keep her hair smooth and untangled. Her own daughters took the girl shopping, paying for a new wardrobe.

"Machelle," Otis said.

"It's Shelly," she snapped back.

"Shelly, I'll not have you call my wife that."

What Otis Sexton didn't know were the words May Sexton had spoken to her daughter two days earlier in the hallway of the Indian cultural center.

"She told me that she missed me and that she loved me," Shelly would later recall. "God, it was the first time in my life she'd ever said that to me."

That evening, Jackie and Otis finished supper. Shelly hadn't joined them. Jackie asked her to do the dishes. Shelly complained, if she didn't eat, why should she do the damn dishes?

Otis was on his way up the stairs when he heard his niece say, "That bitch."

He slapped her once in the face.

"You know, later I really regretted it," Otis would later say. "But we were all under a lot of pressure. It was just one of those momentary reactions."

Machelle Sexton stomped down the stairs and walked out the front door.

Otis watched her from his porch.

She was walking down 15th Street, her handbag swinging in her hand.

7

Melton Fletcher had worked in Indian affairs since the federal government began helping Native Americans relocate from reservations to urban areas in the 1950s. Half Choctaw, an Oklahoma tribe, he'd been a licensed social worker at the cultural center since 1978. He was 70 years old.

Fletcher had investigated scores of claims from people purporting to be Indians. The status often meant federal assistance and special rights under treaty law. Ed Sexton wasn't the first con man he'd dealt with who claimed to be of Indian blood.

"He was a wheeler dealer," Fletcher would later say. "He was a manipulator, all the way."

Both Sexton and his wife were maintaining they were Cherokee. Fletcher had traced the lineage of each and found none of their relatives listed in Cherokee Nation records in the Minneapolis office of the federal Bureau of Indian Affairs.

Later, Fletcher would recall making an appearance before Family Court Judge Julie Edwards. Ed Sexton rolled into court that day in a wheelchair. Fletcher had talked with Sexton four times previously, but he'd never shown any sign of disability. Fletcher said he told the court that the family had no record of Native American blood.

But on July 23, the same day Machelle Sexton walked away from Otis Sexton's house, it appears that Mel Fletcher had assumed a different role.

Machelle had walked to a local liquor store and called her mother at the house on Caroline Street.

"She told me she was divorcing my father, that she was going to get all the kids back," Machelle later recalled. "She kept telling me she loved me."

Machelle told her that her uncle had slapped her.

"I'm going to send someone to get you," May Sexton said.

Soon a car arrived at the store. In it were Mel Fletcher and a friend he'd brought along for company.

In a later interview, Fletcher would acknowledge that he knew the family dynamics, the rape allegations, some of the charges of abuse. Yet, he took Machelle Sexton back to the house on Caroline. The only explanation he could offer was: "We have to, as a social worker, comply, as long as that person is not in danger."

But Machelle Sexton clearly could be in danger. Ed Sexton was still living there.

Clark Hosik, the center's director, later would try to explain. "The only thing I can recall of the situation is Mel felt really bad for the kids and he wanted to help them. Once you get into that mode of trying to keep families together, well, he didn't realize the depth of the problems there."

As Fletcher drove toward Jackson Township, his companion Barbara Booth looked in the backseat and said, "I think we have a problem." She appeared to be having a seizure.

When they reached the house on Caroline Street, Fletcher noticed two boys fishing down by the pond. One was Patrick Sexton, the other his cousin, Willard. Patrick approached the car and looked in.

"Oh, it's just Shelly," Patrick said.

Later Patrick recalled, "She looked like she was faking it. Her eyes fluttering and all that."

. May Sexton came out, peeking in the car. Fletcher suggested the mother call an ambulance.

"It was pretty unbelievable," Barbara Booth would later recall. "The mother didn't even seem to react. Here was this girl, out of it, and she was talking about what a nice day it was outside."

EMS records would later show the ambulance arrived at
8:38 p.m. Machelle told paramedics she'd been struck and
thrown up against a wall by her uncle. She'd been throwing
up, she said.

But months later, Machelle Sexton would say the real
reason she was ill was an anxiety attack. "I kept thinking
on the way over, am I doing the right thing? I knew something was wrong. My mother was saying she loved me, and
she just never said that."

The paramedics loaded Machelle onto a stretcher.
Fletcher later claimed he told EMS workers to make sure
she got into a group home after the hospital. But there
was no mention of those instructions on the EMS records.

They took Machelle to Massillon Community Hospital
where she was examined.

When she was released, May Sexton was waiting to take
her home.

8

The affidavit made its way to Jackson police and DHS
attorneys. It was hand-written and signed, notarized on
September 1, 1992, and read:

> I Shelly Sexton of 8149 Caroline . . . do here by (sic)
> state that I did not make any of the allegations that
> was (sic) brought against my father. To have the
> younger kids taken from the home, my uncle was
> talking to the kids one by one in his bedroom. He
> told them to say they will get to come home soon.
> My uncle is doing this because he is jealous of my
> father and always will be.

Simply, Machelle Sexton had recanted. She'd lived with
her mother a month, then moved in with Pixie and Joel

in Bolivar, then left there after her father ordered Pixie to put her out. Now she was living with one of her women's shelter friends.

Later, Shelly would explain what happened.

Her first night home, she'd slept in her mother's bedroom. Her father had moved out the day she came home. May Sexton also was telling the DHS that her husband had moved out. She'd told her oldest son Patrick they were getting divorced.

But Machelle feared her father would return to the house.

Her mother asked her if it was true. Had her father raped her?

"Yes," she said.

"She said, 'Machelle, I love you. I'm glad you did what you did. Now I just want to get you kids back.'"

She moved back into her own bedroom. But voices downstairs woke her a couple nights later. She came down the stairs into the dark living room. Above her father's chair, she saw the glow of a cigarette.

"That's when I knew my mother had lied to me. She was still seeing him. He sat there for a minute, then it began. What he always said: 'Girls disappear every day.' 'We put you on this earth. We can take you off.'"

Ed Sexton gestured toward the pond and said, "Machelle, there's a lot of lake out there."

Machelle recalled, "I had no place to stay. I had nowhere to go."

He came every night, not always after midnight. Sometimes he brought dinner for her mother, meals he'd picked up or cooked at the camper. Willie picked him up. Other times he'd bring his own car, parking it in the closed garage.

Her father composed the notarized letter, she said. Her mother handed it to her and asked her to copy it exactly in her own handwriting. Then her mother drove her down to the office of her attorney, Pat Menicos.

"I just sat there," she said. "He asked me if I wanted to say anything. I just shook my head, no."

9

Detective Glenn Goe went to the Massillon prosecutor's office with his file on Machelle Sexton's rape. He had no physical evidence, no medical exam and no direct corroborating testimony, he told an assistant prosecutor. He had a good polygraph. But, one more thing, he'd heard the victim had recanted.

"Not a chance," the city attorney said.

The entire DHS case also was in jeopardy. With the Indian issue resolved, a hearing was scheduled at the end of September to decide the custody of the Sexton children. Judee Genetin's staff scrambled to amend the language of their complaint, saying Shelly had alleged abuse, but later recanted.

Otis Sexton told everyone he wasn't buying the news that Eddie had actually left May. He suspected it was a ploy to get the children back. He knew Eddie liked to take the family camping in the summer in an old Winnebago the family once owned.

Otis drove up to Portage Lake State Park, in Medina County near Akron. He'd heard Eddie had borrowed a camping trailer from his brother Orville, who lived in Canton. At the campground he spotted his older brother's trailer. Willie was at the sink in the window. Eddie's two-tone yellow van was outside.

He called Wayne Welsh. Despite his protest, DHS workers were starting see Otis as a valuable source. Ed Sexton had left Stark County, all right, he said, but he was only 10 minutes from home.

"How did you know he was there?" the social worker asked.

"I know Eddie," Otis said.

Social workers started checking on the house.

Genetin would later recall, "Mom and dad were playing the system. Now, we believed they weren't following the no-contact order, but we couldn't prove it, even though we were sending people out there all hours of the day and night to see if dad was there."

At the September 28 hearing, May Sexton told the court she'd been in therapy, and that her own counselor had recommended some of her children be returned. Based on the fact that Christopher and Kimberly had denied all allegations of abuse and the father was out of the home, Judge Julie Edwards returned the two children to the mother. She also awarded May Sexton custody of Charles. He was nearly 18, and still being reported as "on the run" by the DHS.

Four days later, Judee Genetin was back in court. DHS staff had spoken to May Sexton's counselor. He said he'd recommended no such thing. The mother had not attended enough sessions, the counselor said. But Judge Edwards stuck by her decision. With the father out of the home, any prior threat was minimized, she said.

"The judge was going to send somebody home," Genetin would later recall. "Basically, the court told us that mom appears to be doing what she's supposed to do— seeing a counselor, not having contact with dad. And nobody is really saying mom is the bad actor. Dad is the bad actor. Mom is protecting them. Mom wants her children back. We're going to reward Mom for what she's doing, and who do you want it to be?

"So my choice was Kimberly and Christopher. They hadn't disclosed, so they, one, weren't going to get in trouble if Dad was in fact there. Two, they did not appear to have been abused. From everything we were gathering, the mother seemed to protect them, in fact."

Soon, Charles "Skipper" Sexton returned from Indiana,

moving back in with his mother. Then, a month after the hearing, social workers found themselves investigating a new referral. Lana Sexton, while in foster care, was attending a sex abuse victim group. In a therapy session, she'd disclosed that Charles had raped her in the bathroom of the family home.

A social worker named Tracey Harlin was assigned to investigate. She interviewed Lana, age 12. Lana said she was worried about Skipper being home with her younger sister, Kimberly, age 8. Skipper liked to play a sex game she called "The Statue of Liberty Game."

Skipper raped her, she said. James and Matthew had witnessed it, watching from a ladder, looking in the bathroom window. She said her mother had beaten Skipper when her brothers told her about the assault. It was consistent with accounts given months ago.

Harlin asked Lana about abuse by her father.

Lana Sexton lost all expression on her face and her eyes went blank. Then the girl began to digress. She started talking about demonic movies, Satanic rituals, voodoo dolls, and candles.

Then she mentioned an upside-down cross and her father in a hooded robe.

10

Three days later, Tracey Harlin interviewed Kimberly, now 8, at school. She'd not been abused, she said. No, she hadn't seen her father.

Harlin noted: "Kim was quiet and appeared very non-trusting and gave smooth answers like she had been coached."

Later that day, Harlin and James Sexton showed up at the Jackson Township Police Department. James was 16 and in his junior year at a high school near his foster home. The DHS wanted to document his witness statement with police. If Charles Sexton had indeed raped Lana, Skipper would face criminal charges as well. Before the interview, Harlin told Detective Glenn Goe that James—the boy who'd been locked in the dark room as an infant—suffered from autism.

Goe put the interview on tape.

James said Skipper's assault on Lana had taken place two months before they were all removed from the home.

"How did you find out about this to begin with?" Goe asked.

"Well, I heard about it," James said. "I heard everybody talking about it. I knew about it. Then my mom beat him up for it."

"What did she do?"

"Bent him over a sink and started scratching him, punching him, slapping him. Choking him."

"Did you see Skipper rape your sister?"

"No."

"Do you think he did?"

"Probably . . . My sister was crying when she told my dad."

"Did Lana ever tell you?"

"Yeah. She said he stuck his wiener up her butt."

Goe asked, "Did Skipper ever do anything like that to you?"

"Yes."

"When was that?"

"About two months before foster care."

"What happened?"

"He asked me to come upstairs for a couple minutes while I was watching television. I went up there. He says, 'I'll offer you this watch if you lay on the bed and let me do something to you.' I laid down on the bed. He told me to pull down my pants. Then he got on top of me and raped me."

"What did he do?"

"He stuck his wiener up my butt."

"Did you want this to happen to you?"

James eyes widened. "No," he said. For a brief second anger crept into his voice. It was the only emotion he would show during the entire session.

James said Skipper raped Christopher later that night. He witnessed it, he said. Christopher didn't seem to put up a struggle. Chris later denied what happened to James.

"He said I was imagining things," James said.

"Why would he say that?" Goe asked.

"Because I was a little bit retarded, he thought I was seeing things."

Goe asked him about the "State of Liberty Game."

James explained, "Charles was standing up like the Statue of Liberty. He went downstairs, got my two sisters, came back up. Stand again. And he let my two sisters suck his wiener."

"When was that?"

"A couple of years ago."

"Which two sisters?"

"Lana and Kimberly."

"Did he make them do that?"

"No."

"How did he get them to do that?"

"He just asked them."

One of the sisters told their father and Skipper was "whupped."

They talked about beatings of all the children. Goe began confirming details Machelle Sexton had told him before she recanted. Goe wondered why the children always denied problems in the home when they were questioned by social workers.

"Because my dad had a surprise planned," James said.

"Like what?"

"We was going to go to Disneyland."

But the trip never happened, he said.

That same afternoon, DHS returned to Family Court with the new charges by Lana and James. Judge Edwards gave the custody of Charles back to the DHS, but then permitted May Sexton to send her son to an aunt's house in Orville, Ohio. Charles Sexton was to have no contact with any of the children while the investigation continued, she ruled.

Glenn Goe also attended the hearing. He and Tracey Harlin spoke with May Sexton after the hearing. She said James's story was a fabrication. She said, yes, she'd slapped Skipper, for saying dirty words.

"Could you bring Charles in so I could talk to him?" Goe asked. Tracey Harlin wanted to interview him as well.

"Yes," May Sexton said.

When they didn't show up that afternoon at the police department, Goe called May Sexton at home. She'd hired an attorney for her son, she said. The lawyer didn't want Charles giving any statements. She was taking him to his aunt's.

Later, May Sexton told the DHS that complications forced her to send Skipper to her brother's near Jeffersonville, Indiana. At the time, the DHS was not aware that it was the same place he'd stayed while he was on the run.

Eight days later, on Tuesday, November 17, social workers couldn't locate May Sexton or her children. Bonita Hilson called Skipper in Indiana. He said he hadn't seen his mother since he left home. He had no idea where she was. Later, the DHS asked police in Clark County to drop by the uncle's house and confirm he was indeed there.

That same day, a staffer from Jackson Middle School called. Christopher hadn't been in school all week, and most of last week.

That afternoon, Bonita Hilson drove over to the house on Caroline Street. No one was home. She left a note on the door addressed to "Mrs. Sexton." She dated it and noted the time at 3:25 p.m.

"Please call me tomorrow. It is important," it read.

11

A half hour before lunch an assistant assignment editor named Julie Cairelli took the call in the newsroom of Channel 5, a Cleveland station. It was Saturday, November 21, four days after Bonita Hilson had left her note.

"I'm tired of being harassed," said the caller.

He identified himself as Ed Sexton, of Jackson Township.

Ed Sexton said he was being harassed by the Department of Human Services and its children protection workers over bogus allegations. Every newsroom routinely received complaints from citizens facing problems with local, state, and federal bureaucracies. Some were transferred to reporters to investigate. Others were dismissed by editors on the spot, determined groundless or not newsworthy.

Ed Sexton offered an instant news angle. He was barricaded with his wife and children in his home in Jackson Township, he said. He believed social workers were coming to take away his son.

"I've got weapons," he said. "I'll kill any worker or police that pulls into my drive."

Then he hung up.

Cairelli called Jackson Township Police. She'd report Sexton's call then have a reporter keep in touch with the department all day.

Inside the house on Caroline Street, Ed Sexton was ready for battle. Earlier in the week, he and his son Willie had gone to Indiana to pick up Charles after police visited the house there, looking for Skipper. Charles later said they'd returned to Ohio and spent a couple of days in a Canton motel.

"My dad was saying we got to get those kids back," Skipper later recalled. "Me and Willy and my dad, we came up with some schemes for the standoff. So we loaded up the car. Got a bunch of chicken wire, started getting weapons. Canned food. We had food out the ass. A big-ass propane stove. I mean, we was ready."

The plan, as Charlie would recall it, was to force DHS to give all the children back to May Sexton. Then, Sexton would continue living away from home, but return on Christmas, pick up his family and flee the state. He said he had friends in the Mafia. They could get them new identities and jobs. But he wouldn't be taking James, he told Charlie and Willie. He was going to tape James up in the basement and leave him there to starve to death for talking to authorities.

Sexton and his sons prepared the house like suddenly besieged characters in *The Night of the Living Dead*. They jammed mattresses and furniture against the entrance doors. They hoisted heavy tabletops over the picture windows, then drove spikes into the trim. When they ran out of tables, they pulled interior doors off their hinges. They covered one window with maple kitchen cabinet doors. They used the chicken wire for the shooting positions. They stapled the wire across small windows, then hung black garbage bags over them so police snipers wouldn't get a profile from inside lights. They piled the cans of spaghetti, liters of soda, and boxes of dry goods in the den, just under the eagle on Ed Sexton's Airborne flag.

Ed Sexton took a position at a window at the kitchen counter. The house on a hill, he had the high ground and a view of his driveway and Caroline Street. He had a Remington 20-gauge pump with two boxes of deer-hunting slugs. In his pants, he tucked a stainless Taurus .357 revolver. He had five dozen rounds. He placed the boxes and shells on the counter next to a large ashtray and a clipboard with a yellow legal pad.

Skipper Sexton also maintained later that both he and

Willie had pistols and pump shotguns. They were standing guard from the windows above the kitchen, he said.

By 11:40 a.m., two Jackson patrolman in cruisers were dispatched, but they didn't go to the house on Caroline Street. They met at a Dairy Mart on Wales Avenue, a few hundred yards from the property. Instead of approaching the house and possibly drawing gunfire, they used the store pay phone to call the house.

Estella May Sexton answered. Yes, it was true her husband had weapons, she said. He was angry that DHS was planning to pick up her kids.

"Can I talk with Mr. Sexton?" a patrolman asked.

"He won't come to the phone," she said.

The patrolman was able to get from May Sexton the name of the family's personal lawyer. Detective Glenn Goe arrived. He called a worker at child protective services. There was no pick-up order for Sexton children, she said, only the no-contact order already in place for weeks.

A Jackson police captain named Steve Zerby arrived.

"I know Ed Sexton," he said. "Hell, I used to cut his hair."

Zerby had been a barber before he got into police work 22 years before. Zerby fed coins into the pay phone. Somebody would pick up at the Sexton house, then hang up. Zerby called one of Sexton's attorneys who also placed a call to the house.

Zerby talked to May Sexton, asking, does he have weapons?

"Yes," she said.

"Do you think he'll hurt you or the kids?"

"I don't know," she said.

Zerby moved a couple of cruisers to Caroline Street, then went back to the police department where he could try to negotiate with Ed Sexton without having to feed the pay phone.

Sexton finally got on the line.

"It's the system against me and my family," Sexton said.

"They've already taken some of my kids. But they're not going to take Charlie."

It was mid afternoon. Channel 5 still hadn't dispatched a news crew. Zerby decided to make that work for him.

"You know, we're going to have TV stations down here pretty soon," he said. "You're going to have cameras all over, and that's going to be reflected when you go to court. And you will have to go to court, Ed. The smart thing is to handle it in a quiet manner."

Eventually, Sexton began talking about making a deal. He wanted a letter from child protective services that he and his wife would get the kids back now. Zerby passed it on to an on-call worker at DHS. A few minutes later, Judee Genetin walked into Zerby's office.

The negotiations continued for three more hours. Finally, Sexton took Genetin's latest offer. She'd write a letter stipulating that she would remove social worker Bonita Hilson from the case. She would promise not to remove Christopher and Kimberly from the home at this time.

At 6 o'clock, it was already dark when Steve Zerby walked up to the house, floodlights illuminating the driveway, the small square window of Sexton's shooting perch looming just over the captain's head. Channel 5 had just arrived.

Charles "Skipper" Sexton later claimed he and his brothers had two handguns aimed right at Zerby. "I thought I was gonna shoot somebody. You know, my adrenaline was built . . . I was pissed. And then Captain Zerby comes out . . . I thought it was going to be a little fight at least. The old man walks right out. Damn. What the fuck's going on? I mean, if I heard a firecracker or something, Captain Zerby was through. [Or] just shoot a couple times. That's fun—not shooting people. I mean just shooting a gun. It gives you a rush. It's a fun sport."

Sexton and Zerby walked out together. Police would find only a 20-gauge Remington pump and a .357 Taurus revolver, the serial number ground off, considerably less than the arsenal Charles later claimed.

Sexton was cuffed and put in a squad car, his long fingers wrapped around one of any jail's most precious commodities. Two cartons of Camels.

Charles Sexton would later say he and his brother Chris went out that night and beat up a couple of teenage boys on Wales. They needed to blow off steam, he said.

Ed Sexton would be taken first to a county crisis center, then jail, after a psychiatric examination showed he was mentally sound. While he waited for transport in the Jackson Township police station, a Channel 5 crew interviewed him. He claimed DHS was framing him.

Asked why he'd barricaded himself in the house, he said: "I just had to do something. And that was the only thing I could do."

The reporter asked if he'd ever molested his children. Sexton smiled, his eyes twinkling. "No," he said.

Detective Glenn Goe also sat Sexton down for an interview. He wanted to ask him about Shelly's original complaint and Charles's alleged assaults on Lana and James. He read Sexton his rights, then asked him to sign a form acknowledging Goe had read them.

Sexton wouldn't sign the form.

"Can't we talk, Mr. Sexton?" Goe asked.

"Not without my attorney," Sexton said.

The TV station also interviewed Judee Genetin. But the most troubling questions would come much later, the ones she would ask herself.

Letter or no letter, she could have had Christopher, Kimberly, and Charles taken into police custody after Sexton was led away. Then, she could have filed for custody of the children on Monday. After all, Ed Sexton had violated the court's no-contact order by going to the home. And Charles Sexton was to have no contact with minor children as well. Instead, Genetin had decided to leave the kids with May Sexton. Eddie would be in jail, she reasoned. And the kids had faced enough trauma for one night.

"That was the one mistake I've felt guilty about," Genetin would later say. "I could kick myself. As I look back at all my years with the department, it was the biggest mistake I ever made."

Within days, the family would begin to disappear.

vi
Wings

1

The standoff pushed the Sexton story into the stream of news coverage in central Ohio. But Ed Sexton's flirtation with fame quickly began to fade.

One of the last stories appeared December 1, 10 days after the standoff, in the Akron *Beacon Journal,* headlined: ABDUCTION CHARGE IS DISMISSED.

Eddie L. Sexton, Sr., a 50-year-old Jackson Township man, the Tuesday story went, pled no contest yesterday in Massilon Municipal Court. He was convicted of two misdemeanors, child endangering and inducing panic. Judge Eugene M. Fellmeth dismissed the felony abduction charge because police couldn't find Sexton's wife or three children to testify. Fellmeth sentenced Sexton to 180 days in jail and $100 in court costs, but then suspended the jail term, putting Sexton on probation. Sexton got out of jail three days before his hearing by posting a $7,500 bond. The probation stipulated Sexton stay away from his family and workers employed by the DHS.

A Monday edition of the Canton *Repository* carried an interview with Sexton, given before his court hearing. The patriarch denied all abuse and called for Ohio governor George Voinovich to look into his case. "I'm going to stomp the streets and get someone to listen," he said.

Just a week before sentencing, two days after the standoff, DHS legal chief Judee Genetin had rethought her decision and gone once more to Family Court, seeking a hearing to return DHS custody of Kimberly, Christopher, and Charles. May Sexton left a phone message for Genetin, saying she'd see her at the hearing the next day. She didn't show up. Jackson police had been looking for May and her children all week.

In the *Repository* story, Sexton was outright defiant. He announced that he'd told his wife to flee the Canton area.

"I said, 'Go, put your wings around them and go,'" he said. "She's a loving mother. She wants no harm to come to them. She wants to protect them from going back to foster care and going through this again."

TV coverage on Channel 5 also sought out the family's reactions. One report featured an interview with Eddie Sexton, Jr., the namesake sitting on the couch with his wife Daniela and two children.

"It's a good family," he told viewers. "There's nothing wrong with our family. They've got to be making it up . . . because I've never seen anything out of the way when I lived in the house."

The Sexton family was not without silent support and public indifference. May Sexton got a few support letters from other families accused by the DHS. Nobody reading the papers knew the details. The DHS and police weren't revealing most of what they knew about the family's secrets. And bizarre child abuse stories were coming under increasing scrutiny by the national press.

Awareness of the problems surrounding abuse cases was at an all-time high nationwide. Stories were airing on networks about innocent teachers and family members imprisoned by junk science, including memory regression and incessant interviewing of suggestible young children. A study showed children often made up allegations to please their interviewers. Some experts likened the prosecution of "ritual" abuse cases to a collective hysteria not all that different from the Salem witch trials.

There was no such outcry in Stark County. It was Thanksgiving week, the papers soon filling with ads for local Christmas sales. Belden Village sparkled with smart decorations. Downtown brightened a little, but still looked old and tired.

The charges also may have lacked public impact simply because all the victims were among the Sexton's own. The Sextons, originally from West Virginia, were what some locals called "ridge runners." For years, people had been migrating from one of America's poorest states to central Ohio for jobs at Timken, Hoover, and Akron's rubber plants. Some landed work, others a spot on the welfare roll. The poorest lived in the dilapidated shingle-sided houses a few blocks from the Canton courthouse.

Some observers noticed that people didn't want to deal with confronting a universal human taboo. "Somehow, society seems to have granted victim status to everyone except victims of incest," *Beacon Journal* reporter Dave Knox would later say. "There's something about it being 'all in the family.' There's an element that it's somehow their fault."

Family Court Judge Julie Edwards later wondered if all the official secrecy in the juvenile court system somehow contributes. "There certainly doesn't need to be any more punishment for the victims. The intention is to spare the victim the embarrassment. But why should we? They're not the perpetrators. They've done nothing wrong. Maybe in our effort to protect their identities, we encourage the stigma, by keeping it secret."

By late 1992, the secrets—the ones kept by social workers and policeman—were actually working to Ed Sexton's advantage. If the public knew the detailed reports from the house on Caroline, it's doubtful the good people of Stark County would have stood by while Ed Sexton was released.

Judee Genetin later said she had called Captain Steve Zerby, stressing Sexton stay in jail. She'd also dispatched a staff attorney to the hearing. Somehow, the children's interests appeared to have been overlooked.

Part of the condition for probation was that Sexton stay away from his wife and children. Zerby thought the plea deal gave the police more leverage. Any contact and he could be arrested and jailed for contempt. "These hostage situations are not that uncommon in police work," Zerby would later say. "In this case, nobody knew the depth of the situation, other than a few accusations we had."

Detective Glenn Goe attended the hearing. He recalled that he wanted to see Sexton get a jail sentence. Though Machelle Sexton had recanted her charges, he said, the man had threatened DHS workers and cops.

Robert Zadell, the part-time assistant prosecutor for the Massilon Law Department who handled the case, would maintain police never demanded jail time, nor did anyone from the DHS. When they didn't have the witnesses for the felony, they cut a deal on the misdemeanors. It happens in American courts every day. "If somebody would have said jail, I would have said fine," Zadell later said. "But everyone who was there agreed."

Massilon Judge Eugene Fellmeth would later say he freed Sexton on the recommendation of the assistant prosecutor. "They're the ones that investigate the case," he'd tell the *Beacon Journal* months later. "I never question them if I think it's reasonable."

The final installment in the standoff story wouldn't even be covered by most news agencies. Days after the hearing, Ed, May, Christopher, Kimberly, and Charles would take flight from Stark County and the State of Ohio.

2

Teresa Boron did not subscribe to any of the local newspapers. She learned about the standoff from a Channel 5 report she saw the next day at the family machine shop. She watched Eddie Sexton, Jr. proclaiming his "good family."

One of the workers, a Jackson graduate, pointed at Eddie Jr. on the screen and said, "He must have forgot about all those times he came to school with black eyes."

Yes, Teresa had seen black eyes.

Only a month earlier, she was backing out of the shop driveway, heading to lunch, when she saw young men walking toward her in the car mirror, one of them very large.

"That's Pixie's brother, Willie," she wondered out loud. "But who's that with him, and what are they doing here?"

When she turned she recognized him.

God, it's Joey.

He had a scraggly beard, scraggly collar-length hair. Both of his eyes were black, blue, and purple, his cheeks and jaw swelled.

She jumped out, screaming, "What the hell have they done to you? Who did this to you?"

She glared at Willie Sexton.

"I'm all right," Joey said shyly.

Teresa began crying.

"Who did this?" she demanded, grabbing him by the shoulders.

"I don't know."

"Yes, you do."

She turned back to Willie. "Who did this to him?"

"A cousin," Willie said.

The story trickled out. Joey had called a paraplegic girl-friend of the cousin a "gimp," so the cousin beat him up.

She glared at Willie again. "What's the matter with your family? Why don't you just leave him alone?"

Joey put his arms around her, hugging her. "I'm all right," he kept saying. "I'm all right."

No, she thought. Joey would not call someone in a wheelchair "a gimp." She doubted he even knew the word.

"Where was Stella?" she asked. "What did your wife do, sit there and watch?"

He said Pixie had taken him to the hospital. "She was crying, too," Joey said.

Willie Sexton looked at her with earnest eyes. "I told him never to go around them again," he said, nodding. "Don't worry. I won't ever let anything happen to him again."

Now this, Teresa thought, looking at the TV again. The Sextons were making news.

3

Joel Good showed up hours later at his grandparents'. He was soaked to the skin, crying, and clutching a note. He said he'd walked 12 miles from Bolivar. Pixie had thrown him out of the car. She was on her way to visit her father in jail, he said.

"Why?" Lewis Barrick asked.

Joey said he'd asked his wife what she wanted for Christmas. Pixie's answer was in the note he still had in his hand. Word for word it read:

> Joel,
> What I want for Christmas is for you to leave me and the girls to start our life over and you go your way. Then maybe my family can get along with out (sic) you. Right now no one can do + say any thing you being there. Cause we don't know what you are "going" to do in the future. Are (sic) marriage *is* over any way. Which it has been for the past 2 months. Me + you don't get along + neither does the girls.

About the baby you can see it if you want but as far
as raising it I will raise it. I will raise it with the girls
myself. And what ever (sic) you do don't try any thing
(sic). Or your family better not try any thing (sic).
Because I have already talked to dad + his people +
they said any trouble just call + they will help me.

Love
Pixie

The next day, Teresa Boron took her nephew to an
attorney, telling him she'd be paying his legal bill. He'd
decided to file for divorce.

The entire family had suspected the marriage was in
trouble, their troubles beginning not long after the pregnant Pixie began to show. Joel had lost his driver's license
after ruining his uninsured car in an accident. Pixie had
been dropping Joel off to do laundry at his grandparents',
Pixie driving away in her mother's car. She'd leave Joey
with Shasta, telling everyone she was taking Dawn to the
doctor or running other errands. But often she didn't
return until late at night. Sometimes she didn't come back
at all.

"Where does she go?" his family asked him.

"I don't know," he'd say.

Teresa's brother Sam Barrick said one day, "I'll bet she's
seeing her dad still. I'll bet they still got something going
on."

But despite the visit to the divorce attorney, Joel still
defended Ed Sexton against the DHS. He seemed appalled
anyone had even accused his father-in-law of sexual abuse.

After Joel showed up at the Barricks' with the letter,
Teresa sped over to her parents', picked him up, and
brought him back to her house. It was Thanksgiving week.

Soon Teresa's mother was calling. Pixie kept phoning,
she told Teresa. Pixie said she and her brother Eddie Jr.
were trying to raise bail money for their father. They

needed Joel so they could get a security deposit back at a private campground in Bolivar called Bear Creek.

Gladys Barrick wanted to know why they needed her grandson.

Pixie said the camping spot was in Joel's name because he was the only one with a state ID.

"Don't think I'm stupid, Stella," Gladys shot back. "You don't need a state ID. You have a driver's license."

At the time, nobody but the Sextons knew that in September, Ed Sexton had also used Joel Good's name for camping permits at Portage Lakes. He'd also used Pixie's name and the aliases "Franklin" and "Sarah" Sexton to skirt the 14-day camping limit there. He was cited for alcohol in the campground and warned about litter. When rangers warned Sexton for exceeding the limit, he moved to Bear Creek.

After a couple of days, Joey wanted to go back to his grandparents'. Reluctantly, Teresa drove him back.

But by Thanksgiving weekend Teresa Boron was back in her car, looking for her nephew again.

Her father called, explaining what happened. Pixie had spoken to Joey on the phone. Joey asked his grandfather if he could drop him off at Canton Center Mall, where he planned to have a talk with Pixie. A couple of hours later Joey had called from the mall.

"Would you all hate me if I went back with Stella?" he said.

"I told him we didn't hate him, we were just worried about him," Lewis Barrick said.

Nobody had heard from him in a couple of days.

"I'm going to find him," Teresa said.

She recalled later, "I had a horrible feeling he was dead."

Teresa drove to his favorite haunts, then over to the house on Caroline Street. It looked dark and abandoned up on the hill. The handless Jesus waited by the walk, its stone eyes vacant.

She was too frightened to approach the door. She came back later with her husband. They pounded on the door for nearly a minute. When it opened, Pixie poked her head out. Then Joel stepped out.

"What are you doing?" his aunt asked.

"We want to work it out," he said.

Pixie said she'd moved into the house. Her parents were gone.

Teresa said, "If you want to work it out, fine. If you don't work it out, I'll be happy either way." She looked right at him. "Don't you ever do this again," she said. "Don't you ever leave and not tell anybody what you're doing. I thought you were dead in a ditch somewhere."

"Why?" he asked.

"The way they beat you up," she said. "They'll kill you next time."

4

May Sexton would later recall her version of the events surrounding the police standoff.

"Like I've told a lot of people, if they ever heard that Elvis song—you know, walk a mile in my shoes—then they'd know why. If they had the things said to them that were said to me, I didn't want anybody to get hurt. There's so many things that a woman can do now to get out of a situation like mine. I would have done it if I had known then.

"I told Eddie he'd have to get out because I wanted my kids back. Machelle came back, she and I sat down, and she told me about what her father did to her. She said Pixie said Dad had done the same thing to her, too. I said, 'Well, when was this all going on?' And she said, 'When he'd take us to the drugstore.'

"I was shocked, because Eddie didn't let on anything like that was going on. Well, the girls didn't either. And I couldn't understand why, you know, they didn't tell. Unless he was saying, 'I'm going to do this or that if you say anything.' I don't know. I don't know, you know, what was going on. But I believed her.

"But he was sneaking in the house, yeah. And I told him what was gonna happen [with the DHS] and he said, 'Nobody is going to find out.' I said, 'Well, what happened with the bigger ones isn't going to happen with the little ones.'

"When I was on Caroline, when I got custody back of the kids, he was accusing me of having an affair with Pat Menicos, who was my attorney.

"I didn't trust Eddie. I couldn't trust him anymore. In September, he threatened me with a gun while Shelly was there. I called Jackson Township police and they came and I was telling them and they said, well, we can't do anything about it, unless he was there and they seen something and all this stuff.

"The only reason Machelle recanted was because she was threatened by her dad. He asked her how long she was gonna stay with me and I said, 'She's going to stay as long as she wants to stay. You don't have anything to say about it.' He said, 'Well, she better be writing a statement that I didn't do anything to her because I'm not going to have lies told on me.'

"Well, I just wanted to get away from him. Because I had Kim and Chris and I didn't want to lose them over his stupidity—coming to the house all the time. He wanted me to meet him with the kids one night and I told him, 'I'm gonna call social services and have them come get the kids. You don't deserve them.' He told me I was going to pay for it.

"So we packed some things in the van, Chris, Kim, and I, and I went to Elizabethtown, Kentucky. I was gonna get in touch with my brother to help me find a place to hide from Eddie. And I was planning on calling social services. But the van broke. Something happened to the brakes. So

I called my daughter Pixie and asked her to wire me some money. But she let her dad know where I was.

"Eddie Jr. brought Eddie down in his van. They fixed my van and that's when we came back to Ohio, arguing all the way. He brought us back from Kentucky to a motel. And then Willie left in the morning, and when he came back, there were all kinds of wire and stuff in the back of the van. We went to the house and him and William started putting this wire and stuff all over the house.

"After they took Eddie to jail, I took off with the kids again. I moved to Eddie Jr.'s house. But Eddie Jr. wanted to get his father out of jail. He put his dad's rifle to my head, like his dad did, and threatened me if I didn't get him out of jail. He was drinking, and I was petrified. He wanted to sell my van for bail money.

"I wanted to get away from there. So the kids and I went and stayed with this black lady. I don't even remember her name. She'd been at our house before. It was the only place I could figure out to go because Pixie had my Pontiac. I was afraid of my son and afraid of Eddie. Eddie was always talking about, you know, he's got friends here and he's got friends there, and I was a nervous wreck.

"I didn't even know there was a [Family Court] hearing. We stayed with the black lady about a week because we were there Thanksgiving. She fixed Thanksgiving dinner for the kids.

"Then, Eddie [Sr.] come driving up in my Pontiac. And him and the black lady got into an argument. He owed her money, quite a bit, I guess. And he acted like he was gonna stay all night, but as soon as she went up to bed, that's, you know, when he told us to get into the car.

"We went to the Lincoln Motel and we stayed there. Pixie and Joel came there, something about switching the tires on the car. Eddie had a big envelope of money. I don't know where he got it. But it was really full. He left the motel, and Chris and I were talking about if we could just get some of that money his dad had, what we were going to do. But when he came back, he had Eddie Jr.'s motor home. I don't know how he got it. But he had the boys put everything in the motor home.

"And that's when we left Ohio."

5

Augusta Townsend paced the small kitchen in her Canton inner city home, getting ready to tell a visitor about her encounters with the Sexton family and their two-week stay in her house after the police standoff in late 1992.

She was an athletic-looking, blunt-speaking black woman in her early 40s. She said she was on disability for an old steel plant injury. She said she also took care of her 87-year-old husband, a World War II vet she liked to call "Soldier Boy." She liked to wear military uniforms herself, explaining that in her neighborhood, "You dress army-style, they'll leave you alone."

Augusta Townsend said she'd known the Sexton family a couple of years, introduced through her cousin, who hung out with Eddie Jr. Eddie Sr. called himself a "preacher man." When Townsend's cousin's girlfriend committed suicide in her house, Sexton blessed the home, saying, "All the demons are out."

"He said he'd done every sin that was known, but now he was saved," Townsend recalled. "But then he said he worshiped both God and the devil. I'm telling you, he ain't no preacher for God. He is a preacher for the devil. That's for sure.

"See, 'cause I would sneak out there [to Caroline] and they wouldn't even know I was there. One day I went to the open window and Willie was with Pixie and Eddie had a cat on the table, worshipping the cat with candles and stuff. I turned around and left.

"See, I'm a sneaky little bitch, excuse my English. I wanted to know what was going on. So another time I

parked my van about three blocks around the corner. I
was nosey. I caught him fucking this girl in that shed right
when you first come in. I don't know what girl. Sixteen,
eighteen, I can't say. She was not as tall as me. I mean,
the man was a whore to his days, you hear me?

"Then, after he moved out of the house, we used to go
out to the trailer park and see Eddie Sr. He kept moving,
because he was supposed to stay away from his wife. I went
out there, sir, and Pixie come out with some shorts up
the crack of her ass. You could see her pussy. Excuse my
language. You could see her nipples through her shirt. I
went into that trailer and I'm telling you, it smelled just
like good-time pussy.

"I said to my [cousin] we better get the fuck out of here
now. I didn't see any other man around but Eddie, so
evidently there had to be some deep fucking going on.
Before we left, the mother drove up. She spoke to me, and
when she went in that trailer—man, she was throwing
dishes and everything else at Eddie Sexton. She *knew* her
daughter was fucking that man.

"That girl Pixie, I seen it in her a long time ago that
she's very jealous about her dad. She'd come around the
house. Too jealous. I mean, it's just like a husband-and-
wife jealousy. And she didn't want nobody close to her
daddy. It was like: don't get two feet in front of *my* daddy."

Augusta Townsend said it was her cousin and a Sexton
nephew who beat Joel Good, on the street, not a hundred
feet from her door. They jumped him when he stepped
out of a car. Ed Sexton was nowhere around. "He was too
scrawny to beat that boy like that." Eddie Jr. and Pixie
were also there, she said.

A couple of weeks before the standoff, Eddie Sr. had
offered to trade Townsend his Chevy van for her Ford
truck. She signed over the truck, but he never showed up
with his paperwork. Then he landed in jail.

Townsend confirmed that she'd offered May, Christopher, Kimberly, and Skipper a place to stay after Eddie Jr.

put a gun to his mother's head. Soon Eddie Jr. dropped by, trying to raise bond money.

"When you get around Eddie Jr., he was very possessive, just like Pixie was. *Of his daddy.* I said, my God, what did [Eddie Sr.] do? Fuck 'em all? Excuse my English."

She gave Eddie Jr. $500, figuring once Ed Sexton got out of jail, she'd be able to get the van. It had been a relatively uneventful week while the mother and children were there. But then Ed Sexton showed up, out on bond. The atmosphere changed not long after he walked through the door.

At first he bought groceries and had his boys do repairs on her house. Willie moved in as well. Ed Sexton had a .38 revolver with him, Townsend said. "He's the kind of man who push the situation. Aggravate you to do things. Yeah, manipulate.

"I gave the kids clothes and shoes, just to help them out. Because they said they was trying to get an Indian reserve . . . 'cause the Indian reserve was going to give them their freedom. I got the clothes from Soldier Boy. Plus, I had camouflage pants. I said, I'm gonna tell you something, at night can't *nobody* see you in camouflage, you know. So we went to the Army store and we bought different things.

"Okay, and the mother was nervous and all that. But she's just as wrong. Because I'm gonna tell you something, if she was any piece of woman, I wouldn't allow my husband to fuck my kids . . . do that freaky fool shit. He'd have been the hell out of my house and he'd have never come back.

"All of them was [sexual]. I seen his little girl [Kimberly] just crawl, climb, and squirm like some sex maniac on top of her daddy. It's just like you train a dog. If you train a dog to hump, he will. Everybody acted like they was deep in love with that man all the way down to the youngest. And they don't want you around their daddy. They look at you like a demon that's going to kill you.

"But the mother acted like she didn't give a fuck. Excuse my English. All she cared about was Christopher. And she showed me those [family] pictures. She was in the bedroom. She said 'This is Chris, my love.' Something ain't going on right, I thought."

The boys were sleeping in Townsend's living room, Christopher and Skipper on a roll-out sofabed. Kimberly was sleeping with her parents in another bedroom.

"And that night I come downstairs to use the bathroom. And I saw them. The mother was on her knees on the side of the bed, sucking that boy's dick [Christopher's]. Her head was between his ass and going up and down. And Skipper was watching. Willie was asleep in the chair. I crept back up the stairs."

She spoke to Soldier Boy. "I said I don't play that—when I get upset I cuss—I said, 'Soldier, I don't play that bullshit.' I said, I brought those kids back to protect them. I didn't bring these kids here for them to take advantage. Daddy in the bed with one. Mommy on the side of the bed sucking the boy's dick.

"They was going to leave anyway, but I started bitchin'. I said don't nobody pay enough bills in this motherfucker but me. I said, I'm the boss. I said, ain't gonna be no motherfucking shit goin' down in my house. I said, I love kids . . . And they started packing."

They left in the middle of the night. Augusta Townsend lost the $500 for the bail, and never received the paperwork for the van. She found only a hollow point bullet standing on her kitchen counter.

She figured Eddie Lee Sexton was sending her a message.

"Because I seen something happen at my house, I thought I was going to get killed," she said. " 'Cause I'm telling the buck-naked truth, them is some freaky mother-fuckers, excuse my English, please."

6

"An interesting family."

That was the word Canton attorney James Gregg would first use to describe his long-time clients, Ed and May Sexton. Even so, Gregg figured there had to be some kind of foul-up somewhere that led to the standoff.

They first met in the 1960s, when Gregg was a young attorney for Legal Aid. Sexton walked into his office one day saying he needed a divorce from his first wife. In the ensuing years, Gregg had handled general practice work for Sexton—accident claims, title work, and the like. But every visit across 15 years, Sexton would mention it.

"This is the man who got me my divorce," he always said.

Sexton had a couple of other odd routines. Gregg smoked Lucky Strikes, and Ed Camels, his fingertips always yellow with tobacco stain. He always brought Gregg a pack of cigarettes, dropping them on his desk before they conducted business.

Also, he always paid in cash.

Two months earlier, on September 2, Sexton had come in to deed a second home he owned in Canton to his son, Eddie Sexton, Jr. The patriarch didn't want a title search done. That would have guaranteed to Eddie Jr. that he was receiving the home free and clear of liens or other attachments.

Gregg warned Eddie Jr., "You know, I don't even know if your dad owns this. I'm not certifying anything."

Eddie Jr. wanted the deed, nonetheless.

Seven days later, Estella May Sexton showed up at his office. There was a lien on the house on Caroline Street for an unpaid hospital debt, she said. She wanted to know what could be done. She wanted to sell the house. The bank was also foreclosing on the mortgage. Gregg was able to prevent the foreclosure, but the title could only be cleared by paying the debt. Records later showed the title was clouded by nearly $7,000 in liens from clinics and hospitals.

When the DHS came against the Sextons, Gregg referred the case to attorney Pat Menicos. "Luckily, I was just heading out for a vacation at the time," he would say later.

Sexton's defense in Massilon Municipal Court was handled by another lawyer as well. That attorney wasn't paid in cash. "He ended up stiffing the defense attorney for $2,500," Gregg later said.

But for Gregg, Ed Sexton was the perfect client. Once, Ed and his brother Otis were in a car accident together. Ed Sexton accepted the insurance company settlement without protest. Otis wanted to hold out for more.

"The reason I liked him was he never gave me any problem," Gregg would recall. "He never second-guessed me once."

The only difficult case Sexton ever faced was back in the mid-1980s when a paternity claim was filed against him by a niece who'd lived with the Sextons while she was finishing high school. Sexton denied the baby was his child. A blood test was planned. But then the girl dropped the case.

There was another oddity. Ed Sexton told Gregg once that he was expecting a very large contract with Burger King restaurants to do a promotional tour. The money was coming any day, he said. He wanted the attorney to help him set up a company with the assets. But the money and the company never materialized.

On the Thursday before Sexton made bail, Eddie Jr. had stopped in Gregg's office, trying to raise money to get his father out of jail. Gregg tried to counsel him, saying it wasn't worth the time or expense. The hearing was scheduled for Monday. If they all just waited four days, Gregg said, the judge would probably let his father out of jail.

There was one more thing about the Sexton family.

James Gregg would notice it every time Ed and May Sexton came through the door. They smelled.

"Maybe *interesting* isn't the right word to describe them," Gregg would conclude one day. "Maybe the word I'm looking for is *macabre.*"

7

Otis Sexton held all of them responsible: the Jackson Township police; the Massilon prosecutor; Indian social worker Mel Fletcher. If Glenn Goe had pursued Machelle's charges, if Goe and Steve Zerby had lobbied Massilon's attorneys, if Mel Fletcher had kept his nose out of a DHS case, Otis reasoned, Eddie might have been in jail and future problems avoided.

Otis wondered if the Jackson police would have dragged their feet with other families in the township, particularly the ones who lived in the quarter-million-dollar homes. He reasoned: The department has a long file on the family. A girl from the family says her father raped her. The girl passes a lie detector test. Her brother and sisters reveal horrors.

Even an old hillbilly could figure that one out.

"And what do they do? *Nothing,*" he told friends.

The DHS wasn't entirely off the hook either, he'd later begin to say. While it's not shown on the DHS summary of the Sexton case later filed in court by the agency, Otis Sexton would eventually claim he'd made nine complaints about his brother's treatment of the children between May of 1979 and April of 1992. He also would say he complained to high school and grade school counselors and several police agencies.

He'd recall, "It was always the same answers: We're short on staff. Or the kids have to admit the problem themselves."

Now they had, he decided, and still nothing.

Judee Genetin would later say DHS had not received the Otis Sexton referrals.

"If nobody believed me, that makes me a liar, doesn't it?" he would later explain. "And I'm not a liar."

Ten days before Christmas Otis heard rumors in the family that May Sexton was living with his brother Dave near Tampa. He called DHS, which contacted Florida officials, but May was not found. A few weeks later, Otis's daughter called, saying she'd just spotted Eddie, May, and Kimberly in a Giant Eagle grocery store where she worked. Otis called DHS. DHS called Jackson police. But the family was already gone.

He'd later explain his passion this way.

"Everybody has somebody. I've got my wife and daughters. The police and social workers got to go home to their families. But what did those kids have? Nothing. Now they didn't even have each other, all spread out in those foster homes, or out there with Eddie on the run.

"It just kept going through my mind. Over and over. Who did *they* have. Who was going to stand up for those kids?"

There was one more event that made him furious. A few days after Machelle had left his home, he called Wayne Welsh.

"I'm surprised you're not in jail," Welsh said.

Machelle Sexton had been in the prosecutor's office. She signed paperwork claiming Otis had not only beaten her, he'd sexually abused her as well.

8

Four days after Christmas of 1992, a Stark County sheriff's detective named Steve Ready swivelled away from a pile of police reports and asked Judee Genetin to clarify what she was saying.

"Now, Judee, who did you say was out there?" he asked.

"One of the Sextons," she said. "Steve, we need you to sit in with us on this."

She'd walked down a flight of stairs, not waiting for the elevator. She looked worried. Ready knew everyone on the floor above him was on edge. They were worried that Ed Sexton was going to show up at the Renkert Building and start blasting away. Genetin had ordered every office door locked and extra security posted. Everyone had seen Eddie Jr. on TV supporting his dad.

Now he was outside, Genetin said, brooding in the hallway.

Ready sighed, looking straight ahead. At an inch over six feet, he wasn't sure if these DHS women wanted him for his interview skills or his muscle. He knew little about the Sexton case.

A month earlier, Ready had caught the TV coverage as he sat in his living room with his wife Judy in their North Canton home. It was the first time he'd heard the name Sexton. He thought, what an *asshole*. Holding hostages. Going to shoot people. Shit, the guy can't win that fight.

That's about all he knew about the Sexton clan.

A uniform and 13 years of cruising the streets of Stark County had produced a soft-spoken mix of humor and cynicism in the 41-year-old deputy. Before, Ready shipped ingot in a steel mill, sold insurance, pushed paper at a rental car agency, and guarded courtrooms as a bailiff in Canton Municipal Court. He got his chance to be a cop in 1978.

"As long as I can remember, that's all I ever wanted to be—ever, ever, *ever,*" he'd later say. "You want to say it's because you wanted to help people. But, shit, it seems all you do is get spit on, so I don't know if that's still it."

Ready had made detective. He was working in a suit and tie. He had a cubicle in the DHS. He investigated child sexual abuse. He'd picked up the pathology of pedophiles in seminars and from social workers. It was work a lot of cops didn't have the stomach for very long. Ready was still optimistic about the job. It felt good to be out of uniform. He'd had the assignment only eight months.

Canton was a friendly Midwest town where people made eye contact and thought nothing of striking up conversations with strangers. Ready knew that also worked in most interviews. He considered himself "a hands-on kind of guy." He'd cozy up, rubbing a suspect's shoulder, giving an appropriate pat on the back. Recently, a 52-year-old pedophile who'd stonewalled social workers had confessed to a dozen felonious counts after a couple of hours alone with the detective.

"You catch more flies with honey," he'd say.

If that didn't work, Ready figured, then you took your last shot by raising a whole lot of hell.

They gave Ready a quick briefing on the case. He sat at a table with Genetin, social worker Tracey Harlin, and a DHS supervisor as Eddie Sexton, Jr. was shown into the small conference room.

Eddie Sexton, Jr. looked like somebody begging to have his car searched, somebody trying to look hip, but badly missing the mark. Almost six feet with a scraggly goatee and ragged sideburns. Black hair cut short on the top. Six-inch locks behind his ears, falling to his shoulders.

The young man was upset, Ready quickly determined, but not at the women in the room. His old man had taken him for thousands, he claimed.

Eddie Jr. said he'd put up $7,900 of his savings to get his father out of jail. He claimed the money came from an insurance settlement for a back injury. After his father was sentenced, Ed Sr. told him he couldn't get the bail money back until 170 days after his release. But after his father left town, Eddie Jr. checked with the Massilon clerk and found the money had been given to his father the very day of the hearing.

"I want to find him so I can get my money back," Eddie Jr. said.

Ready had seen it hundreds of times over the years:

people who want nothing to do with police, until they were the ones who got screwed.

Later, Eddie Jr. would tell Ready and others another version of the rip-off, the true story he'd held back because of pure embarrassment. He and his wife Daniela had two children under five, Elizabeth and Eddie Lee Sexton, III. Daniela had received an inheritance from her grandmother. They had a Mercury Mekur XR4TI and just bought a Dodge van. They also had a 24-foot '73 Dodge Challenger motor home they'd loaned to Eddie Sr. while he was staying in campgrounds that year. From jail, his father put him to work raising the bail money, he said. He'd gotten the bulk of it by taking the Dodge van and the Mekur to Johnson Motors, the owner agreeing to give them half their value, but would hold the vehicles until Eddie Jr. brought the money back. Eddie and Daniela also sold furniture, a $1,500 stereo system and a new clothes dryer hardly out of the shipping box. Daniela cashed a couple bonds. Finally, he'd also testified at the bond hearing to his father's good character.

Minutes after he was sentenced in Massilon, Eddie Sr. told his son to go outside to talk to a TV news crew outside, to voice his support. Eddie Sr. said he'd go upstairs and get the bond money. When the father came downstairs he said he'd been told by officials he couldn't get his bond money until his probation was over.

Ready thought, the old man had ripped him off, getting paid in cash, while Eddie Jr. was outside pleading his case on TV.

And that wasn't the only money his father owed. Eddie Sr. had borrowed a $1,000 a couple months earlier. Eddie Jr. also had dished out $5,000 for the house he lived in, but then found out his father only had a land contract on the property. His new deed wasn't worth a damn.

His father had taken off with his motor home, Eddie Jr. told Ready and the DHS staff.

"Any other vehicles they might be operating?" Ready asked.

Eddie Jr. said they had a grey '83 Buick Electra, a four-door he believed was registered to his sister, Estella Good.

Both Ready and Genetin began asking the young Sexton about reports of abuse in the household.

All the children were physically abused, he said. He'd never been sexually abused, he added, but he suspected his younger sister Sherri had. He told them how his father had shipped Sherri to Florida to stay with their uncle Dave. Eddie Jr. had visited her there. She'd told him her son Christopher was her father's child.

Some family, Ready thought.

He also detailed a story about his father taking Sherri for a ride in the family van a couple of years ago. Eddie Jr. drove to the same store a few minutes later and saw the van parked in the back. No one was sitting in the seats, but the van was rocking.

He also believed Pixie had sex with her father. "But I can't prove it," he said.

Ready asked him to speculate where the family might be now.

Eddie Jr. said probably on a Cherokee Indian reservation somewhere.

Ready looked for more possible leads.

"Has anybody been in contact with your father?" he asked.

Eddie Junior said he suspected his sister Pixie had been talking with him by phone from the house on Caroline. His father had an AT&T calling card billed to that number, he said.

Ready could see a few possible skip trace leads: phone bills, vehicles, an uncle's name. He'd have to ask a county grand jury for a subpoena on the phone bill.

"If he calls you or your sister," he said, "I want you to call me."

Eddie Jr. had one more thing to add. His father also

knew how to find people, too. "He knows where all those kids are at," he said. He was talking about Matt, James, and Lana, the remaining children in the foster homes.

He also predicted that his father would be armed.

Before he went back downstairs, Ready told the DHS staff he'd look into it, but he also reminded them: downstairs, on his desk, he was looking at one hell of a caseload of his own.

9

They had a big Christmas dinner. Joey was there, but not Pixie. He brought Dawn and Shasta. Joey said Pixie was celebrating the holiday with aunts and uncles. One of Teresa's daughters tried to teach Dawn to roller blade in the basement, with little luck. But at least the little girl was talking now.

In early January, 1993, Joey and Pixie showed up at Teresa's parents, Pixie apparently in labor. They wanted to leave Shasta, but take Dawn to the hospital. Gladys Barrick warned them. They wouldn't let a 4-year-old in the maternity ward.

"Then we'll just have to keep her in the lobby," Pixie said.

Later, Gladys Barrick would say, "Shasta couldn't talk. Dawn could. I think they were afraid Dawn was going to tell us some of the things that were going on."

Shasta cried for hours, bawling from the time they left. Gladys Barrick couldn't comfort her. She finally cried herself to sleep.

It was a false labor.

In mid January, Joey disappeared again for a couple of weeks. No one answered the phone. No cars were parked outside the Caroline house. The entire family worried again. One day, Pixie finally picked up the phone.

"We couldn't get a hold of you," Teresa said.

Pixie said they were visiting her relatives in Kentucky.

Later Teresa asked Joey, "What family?"

Joey said he didn't know.

But they had good news. Pixie's baby had been born on January 17. They'd named the child Skipper Lee, after her brother Charles "Skipper" Sexton.

But it wasn't until a couple weeks later, in early February, that anyone saw the child. Teresa came home from the grocery store to find Joey, Pixie, and the children there. They all sat around the kitchen table, drinking soda and coffee.

Baby Skipper was a cute child, Teresa decided. He had sandy brown hair and an acorn-shaped face. The infant looked healthy and active. Teresa studied the eyes, baby blue and as focused as any 3-week-old infant's. Later, she would pull out Joey's hospital baby picture. Little Skipper was the spitting image of his dad. And he was born on Joey's father's birthday, two days from Joey's own birthday on January 19. Teresa wondered why they didn't incorporate the name "Joel" somewhere in the child's name. Joey, too, was named after his dad.

One thing about the infant did disturb her. Little Skipper smelled. Not because he'd soiled his diaper. She thought, this baby needs a good bath. She said nothing. She didn't want to offend the new parents.

Teresa wondered about baby pictures.

They didn't have any.

She asked, where was the baby born?

"Mercy," Pixie said.

Teresa gave them all the baby clothes she could find.

Pixie said they were going to be moving from the house on Caroline. The house and its contents would be auctioned on February 18, she said. They were staying there to keep it clean for realtors.

"Where are you moving?" Teresa asked Joey.

He looked at Pixie.

She answered, "Back to the apartment."

"In Bolivar?" Teresa asked.

She nodded.

"You've been paying rent for all this time?"

"Yes," she said.

When they got up to go, Joey walked over to Teresa and gave her a big hug and kiss.

"I love you, Aunt Teresa," he said.

She thought, why's he doing this? He hadn't hugged her like that for years.

The same day, Joel Good stopped by his grandparents'. He'd called earlier, but Gladys Barrick had told him she had the flu. Give her a couple of days to get better; it wouldn't be a good idea to expose the baby, she warned.

They showed up anyway.

Gladys Barrick decided she better not hold the infant.

"Next time you come over, I'll be better and I can hold it," she told Dawn, who wanted to bring her the child.

The grandmother later told Teresa that she couldn't understand why they'd ignored her warning and come over.

"We didn't realize it at the time," Gladys Barrick would say many months later. "But Joey was telling us all goodbye."

vii
New Rules

1

Every big family had one: the family character, the odd duck. Tuck and Colleen Carson would say Tuck's sister May Sexton and her husband Eddie were all of that, and more.

Tuck had not laid eyes on May for years, until she and her family showed up at their father's funeral in Indiana, then their mother's burial in Steubenville, Ohio, in 1991.

"They looked like gangsters," he'd later recall.

They rolled up to the funeral home in a big black Cadillac. Eddie and all his boys wore dark suits with dark shirts and ties. They all wore sunglasses. They all stuck together, hardly mingling with the rest of the mourners. Outside of the funeral home, one of the teenage boys pulled out Eddie's pistol from under the car seat, eager to show it off. Tuck Carson respected firearms and the right to carry them. And that meant you did not wave them around in a public parking lot.

Tuck and Colleen lived in a small, well-kept ranch house

between Jeffersonville and Charleston, just down the road from grazing cattle, blackberry patches, and soybean fields. Louisville was a half hour away. Tuck saw more of the highway than his doorstep. He was on the road five days a week, logging two to three thousand miles hauling Fords and Chevies and luxury cars to dealerships from Detroit to Florida, and most of the states in-between.

After the funeral, May started getting friendly, calling periodically. Wanting to keep in touch. Colleen talked to her mostly. Tuck chatted with her when he wasn't on the road.

May had been through a lot of changes.

As youngsters, Tuck Carson remembered his younger sister as their father's favorite girl. In her late teens, when the family lived near Toledo, she was a beautiful teenager with exotic dark features. She spent hours on her hair and makeup. She was a high school cheerleader in Toledo, another stop during a string of stays, mostly at bases like White Sands and Fort Knox as their father soldiered his way through three wars. Like a good Army brat, she learned to make new friends quickly.

"When it came to going shopping or going out, she was the first one out the door," he'd later recall. "She was the leader of the pack."

An all-American girl.

The woman who showed up at his parents' funerals bore no resemblance to the sister he'd known before he joined the service. She'd gained weight, had little energy, and seemed to have lost all the light that used to beam from her eyes. May also had become a silent follower. She offered few opinions. She rarely smiled, let alone laughed. Before she answered a question, her eyes often went to her husband Eddie. She seemed to have no identity of her own.

Their father tried to warn her, as Tuck remembered it.

"There was something about Eddie that Dad didn't like," Tuck later would recall. "He said, 'He's nothing but trouble.' And in the beginning, he was right."

Tuck remembered coming back on leave after his father Clyde had retired to Wellsburg, West Virginia. The visit was like walking into a hornet's nest. He found his father rummaging through the house, looking for his rifle.

"No sonovabitch is going to shoot at me without getting shot at back," the retired Ranger was shouting.

May had fled to their parents' house, running from Eddie. But Eddie had shown up at the house.

"Eddie had a rifle and had threatened May," Tuck recalled. "If she didn't come and get in the car with him, he was threatening to shoot Dad."

Their mother had hidden the gun. As his dad searched, May left with Eddie.

Later, Tuck's father had news about Eddie Sexton. The retired master sergeant had done a little checking into Eddie's military background. Eddie was no Green Beret, as he'd claimed to the family. He'd been booted out of the Army. He tried to convince May to dump him.

"But she wouldn't listen," Tuck recalled. "She was already under his thumb."

A dozen years passed before Tuck saw the couple again—at the funerals. A year after the last one, the Carsons found themselves with May's son Skipper living in their house.

It was May's idea to send the boy over the summer of 1992. May talked to Colleen, saying, "He'd just like to spend some time with his uncle on school break." But with Tuck on the road, he'd spend more time with Colleen. Skipper was there almost two months.

Colleen was happy to have Skipper. The Carsons were in their mid 40s now. Colleen's three daughters were grown. She'd never had a boy around the house. Colleen provided nursing care for a 90-year-old woman she'd had in her home for a dozen years. She'd taken custody of the woman when she quit a nursing home job, after promising the woman's dying sister she'd always provide her care.

Skipper was helpful and attentive. "He was as nice and

polite as can be," Colleen would recall later. "And we treated him like a king."

They put Skipper in a vacant bedroom. He seemed thrilled to have his own room. He helped Colleen with dishes and housecleaning and yard work. He wanted to go with her on grocery shopping trips. He wanted to go everywhere. They'd drive up the road to Charleston. The town had a water tower, a couple of church steeples, and a burial vaults manufacturer. But for Skipper, the outing was like a trip to the Vegas strip.

In late summer, Skipper got a temporary job striking tents at the local 4-H grounds for the annual fair. The Carsons provided for all his meals and other needs. Skipper was all pumped up about having his own money for cigarettes.

It was Colleen's daughter Bonnie who first heard the stories. Bonnie spent the night at the house sometimes. Skipper seemed eager to impress her. He told her he lived in a $200,000 home with a pond. They had a big-screen TV, a state-of-the-art stereo system, new cars, and a Winnebago in the drive, he said.

"It doesn't make sense," Bonnie told her mother. "Just look at the clothes he wears."

Skipper wore T-shirts and baggy jeans and unlaced old tennis shoes. One time he wore his jeans backwards.

"He was trying to look like he belonged to something, but he didn't," Colleen later would recall. "He also wanted to be a part of our family. Once, he said he wanted to live here with us for good."

They began to notice strange things about the boy.

One time, Colleen and Skipper were sitting on the living room couch watching TV. It was something on one of those learning channels, a documentary about the occult.

"My dad did that," Skipper said.

"Did what?" Colleen asked.

"Killed a cat. We sat at this table, with lit candles."

Colleen turned, a little shocked. "You mean you did this in your house?"

Skipper immediately dropped the subject.

Then, the strange sleep behavior started. Bonnie could hear him all the way downstairs, while she was sleeping on the couch. She'd hear him talking loudly in the dead of night.

"Who's he talking to up there?" she asked her mother.

"God knows," Colleen said.

Sometimes the night talk turned traumatic, Skipper screaming, "Stop it! Stop it! No, don't! Stop it!"

Colleen would rush into the bedroom. Find him sitting up in bed, his eyes glazed with terror. She'd calm him down, telling him it was just a nightmare.

Something traumatic has happened to this boy, she thought.

"Skipper, if there's something wrong, you can tell me," she asked him one night. "You know, I can help."

She asked him a dozen different ways a dozen different times, but he'd clam up as soon as he got his wits.

Tuck took Skipper on the road for a couple trips, hauling cars. He showed him how to handle a big rig, how to handle the gears through the mountains, how to spot the crackpot drivers on the interstates.

On one trip to Florida, they met May and Eddie at a restaurant for lunch. The Sextons said they were down there visiting relatives.

As they talked over coffee, Tuck had a hard time believing Eddie Sexton was the same man who'd pulled a gun on his sister years ago. He was so laid back, so exceptionally polite.

"Yes, ma'am," he'd say to the waitress. "No, ma'am, that's fine."

He gave Skipper some spending money before they left.

Tuck and Skipper had a few good talks in the truck. Skipper soaked up information, asking about the trucking business and ways to deal with life on the road. He said little about his family. But during one trip, Skipper mentioned "welfare" had taken some of his brothers and sisters from his house. They were accusing his father of all sorts of lies, he said. When Tuck pressed for details, Skipper clammed up.

When the school year started in September, Colleen became concerned. She called up May.

"May, I think you need to come and get him," she said. "Or, if he's going to stay here, I need to get him registered for school."

The Sextons picked him up the next day. But two weeks later, Colleen returned from a trip to town and found Skipper Sexton sitting on her doorstep, a big bundle of clothes in his lap. He looked depressed.

Tuck was on the road.

"Skipper, what's going on?" she asked. "What's wrong?"

He wouldn't say anything.

"If you can't tell me what's going on, then you're going to have to leave."

"They're gonna pick me up in a couple of days," he said.

Later, Colleen Carson would maintain she couldn't get any information out of him. What happened a couple of days later, she described this way:

The two of them were sitting in the living room watching TV when a sheriff's deputy and another man knocked on the door.

"Is Charles Sexton here?" the deputy asked.

Colleen told him she knew the Sexton family, but she didn't know any Charles Sexton.

After they left, she turned to Skipper, saying, "Who's Charles?"

"Whew," he said, lighting a cigarette and exhaling. "That's my real name."

Colleen later recalled being angry. "This is my house," she told him. "There's something going on."

She said she called Ohio and May Sexton picked up the phone. She demanding he be picked up at once. "Whatever is going on, I don't want to be in the middle of it," she said she told her.

Two of his brothers picked him up the next day.

Then, in the weeks around Christmas of 1992, the Sexton family began circling again. May Sexton called Colleen first, while Tuck was on the road. She said she was calling from a local motel.

"We thought we'd stop by for a visit," she said. "We're kind of tired of Ohio."

Colleen thought, which is it? Something was going on.

May told her they might head out to Oklahoma. Then, the Carsons didn't hear from them for a couple of weeks.

May called again, saying they were back at a nearby motel on Highway 62. Tuck drove up to visit. Both May and Eddie were there. The family looked as if it were on the move. They had an old Buick Electra. Kimberly, Christopher, Skipper, and Willie were with them. They had a Dodge Challenger motor home.

Eddie said they'd just been to Oklahoma, trying to document the family's Indian roots. Tuck didn't question it. The way he understood the family tree, his grandfather was pure Wyandotte, his mother part Cherokee. One of his brothers, in fact, had legally changed his name to a tribal name.

Eddie had mounds of paperwork he wanted to show Tuck. He'd been having trouble with welfare officials in Ohio, he said, but the matter was straightened out now. He laid out letters and documents with legal letterheads on the motel bed. He pointed to one, showing where the children had been released back to him.

Tuck wanted to know what the problem was.

Eddie said welfare officials in Ohio were accusing him of incest. His brother Otis was behind the whole thing.

"Can you believe that?" Eddie asked. "That I'd do something like that to my own children?"

"No, not really," Tuck said. "It would take a sick sono-vabitch to do that."

Eddie wanted the dispute settled by the tribe, he said. But they hadn't been successful in documenting their heritage in Oklahoma. He talked about going back to Ohio to research graveyards where May's grandparents were buried. He also wanted to make a quick trip back to Canton to pick up his disability check, then get the rest of his kids. He was selling his house, he said. He asked Tuck if he knew where they could find a place to live locally. They needed a temporary place to stay until the deal went through.

"I'll check around," Tuck said.

As they visited, somehow the subject of guns came up. Tuck was a hunter. He appreciated a good shotgun when he saw one. Eddie said he'd brought his guns with him. He began pulling out cases and laying weapons on the bed: a 30-30 lever action rifle; a riot shotgun; a .357 magnum revolver; a .45 semi-automatic pistol; a big .44 magnum revolver, like the kind Dirty Harry had.

"He had a goddamn arsenal," Tuck would later recall.

Later, Eddie demonstrated how his kids could handle firearms. All the boys could break down the pistol. Then, little Kimberly, hardly 10, demonstrated, taking the handgun apart for inspection and cleaning, then assembling it.

"Why have they got all those?" Colleen asked him later.

"They're moving," Tuck said. But certainly not in with them.

Later, the Sextons visited their house. Eddie sipped coffee and talking about how important it was to keep his family together. Kids need a parent's love, he said. Bureaucrats had no business meddling in a family's affairs.

When he left he told Colleen, "We sure appreciate your hospitality, ma'am."

But later, Colleen would say there was something she didn't like about Eddie Sexton. "His eyes are weird," she said.

Soon Tuck gave them a lead for a home rental, a place about 20 miles up the road, off Highway 62. Everyone called it Bushman's Lake. It was a summer resort community of mobile homes on the Ohio River. In the winter months, he'd heard they always had plenty of homes to rent.

The Sextons picked out a home, but it was mobile, a trailer on a lot with the Ohio River as its backyard. Soon the family grew considerably. The Carsons met Pixie, her husband Joel, and their three kids.

When Colleen saw the setup she found it pretty amazing. That little two-bedroom trailer. Little children. Teenagers. Adults. Eleven people in all.

Later, she would say she felt sorry for them. How were they going to get by with so little room?

2

One of the few times Clyde Howard Scott, May Sexton's father, had contact with his daughter May and her husband Ed was later documented in a 1982 FBI report. Clyde Scott called a Jackson Township arson investigator, claiming his son-in-law was an arsonist. The Jackson investigator involved the FBI. The agent interviewed Scott, who was living in Indiana at the time, then filed his report:

Scott advised that a couple years ago, he and his wife moved to Jeffersonville, Indiana, and have continued to live in this area since that time. About July of 1981, they were in Massilon, Ohio, visiting with their daughter ... and Eddie Lee Sexton. At that time, Scott's daughter and Sexton were residing at 8149 Caroline ... While they were visiting, Sexton asked Scott if he would set fire to the residence. Sexton told Scott that he would give him $10,000 from the insurance money if he would set the fire.

Sexton also told Scott that he wanted four or five of
their children in the house at the time of the fire
and for them to be burned up in the fire . . . During
his conversation, Sexton told Scott that he gets chemicals out of Detroit, Michigan, through Mafia connections, and uses these chemicals and places them on
the wiring in the center of the house. Usually, he
tries to put it on the wiring underneath a stairwell.
The chemicals eat through the insulation of the wiring and cause an electrical fire. Sexton told him that
by using these chemicals, there is no way to determine
if a fire is an arson. Sexton also told Scott that he
has set fires to his residences in the past and that he
and his two nephews . . . set the fires. Sexton told
Scott that he usually is out of the area at the time of
the fires and makes sure someone can vouch for his
presence at the time of the fires. Scott stated he was
very upset when asked to do this by Sexton, and told
him he wanted no part of anything like this.

Scott stated he was not sure if Sexton was actually
serious about burning the residence . . . until he
learned this house did burn approximately two to
three months ago . . . It is his understanding that
Sexton (and his wife) took their favorite children
and went someplace and left the other children at
the residence with the baby-sitter . . . Scott advised
he feels that Sexton probably wanted the baby-sitter
and the children to be in the residence at the time
of the fire.

That fire was May 30, 1982. Firemen had already determined the blaze began in the stairwell, spread upwards and
caused nearly $50,000 in damage. The arson investigator
never was able to prove how the fire began. Nor did he
have the evidence to charge Eddie Lee Sexton.

Ed and May Sexton were not home. A couple who'd
been staying with the Sextons were baby-sitting. Four chil-

dren were home at the time of the fire, including Machelle, Sherri, and Willie. They were not hurt. The baby-sitter had taken them out for ice cream moments after the fire began.

3

She was running from crisis to crisis. She ran from her uncle Otis's back to the house on Caroline, then ran to a friend in Bolivar's, then to Pixie and Joel's. Now she was living in a small mobile home in Bolivar. Along the way, Shelly had fallen in love at least twice. First to a married, 26-year-old park worker at a campground where her father stayed. He'd dropped her after she'd gotten pregnant. Now she was in love with a used book dealer twice her age. In the early months of 1993, Anne Greene was feeling less like a mother figure and more like someone who handed Machelle Sexton water and towels in a marathon race.

"When she'd get in trouble, she'd call," Anne would later recall. "We'd jump and put a temporary fix on the problem, then wait until next time."

But, Anne thought, why should that come as a surprise?

After all their nail-painting chats together, Anne believed she had a pretty good family portrait. Ed Sexton, the patriarch, ruled his household with iron authority. But unlike the great fascist dictators, stability wasn't the order of the day.

Interpersonal relationships among family members were entirely mercurial, Anne learned. They changed from day to day, hour to hour, moment to moment. Everyone courted *Dad's* favor and *Dad's* attention. It was the prime motivation for ratting on each other. They tipped him when a sibling crossed the street without permission. They squealed when a brother or sister talked to a neighbor. They courted favor with each other and tried to build favors, particularly with Pixie, hoping for enough immunity to attempt a brave jaunt to the local convenience store.

May Sexton was right in the middle of the competition among the girls, Shelly would explain. "My mother never supported me," she said. "She was always on his side. She loved to lie, especially on us older girls. She'd lie on the older girls to get his approval, too."

The mother and father also battled. Anne heard about yelling matches and flying dishes and ashtrays. The mother didn't seem to fear getting in the father's face. And once, during a fight between the parents, some of the kids jumped the father, injuring his arm. The next day, May was back on her husband's side and the children were beaten for the brief rebellion.

Ed Sexton also courted his children's loyalty individually, Shelly saying, "He'd tell each of them separately, 'I love you most. You're the one.' He'd tell Pixie and Sherri the same thing, then say, 'But you can't say anything about it. It's our secret.'"

There seemed to be a hazy pecking order:

Skipper appeared to have some freedom. Skipper was allowed to wrestle at school.

Willie, the muscular, stuttering older brother was very restricted, the father often calling Willie "little dick."

"Willie was always downgraded," Shelly said. "He was always [called] a wimp. And my dad was always stronger. He'd always slap him around. Make him feel small. And yet, Willie would do anything for him."

In his teens, Willie tried to run once, taking off on his bike. He didn't get far. Shelly said her father took off in the family van and saw him riding. He jumped the curb with the van and pinned him against a brick wall, tearing the flesh on his arm.

Kimberly, the youngest, was coddled, which in the Sexton definition of the term, meant she got less "whuppings."

Christopher was Mother's favorite. He was allowed to join the junior high school football team.

Matthew was the stealth sibling. He'd perfected to an art form the ability not to draw attention to himself.

Lana was the Futuretron. Her father rehearsed her on how to pose before cameras and the public appearances that never came.

James was always the butt of jokes from both parents and siblings because he was slow.

Sherri alternated between being a favorite and being in the doghouse, particularly when she refused to slow dance with her father at the weekend house dances.

Estella "Pixie" Sexton, the oldest girl, was her dad's eyes and ears, and perhaps his most regular sexual partner. She was their primary baby-sitter when they were young. She barked orders with her father's authority and had a direct pipeline to the patriarch. "If I got mad at Pixie, she'd try to get me in trouble in any way she could," Shelly said.

Shelly had seen one of their first sexual encounters on the couch, but didn't believe Pixie remained a victim of rape. She was in love with her father, she said. "She had gotten really involved. She wouldn't talk about it. It's just the way she acted, always wanting to be with him, not wanting to date anybody, then finally being interested in Joel. Because she knew she could control Joel. He was very mellow."

In the fall, after leaving Otis's, Shelly had accompanied her mother on a visit to her father at the campground. Pixie and Joel were there. Shelly talked to Joel alone. He said he'd had sex with Pixie when they first got married, but now she'd cut him off.

"He asked me what was wrong with Pixie, why didn't she want to have sexual intercourse. We were good friends. He could talk to me. I told him I didn't know . . . I didn't want to get involved in that area. I said to keep trying. I knew in the back of my mind it was because of my dad . . ."

One day, Shelly watched Pixie's children, so Joel and

Pixie could have the camper alone. Later, Joel emerged smiling, saying they'd made love.

Shelly heard from siblings that her father had ordered the beating of Joel, though she didn't know the reason. His father also barked orders at him. Joel told her he didn't like his father-in-law. But, "Joel was just like Willie. More or less what you told him to do, he would do to please anybody. He wanted to be wanted."

Other revelations Anne found even more disturbing. She heard of animal torture, the occult, and some kind of distorted Christianity Ed Sexton apparently preached.

Shelly said her father had killed the only pet she ever had, a rabbit. He called to her from outside her bedroom window and slit its throat as she watched. Then bolted up the stairs to torment her with it, its severed head and cape draped over his hand like a puppet. She was forced to eat it with the rest of the family for dinner that same night.

Ed Sexton held candlelit seances around the dining room table. Her father's mother would talk through her brother Eddie Jr. in a strange voice, Machelle said.

Ed Sexton claimed to be a mystical figure. He read Bible passages and spun his own interpretations. He seemed to be operating from some kind of Pentecostal foundation, which included speaking in tongues. Anne heard about the Futuretrons. "He said he was *the* person with special powers because of the mark on his hand," Shelly said. He was both God *and* Satan. He would have children look in his eyes until they saw Lucifer. He claimed he could take their souls with him, that he knew all their thoughts.

Anne wondered if Ed Sexton really believed that, or was just using it to forge fear and control. Shelly told her about going to a Canton cemetery with her father when she was 15. He brought her brother Willie, then 17, along. He found a newly dug grave. She had to crawl into it and pull a big piece of cardboard over her. The idea was to test her courage. She stayed in the hole a half hour while he made weird noises nearby. Willie, frightened, refused. Her father teased him for days.

No wonder Shelly couldn't seem to form responsible, permanent relationships, Anne thought. They were as foreign to her as life in a distant galaxy.

Shelly told her how she met her new boyfriend, the book dealer. His name was David Croto. His family owned a vintage bookstore near Bolivar. He dealt in wholesale books and eventually would open a vintage comic and collectibles shop in Canton Center Mall. When Shelly was living with Pixie and Joel, Croto's grown daughters were living in an apartment upstairs. Shelly said her father ordered Pixie to put all of Shelly's belongings in the hall. She knocked on the door of Croto's daughters. They called their dad. He offered to let her stay in a vacant mobile home he had in town. Then his daughter and his ex-wife offered Shelly $20 to go out with him. He'd been divorced 12 years. They wanted her to report back to see what he was like on a date.

They went to the Athens Restaurant in Canton for breakfast. A couple of days later, she soon told him she was pregnant by the park worker. He didn't seem to care.

"On our first date I should have realized I should marry this guy," Shelly would say.

It didn't take long. Shelly and Dave went to the February 18 auction at the house on Caroline Street. They bought her parents' refrigerator, the one that had been kept padlocked in Eddie and May Sexton's room.

They would be married on Anne Greene's birthday in the month of June.

4

One more police report was filed in Jackson Township regarding the Sexton family, this time by Eddie Jr.'s wife, Daniela Sexton, on February 24, 1993.

Daniela told police she and her husband had stopped at the house on Caroline Street to check the house and pick up a couch they'd bought at the auction. Joel and Pixie Good came in just after they arrived. Soon she was on the phone with her dad. Then she ordered Daniela and Eddie Jr. out of the house.

They all went outside. Pixie went to her car. When she emerged she was holding a .357 magnum revolver. She told them she'd shoot them if they didn't get in their car and leave.

5

The rules changed, many who left in the Challenger motor home would later recall.

For years the boys rarely left his sight. Now Skipper and Willie and Christopher had the Challenger to themselves when their parents booked into motels. It was in mint condition. A dinette in the back converted into four bunk beds. There was another bed above the driver's cab, and a couch behind the driver became a full double mattress. There was a kitchenette and small bathroom. Their father hung a crucifix over the driver's seat when they left. It would hang for the entire trip.

Years ago, Skipper's father slashed the tires of his bike for riding without permission. Now his parents said they'd be giving him the Pontiac, just as soon as things settled down.

"He did a 360," Skipper said. "I mean, he was a new man."

They began calling him Pops, or "Didi," something little Dawn, or Cockroach, had come up with before they left. Before their father had demanded "Dad." He no longer yelled at their mother. They were walking hand and hand, kissing, gazing into each other's eyes.

"Like two couples out of a movie," Skipper said.

May Sexton also put her thoughts about her husband in words. In October, while he was out of the house, she'd sent him a Sweetest Day card, signing: "I'll always love you, Sweetheart . . . Love always, May."

And, before they left for Indiana, she'd told Ed Sexton she was pregnant, writing, "Our new one is doing pretty good . . . I hope you are truly happy about it, not just saying you are because we just goofed up and caught an egg." She promised she would love him "even after death." If she died before he did, she promised to come back "and cut something off of you" if he ended up with anyone else.

When they drove to Oklahoma, Ed Sexton didn't announce their destination until they'd crossed a couple of state lines. They'd log some 1,600 miles on the motor home with Ed or Willie Sexton driving. The patriarch's constitution seemed nourished by the highway. For years Ed Sexton had been taking pain medications. Sometimes he administered drugs to himself with a syringe. On the road, they saw him popping small white pills.

Skipper recalled, "I said, 'Where the fuck we going?' He told us, Oklahoma. I said, 'What the fuck are we going to Oklahoma for?' He said he was going to get us all put on an Indian reservation. I said, 'I never seen an Indian with blue eyes.'"

Skipper, Shelly, and Matt were the only kids with blue eyes. His mother certainly could pass for an Indian.

"And my dad has black eyes. So I said, 'What am I, the milkman's or something?'"

His father laughed hard, saying, "Probably so."

Before the profanity and irreverence would have meant the belt. Now the whippings had stopped. The only one who got bossed around now was Willie. If he didn't follow orders, he got the fist.

"Me, Willie, and Chris, we was close," Skipper recalled. "Bossing Willie, that got me mad. I hate when somebody does that. And Willie would do it. 'Cause he's slow. That's what ticks me off.''

The boys were together, and they were Army. They had regulation pants, shirts, jackets, belts, and hats. That wouldn't be the only combat gear their father would buy. In the Challenger, he had a catalogue subtitled: "A complete guide to 2,000 military surplus stores in the United States and 11 foreign countries." He told them stories about Airborne and Special Forces and the Rangers. At one time or another, he was a member of all three, he said.

"All the way!" That was the Airborne motto.

That included the way a soldier had to keep his uniform. He taught them how to spit-shine their boots and pass inspection. He gave two of them new ages. Chris, 16, was supposed to be 19. Skipper, nearly 18, was supposed to be 20. Willie looked all of his 22 years.

"We was supposed to act like we was in the military— just out of the military and going home," Skipper explained. "We played it off and everybody believed us. People stupid enough to look at a 16-year-old and believe he was just out of the Army."

The boys remembered staying at a motel in Oklahoma. Sexton was looking for Indian records for his and May's family. Exactly where would remain unclear. The Cherokee Nation of Oklahoma was just outside Tulsa. There was no Cherokee reservation in the state, only tribal services such as housing, travel, and education assistance. Wyandotte, Oklahoma, was the official home of the federally recognized Wyandotte Tribe. Both tribes had migrated west in the 1700s, the Cherokees from North Carolina, the Wyandottes from Ontario, through Michigan and Ohio and finally the West. May Sexton later couldn't pinpoint where the research was done.

"He wanted to find my heritage number, when the different tribes would give those numbers years ago, and he wanted to find out where mine was. And he thought if he proved he was Indian then he wouldn't have to go to court in Ohio. But the only trouble, everybody says he's not Indian, but I don't know . . . And I couldn't get any information that he was. But he was asking about my relatives, not his, so I don't know."

During another interview, May also would recall she doubted her husband was Native American. "He kept calling me a dirty Indian . . . because I wouldn't celebrate Columbus Day."

Across from the motel was a buffalo ranch and a gift shop. The boys stayed in the camper, the parents and Kimberly in the motel room. The boys roamed the street at night. Sometimes looking for trouble.

"We'd go out every night trying to derail trains and shit," Skipper said.

When they left Oklahoma, his father didn't leave entirely empty-handed, Skipper recalled. He bought some kind of assault rifle. On the road, he made threats about people in Ohio. He said he planned to kill a dozen officials and potential witnesses—among them, social workers, Machelle, his brother Otis, and even his namesake, Eddie Jr.

"A good snitch is a dead snitch," he said.

Within two weeks they were back in Clark County, Indiana. It was the perfect setting for developing a military mind-set. As they drove up Highway 62 to their new home on Bushman's Lake, they passed the Indiana Army Munitions Plant. It was the biggest property in the county. The massive complex stretched for 20 miles along the highway. In World War II it built rounds for mortars and eight-inch howitzers. Nearly 19,000 people worked there during Vietnam. Now its endless perimeter fence was rusted, many of its 1,600 buildings decaying. But reminders of the armed services were everywhere.

Bushman's Lake itself was little more than a pond dug out a few hundred yards from the wide, muddy Ohio River. The resort was at the end of a narrow country road that cut through four miles of cornfields then wound down the riverbank to the resort. There were a hundred small houses and mobile homes. In the middle of winter, less than a third were occupied.

There, the boys spent much of their time being trained from furloughed soldiers to sentries. They had to be prepared in case the authorities came. Ed Sexton hatched an escape plan in the new trailer. They were to escape out back windows while two remained behind and shot it out with authorities, then regroup in a secret meeting place.

He began drilling them in the ways of war and survival, gleaned, he said, from two tours of jungle duty in Vietnam. He showed them hand-to-hand combat. There were specific maneuvers. How to sweep a man off his feet by chopping him in the legs. How to do choke holds. How to do kidney hits and jugular hits. How to break a man's nose, then drive it into his brain with the heel of the hand.

Sexton gave his sons handguns to carry when they were on watch. He vowed his enemies would never take him in again alive.

Sometime in February, Joel and Pixie arrived. Actually, it was their second trip to the Hoosier state. They'd visited in January, the time when Joel's family couldn't determine where he'd gone. On January 16, 1993, Ed and Pixie were driving on Highway 62 in Tuck Carson's car when they were rear-ended by a driver who claimed he fell asleep at the wheel. A Clark County sheriff's deputy filed a crash report, but Sexton's name would not have alerted any law enforcement data base. There was no warrant pending at the time.

Hours after the accident, Pixie was in labor. She'd had her baby Skipper Lee the next day in a hospital in Louisville. Ed Sexton got more than a new grandson. Family members later said Ed Sexton collected $5,000 from an insurance company for the crash.

When Pixie and Joel showed up a second time, some of the new family chemistry changed. Skipper said it was difficult to miss that something was going on with Pixie and his father. One day, in the trailer they were renting, his father and Pixie played what became known as "the chocolate kisses game." Skipper had seen it before over the years, using Hershey Kisses. His father played it with his mother and all his sisters.

"He and Pixie were eating these little cherries in chocolate with white shit inside them, like you might get your old lady on Valentine's Day," he explained. "He put one in his mouth, and I thought he was going to eat it. Joel was in the living room. I was sitting right at the table. And Pixie was standing there. And he put his mouth up to her mouth, lip to lip, and passed it. Like you're French kissing your old lady. That shit was sick. I got up and walked out."

Soon the relationship between his father and mother changed. "My father started getting on our nerves. See, Willie could go in the camper all the time. And Pixie and Joel and the kids came. I'm thinking, damn, it's crowded as a motherfucker in here. It's a two-bedroom trailer. Two little kids crying and then my mom and dad are getting into arguments. A week after Pixie came they got into an argument. My old man is calling my mom a whore. But my sister was the one who was a whore, you know, fucking around with her old man. And liking it. And my old man liking it."

Still, on April 12, May sent her husband an anniversary note, writing: "This is a time for loving. A time for caring. A time to let our feelings flow and to let our love for each other glow . . . yours forever."

As far as Skipper was concerned, he could take or leave Joel and Pixie. However, he was enamored with his namesake, their new son, little Skipper Lee. He called the baby his "godson." He held and fed the infant, tried to teach it baby talk.

Joel Good, most family members would recall, did most of the child care for his family. He played with the girls and took them for walks. He fed and diapered and bathed the new infant. He seemed to worship the new child. The

Goods had come up with a nickname for the baby, "Ewok," after the strange speaking midget characters in *Star Wars*.

Ed Sexton wasn't particularly fond of the addition to the family, though by most accounts, Skipper Lee was a quiet, lovable child. Ed said he was "below average." He refused to hold him. He also began distancing himself from Dawn and Shasta. He didn't like it when they referred to Joel as "Dad."

Every two weeks the patriarch would leave Indiana with Willie and Pixie. They'd drive back to Massilon to a post office box to pick up Sexton's disability, Willie's SSI checks, and the last of Joel Good's unemployment payments. During one trip, Pixie and her father had sex in the backseat as Willie piloted the Pontiac up the interstate.

The boys found trouble on their own. One night Skipper crawled through a window of a house at Bushman's Lake and stole a computer, an answering machine, and a couple of rifles. His father found out. He said they didn't need that kind of heat. He made him break back in and take the items back. The FBI was probably on their trail already, he said.

Another night, Skipper and one of his brothers broke into the small resort liquor store and bar that was closed for the season. They took cigarettes and booze. Their father found out about that, too, Skipper recalled, but helped them stash the goods in the woods. Sometimes their father was drinking, something his family had only seen him do before on New Year's Eve.

Joel Good was the odd man out in the male group. He wasn't allowed to take part in the drills or guard duty. Sometimes the Sexton brothers teased him. One night in the trailer, Christopher kept waking Joel up from his sleep. Joel made a stand. He grabbed Christopher's shirt and said, "I'm going to beat your ass next time you do that." They wrestled briefly, and it was over.

The next morning, Christopher told his dad. Sexton

stormed into the little bedroom, threw Joel against the wall, and cracked him across the face with his hand.

"You want to beat somebody's ass, beat mine," he said.

Recalled Skipper, who watched the attack, "Joel was never the same after that. He became just like a little kid."

Joel spent most of his time catering to Pixie and the children. But he also ignored camp rules. Their father wanted the boys out of sight in the daylight hours. He didn't want the landlord to see how many people they had living at the property. Joel kept wandering out of the mobile home.

Willie came up with the idea first, Skipper later recalled. "Willie came to me and my dad and said, 'We should take out Joel, because you know he has a lot of problems.' My dad told Willie he was crazy."

Later, Skipper heard his father and Pixie discuss the idea further at the dining room table. Joel was outside. Pixie complained her husband was "getting on her nerves." Pixie suggested they get life insurance on Joel, Skipper recalled.

"Now that's a good idea," the patriarch said.

Skipper recalled, "It was him and Pixie talking, with their little love affair going. They were gonna have Joel have a freak accident, have the brakes go out on the car. They was going to use my car for it. Gonna pop the brake line. I'm going, c'mon that's my first car. Why the fuck do you want to take him out? Why don't you just take him back to Ohio . . . just drop his ass off somewhere? They was just going to kill his ass."

Soon, the patriarch came up with a new mission. He wanted Skipper and Willie to drive north with him. He was heading north again to Ohio, but this time it wasn't just to pick up some checks.

6

Stark County detective Steve Ready heard about the February 18 auction on Caroline Street through the department grapevine. There had been an advertisement in the paper by auctioneer Ed Fernandez. Ready picked up the phone and called the auctioneer.

Yes, Ed and May Sexton were selling the house and belongings. He'd gotten a call or two from Sexton himself, but mostly his daughter Pixie was handling the details.

"We're looking for Sexton," Ready told him. "He shows up or contacts you, I'd appreciate a call."

Already, Ready was limited by logistics and law as to what he could do to find Ed and May Sexton. Because there was no armed robbery or break-in involved, Eddie Jr.'s loss of the bond money was a civil matter. Eddie Jr. would have to file a lawsuit to get his money back. The Sextons no longer had representation in Family Court. On January 5, their attorney Pat Menicos had withdrawn from the case.

The DHS put out what it called a "protective services alert." It went to police departments in nearby states, stating that Stark County was looking for the minor children. But from experience, social workers knew the notices weren't taken very seriously by many departments around the United States.

Ready checked Sexton's status on his misdemeanor conviction in Massilon. He discovered that the father really wasn't on probation, but good behavior. He didn't have to report to a PO. To stay clean he simply had to avoid appearing again on another crime. They had no proof May Sexton and the children had been kidnapped. In fact, she'd disappeared before her husband. They had only a no-contact order from Family Court.

"If I spotted him in Stark County I had the authority to

take the kids from him," he later explained. "I couldn't even arrest him unless he interfered."

Legal chief Judee Genetin later explained constitutional law prevented them from seeking a bench warrant from Family Court. May Sexton disappeared before they could legally serve her with notice of the last custody hearing. Because she hadn't been legally notified, she technically wasn't breaking the law when she didn't show up.

Even if Steve Ready had a warrant, he'd also be limited on two fronts. The sheriff's department wasn't about to let him go chasing the Sextons cross-country. Everyone in county criminal justice was short-staffed and penny-wise. For years, county law enforcement and prosecution had faced slashed and uncertain budgets. For 10 years, the county had been trying to get a small sales tax enacted to increase crime-fighting revenues, but the effort had been derailed by public referendums and successful recalls of county commissioners who supported the tax. Even if the sheriff sent him on an out-of-state manhunt, he'd have to arrange for local out-of-state authorities to make the arrest and wait out an extradition hearing.

It was too bad Sexton hadn't jumped bail, Ready thought. A bail bondsman could hunt Sexton down, toss him in his trunk, and bring him back from any state with legal immunity. And they often did.

Ready called Ed Sexton's brother, Dave, in New Port Richey, Florida. He'd been told by the DHS that Sherri Sexton was staying with the family. When he called, David Sexton told him she was staying there, but wasn't at home. He got the same answer for the next eight months. Sherri never returned his calls.

Somebody in DHS came up with the idea of chasing the Sextons down through Ed Sexton's disability payments. Judee Genetin called the Bureau of Workman's Compensation in January, requesting information. The bureau reported that Ed Sexton was no longer receiving checks.

One solution, Ready told Genetin, would be the federal Unlawful Flight to Avoid Prosecution warrant, worked through the FBI. If they could indict Eddie and May for felony crimes they could get the UFAP warrant. But with Machelle Sexton recanting, they had no felony.

"The FBI isn't going to get involved over some Family Court bullshit," Ready said.

If some of the other children would only disclose rape or other forms of sexual abuse by the father, they might be able to go before a Stark County grand jury and get indictments. Some of the children were in therapy. But certainly nobody wanted to push the children with repeated interview sessions. Genetin had taken a 30-hour seminar sponsored by the American Prosecutor's Research Institute. She'd learned about the kind of questionable methods used in other flawed cases. For the sake of both the case and the mental health of the children, disclosure had to come naturally.

If sex abuse happened at the hands of the father, one of the children would eventually disclose, Genetin predicted—*if* the children felt they were safe in the foster homes.

Ready called Ed Fernandez again. No, Ed Sexton hadn't shown up for the house sale, the auctioneer said. His daughter Pixie was handling all of the family's affairs.

Months later, Steve Ready would second-guess himself, wondering if he couldn't have done more through the spring and summer of 1993. Maybe he should have attended the auction himself. Maybe he should have interviewed every Sexton relative he could find. Maybe he should have studied every page of the growing Sexton case file at the DHS.

But hell, it wasn't even his case, not yet anyway.

"I beat myself up a lot over that," he would say. "Maybe if I'd done more, some people would be alive."

7

The first thing the girl said when she walked through the door was, "Hi, Mom." It was the day before Valentine's Day, 1993. Twelve-year-old Lana Irene Sexton carried Valentine cards and decorations she'd made for the visit.

Tabatha and Ted Fisher, childless and in their 20s, were getting their first foster child. For Lana, it was one more move. Already, she'd been in seven foster homes. Her father had somehow discovered the location of several of them. She'd also run away from two.

East Liverpool, Ohio was one hour east of Canton, built on a bend in the Ohio River, a bridge to the northern tip of West Virginia leading out of the town. Population 16,000, not a building over three stories. Chalking street signs. Rusty stop-lights. Ancient Mail Pouch ads hand-painted on brick buildings, now faded by weather and time.

But Tabatha and Ted Fisher had found a good life there. Ted worked for a church supply company, maintaining the machinery that made tithing envelopes. The Fishers had a neatly kept, two-story home near the small downtown. Tabatha played piano, Ted, the trombone. They both were non-denominational Christians, active in their local place of worship, the New Hope Community Church.

The Bair Foundation had arranged Lana's visit and prepared the Fishers for foster parenting. They'd attended 20 hours of training. They'd be required to take another 20 every year. They wanted to specialize in therapeutic foster care, working with children with special problems.

With Lana Sexton, they would have all that, and more.

She was from a special situation, the Bair counselor told them. She was a victim of extensive physical, sexual, and ritual abuse. Her first visit would be one weekend. A trial period. Then, they could decide whether they wanted to have the girl.

"We were told from the very beginning she was very difficult," Tabatha would later recall. "But we thought, heck, we'll give it a try."

Those two days, Lana Sexton was an absolute darling. She was pretty, bright, and talkative. They went bowling and rented movies. They played "Uno" and "Sorry." And Lana attached herself to Tabatha as if they'd been separated at birth. She followed her from room to room. She sat with her on the couch. She snuggled up next to her in the easy chair. She didn't seem frightened of Ted, but she kept her distance. Tabatha figured that was because of what counselors had told her about Lana's dad.

When the agency car came on Monday, Lana cried. The Fishers didn't take long to make their decision. Seven days later, Lana Sexton moved into their home.

Lana arrived with an impressive Barbie collection. She had dozens of outfits. She had the house and the car and a half dozen dolls, including Ken. Tabatha didn't know if the load came from her original home or from previous foster families. Lana Sexton didn't talk about her original family, and the Fishers had been counseled not to push the subject.

Tabatha wanted to give some stability to the girl's life, let her experience a household with nurturing guidance and love. Lana enrolled in the local middle school. Tabatha gave her only a couple of minor chores around the house. Lana liked to bike and go bowling and play on a pogo stick.

Then it started.

Soon the girl was having difficulty with her studies. She didn't want to do homework. She wanted to play with her Barbies instead. She recoiled from any positive habit Tabatha tried to show her. She didn't want to bathe or brush her teeth or comb her hair. She didn't want to clean her room. She wanted to take piano lessons, but refused to practice. Tabatha might have written it off to puberty, had it not been for those Barbie dolls. Tabatha's sister, another 12-year-old, stopped playing with Lana because she told Lana that Barbies were for younger girls.

"It was absolutely all Lana wanted to do," she later recalled. "And I'm not exaggerating. If she could, she would sit and play with those Barbie dolls for twenty-four hours a day."

Her attitude seemed to get worse after visits arranged by the DHS with her older brother James. Normally, the agency tried to encourage siblings in separate foster homes to have contact. Soon, counselors decided to have the visits with James stopped.

In time, it became clear that Lana Sexton had a strange mix of personality traits. She was very immature, but also was capable of a maturity well beyond her age. She could be very blunt. She'd rib waitresses, crack inappropriate jokes, and treat the Fisher's adult friends and family as if they were contemporaries.

And she had a favorite word: "Penis."

"He's such a penis," she would say.

"Why are you using that word, Lana?" Tabatha would ask. "You know I don't like it."

She used it for everything:

"He's such a penis."

"That movie was a real penis."

"Don't be such a penis."

Alone with Tabatha, the acting out diminished. Lana loved to cuddle with her in the easy chair. An hour before bed, Tabatha came up with a quiet, sharing time. They read together or talked in Lana's bedroom. Tabatha had learned the practice from her own mother, a special time she remembered as a child.

At night, Lana talked about her sisters. She missed her younger sister Kim. She said they had a little white Bible they used to read in secret. Their father didn't allow them to worship or go to church, she said. Tabatha never pushed church or Christianity on the girl, but she seemed to clamor for it. She wanted to attend church and Bible studies with them. She liked contemporary gospel music and read the Bible before bed.

One night in April, Lana began talking about her brother, Charles, the boy she also called Skipper. She disclosed Skipper had raped her.

"I'm afraid of him," she said.

Tabatha held her close. Lana liked to be hugged when they had their talks.

A few nights later she revealed her dad had sexually molested her. "Dad hurt me," she said. "I don't ever want to be with my dad."

Tabatha held her closer. "You don't have to worry," Tabatha said. "You're with us now."

"No, you don't understand," Lana said, shaking her head. "You can't say *anything* he won't know."

Tabatha reported the disclosure to the Bair Foundation, which passed it on to Stark County DHS workers handling the Sexton case. One week later, as Tabatha picked Lana up from the school, Lana's eyes were wide with fear. She hurried into the car, saying, "I saw Skipper on the playground today."

Lana believed he'd come from a blue truck with Massilon Tigers bumper stickers on it. She'd seen it around the school that day. Skipper, she said, gave her a phone number and said the family was in Salem, West Virginia, 60 miles away.

"I'll be back with Dad, and you better be here," Skipper supposedly said.

Tabatha Fisher remembered seeing a truck like that. It was hard to miss anything new in their small town. The Fishers called the Bair Foundation again, reporting the contact. A foundation worker said he'd request a mug shot of the father from Stark County so the Fishers could identify him. A few days later, Tabatha saw the blue truck at a stoplight, but it turned before she could see the plate.

One week later they were driving away from the school when Lana suddenly ducked, lying down on the backseat.

"He's back there," she screamed.

Tabatha saw only a motorcyclist behind them. "Who's back there?" she asked.

"That's my father on that motorcycle," Lana said.

The cyclist turned. Tabatha wondered if Lana's fears were kindling her imagination. She wished she had that mug shot.

Still, the bed-time talks continued. Lana was convinced now that her father knew she'd told family secrets. "He can talk with us anywhere we are," she said. "You can't hide."

"He's Satan," she said. He had special powers.

On April 29, seven days after Skipper had approached her on the school yard, the Fishers and Lana Sexton arrived home on a Friday evening to find their door wide open, a chilly breeze blowing into the house. The door handle was busted off. Lattice work on the porch was shattered. The neighbor said her dog had been barking earlier.

Inside, they found nothing missing or disturbed, not even Lana's school pictures on their mantel.

"It's my dad," Lana kept saying. "It's my dad."

They spent the night at their pastor's house. Tabatha called the Bair Foundation to report the break-in. By the next morning, both Tabatha and Lana were crying when the foundation car came to pick her up.

8

Ed Sexton seemed to be having little trouble discovering the DHS's secrets.

On January 7, 1993, a worker in the Stark County office received a call from Andover, Ohio. Sexton and his son Skipper had shown up the day before in town, trying to talk Matthew into getting in the car with them. Later, at

midnight, Ed Sexton was spotted outside the foster home.
Detective Glenn Goe sent a mug shot of Eddie Lee Sexton
to Andover police. He also sent one to Salem, West Virginia, asking both departments to be on the watch for the
patriarch.

Three months later, on April 22, the DHS motioned to
terminate its custody of Charles "Skipper" Sexton. He'd
turned 18 and now was a legal adult. That same day, DHS
received a call from the Bair Foundation about his contact
with Lana at the school in East Liverpool. The motorcycle
sighting and the break-in also had DHS workers concerned.

"We had the kids pretty well spread out around the
state," Judee Genetin would recall later. "But it wasn't
spread out enough, obviously. And then you face another
dilemma. One of the things you're supposed to do with
the children in foster care is not move them from home
to home. The more placements, the more detrimental that
is. But we were confronted with real fear for them."

On May 10, the legal staff went back to Family Court
with a new legal angle. Since the Indian pleadings, a four-
year staff attorney named Edith Hough had been doing
the legal trench work on the ongoing Sexton case. Hough
filed a motion seeking permanent custody of James, Christopher, Matthew, Lana, and Kimberly. Hough and Judee
Genetin reasoned that if DHS had permanent custody of
the kids, they could surpass confidentiality rules. They
could identify the children publicly, put out missing fliers,
and maybe even involve "America's Most Wanted" in the
search.

In reality, DHS only had physical custody of Lana, Matt,
and James. But unlike getting a warrant, the court rules
would allow DHS to proceed without serving the Sextons
with hearing papers. They could simply publish a notice
of the proceedings in newspapers. "What we were trying
to do is make them surface," Genetin later explained. "We
were hoping they'd surface to fight it." The notices were

published in the Canton *Repository* on May 18, announcing a hearing date set for August 4.

The Sextons did surface, but not to file legal briefs.

Four days later, an on-call worker at DHS received a late evening call from the Bair Foundation. Andover police were searching for Matthew Sexton. He'd run away from his foster home just after dinner.

Now, as DHS waited for its custody hearing, Eddie Lee Sexton seemed to be picking them off one by one. By Memorial Day, only James and Lana were left under the agency's vulnerable wing.

9

It went down real smooth, Skipper said. They parked near the Andover foster home. Skipper got out of the car. He saw Matt in the yard.

"I got Matt's attention, told him, 'Let's go.' So we picked up Matt and we jetted. We were gone."

But back in Indiana, the family appeared to be increasingly restless. The cramped conditions in the motor home and trailer were taking their toll. They watched TV and listened to the patriarch read Bible verses. He marked dozens of his favorite passages with family photos between the delicate pages of a black King James edition. None of the children went to school. The only relief was periodic trips to town, their own midnight excursions, or their father's combat drills.

Ed Sexton apparently also came up with a method to still the younger children—Dawn, Shasta, and Kimberly—who sometimes became restless at night. It was called Nyquil, a potent mix of alcohol and cold drugs. May Sexton would later claim she and 9-year-old Kimberly took Nyquil nightly because of asthma. But some Sexton children said it was routinely given to quiet the younger ones before bed.

One night, Skipper, Joel, Matt, and Chris were sitting around the trailer. They began talking about a plan to leave. Skipper said he knew about a cave in the area where they could spend the first night. During his summer stay with his aunt and uncle, he'd learned local teens partied there. All they needed was food and cigarettes, and they could jet, he said.

"Joel was in for it at first," Skipper recalled. "Then he says, 'Well, what about Pixie?' I'm like, well you see what's the matter with Pixie. She's in love with the old man.' He says, 'Don't talk about her that way. She's my wife.'

"I'm thinking, well, believe what you want to believe. We had the shit packed. Was ready to go. And then we thought about it. I'm like, damn, you know, we're running away. We're gonna leave 'em. I said fuck it, and went back to bed."

10

Diane Beckort, the 50-year-old manager of Bushman's Lake and Marina, remembered the day Ed and May Sexton drove up to her office, wanting to rent a mobile home on the river, just five months before.

May Sexton said she was pregnant. Beck looked her over. As far as Beckort was concerned, she was too old, and too heavy to really tell.

They had a young brown-haired girl with them, Kimberly. Sexton said he was selling his home in Ohio. Beckort had a mobile home for $300 a month, plus a $300 deposit, the first month paid in advance. The mobile home was unfurnished.

That's okay, Sexton said. He had some furniture he was going to bring from his Ohio house.

Sexton peeled off $600 in cash. She asked for no references. She had four rental homes of her own and managed rentals of another two dozen in the resort. She'd learned references were unreliable. Beckort had too many great recommendations from other landlords who lied to help move their bad tenants out.

Bushman's Lake included a little bar and burger stand, but Beckort never opened it until Memorial Day. When it was broken into one night, the last people she would have suspected were the Sextons. "He was so polite and so nice," she'd later recall.

But just before Memorial Day, Beckort noticed that the Sexton family seemed to be growing. She lived on the other end of the road along the river, far from the Sexton trailer. Now she was noticing other vehicles. She saw several young men and boys around the trailer.

She approached Sexton. "I never would have rented the trailer if I knew you were going to have this many people," she told him. "The septic tank can't handle it."

"I understand, ma'am," he said. "It's no problem. We'll just move."

He asked for a week. She saw the family moving out furniture over the next few days. He came by, asking for his deposit. She inspected the trailer. They'd left it spotless.

She gave him back $300.

"You couldn't ask for a nicer tenant," she said.

11

Two months after the February auction, the couple who'd made the winning bid of $67,000 for the house on Caroline Street still had nothing to show for their earnest money. Veteran auctioneer Ed Fernandez had finally arranged a clear title. Now Ed Sexton wouldn't return to Canton close the deal.

Sexton wanted Fernandez to give the paperwork to his daughter Pixie.

"I can't do that," Fernandez said. "You've got to take care of it personally."

Sexton stopped calling. Then Pixie phoned repeatedly, trying to convince him to release the paperwork.

The buyers tired of waiting. The sale fell through.

The entire auction had been a bust, as far as Fernandez was concerned. He'd sold the house's contents to a crowd of 50 people, calling bids from the home's open garage.

"I hated bringing my crew into that garbage pit," he'd say later. "That filth. That stink. Most of the stuff was just junk."

The contents brought only $700, not enough to cover the auctioneer's expenses.

It was the second time Ed and May Sexton had burned him. He'd signed a contract to auction the house a year earlier, in the late winter of 1992, but Sexton had changed his mind.

Ed Sexton was a low-rent hustler, Fernandez thought. He, too, had heard the talk about some big promotional deal Sexton said he had with fast food franchises.

"He was an ugly manipulator," Fernandez would later recall. "He thinks he's smarter than everybody, but he surrounds himself with losers. He was a con man. Lazy. One of those procrastinators who always had something coming down the road."

Now Fernandez wished Sexton would show up. He'd relish calling up the detective named Steve Ready at the sheriff's department. He'd enjoy turning the con man in. Pixie and that husband of hers had also been no help. She was clueless. The husband was a mute, he figured, maybe an IQ of seven.

When it appeared no one was staying in the home anymore, Ed Fernandez went over to inspect the premises. Inside, he found the place gutted of remaining furniture, garbage all over the house. The bathroom toilets were filled with human waste, like some kind of sick, defiant goodbye notice.

He called his lawyer and turned over all the paperwork.

As far as he was concerned, Ed Fernandez would count himself ahead if he never saw another Sexton again.

12

Tuck and Colleen Carson had visited the trailer at Bushman's Lake a couple of times. They had seen the crowded conditions and the older boys with handguns tucked in their belts. On one visit, Eddie showed Tuck his hand and pointed to what he called "a continuous life line" in his palm.

"You know what that means?" Sexton asked.

Tuck shook his head.

"It means I'm destined for life in the hereafter."

He may have calmed down compared to the early days, Tuck figured. But Eddie Lee Sexton was still as weird as all hell.

Colleen was struck by the boy named Joel. "He acted like he was even scared to talk," she'd recall later. "Like they were going to bite him or something."

In late spring, Eddie and May announced they were moving to Florida. The sale of their house in Ohio was almost wrapped up, they said. They had a new couch and love seat. They wondered if they could store it at the Carsons' house until they sent a truck to pick it up.

They left in the Challenger motor home, Pixie and Joel following them in the Pontiac. There was a 1993 Fraternal Order of Police sticker on the Grand Prix's chrome bumper, and a red-white-and-blue sticker on the trunk. It read:

GOD, GUNS & GUTS MADE AMERICA
LET'S KEEP ALL THREE!

viii
Dream Reaching

1

After the break-in in East Liverpool, Tabatha and Ted Fisher eventually convinced social workers to let Lana Sexton return to their home—but only for weekends, when they were free to watch her every move. Considering Ed Sexton's savvy, workers worried Lana could be kidnapped from school. During the week, she lived in a second foster home in Canton.

Lana made no secret of whom she preferred. She wanted Tabatha and Ted as her parents. She began calling them Mom and Dad. But every Monday, after they took her to counseling, they drove the girl back to Canton. The Fishers also had taken four other foster children into their home.

Even with the weekend visits, the disclosures continued throughout the summer, and turned more bizarre. One night, during their bedtime sharing, Lana showed Tabatha the line in her hand.

"I'm the only one who has this line," she said.

Tabatha squinted at her palm. She'd never paid any attention to the lines on people's hands.

Lana took Tabatha's hand and pointed. "See, Mom, you don't have a line like that in your hand."

She talked about going to "Futuretron meetings" in Florida and New York with her father. She and her father stayed in a hotel. During one Florida visit he took a lot of pictures of her, having her smile "for the Futuretrons."

"Did you meet the Futuretrons?" Tabatha asked. "What are they?"

"No, he met with the people," she said. "I stayed in the hotel." Lana couldn't seem to explain who exactly these "Futuretrons" were or what they did.

Other stories were more dark. She heard about the beatings and being kept home from school. She said her father once made her wear a transparent white dress and dance around a table lit with candles. She told that story often, but it was pale compared to other disclosures.

One day, when they'd gone swimming, Tabatha noticed a large scar at the base of her spine. "That looks pretty painful," Tabatha said. "You get that from a fall or something?"

"No, my dad cut me," she said.

That night she told her more. Lana said she'd been born with a twin sister. But her father separated them at birth, then killed the other twin.

Lana eyes welled with tears. "That could have been me," she said. "I could be dead."

"How do you know that?" Tabatha asked.

"My sister told me," she said. She wouldn't say which one.

Another story about miscarried babies unfolded. Lana said her father would hit her mother in the stomach when she was pregnant. He did this several times.

"Then the baby would die," she said.

And, Lana added, she had to drink its blood.

"Did you ever see the baby?" Tabatha asked.

Eddie Lee and Estella May Sexton,
patriarch and matriarch of
"America's most dysfunctional family."

Sexton's parents, William and Lana. He disciplined the boys, she the girls.

Otis Sexton during his days as an evangelical minister.

Sexton's birthplace in Baisden Bottom, near Logan,
West Virginia. His father preached and worked the mines.

The gas station in Naugatuck, West Virginia that Ed Sexton
robbed the day after he was married in 1963.
He spent the next five years in prison.

"Your family is your country." The young Sexton siblings: (*top row*) Eddie Junior, Patrick, Sherri; (*middle*) Willie, Charles, Pixie, Machelle; (*bottom*) Matthew, James, Christopher, and Lana.

Machelle Sexton in a rare photo from her early teens. Police called her a hero.

Lana Sexton. Her father said the life line on her hand gave her mystic powers.

The Sexton Stare:
Police snapshots of Sherri, Matthew, Christopher,
and Eddie Junior, just after their father and mother's arrest.

Christopher Sexton was allowed to play football. He was his parents' "favorite," siblings said.

Charles "Skipper" Sexton as a young Jackson wrestler.

Sexton's "marriage" ceremony with his daughter Lana in the family living room.

Ed's "marriage" with Sherri the same night. She later would carry his child.

Shelly's drawing of the Futuretrons.
The patriarch said in the future all people will look alike.
(Use of Burger King logo is unauthorized by Burger King.)

The former family home at 8149 Caroline Street NW.

Armed with an arsenal of guns, Sexton kept a ready supply of ammunition by the window in preparation for his battle against the outside world.

The house on Caroline in flames, one of several fires police suspect Sexton set in the 1980s for insurance money.

The beginning: Joel and Pixie
on their first date, the senior prom.

Joel Good as a senior in high school,
before he became part of
the Sexton family.

Joel Good after one of many beatings
he endured by the Sexton boys.

"He always wanted a family." Joel, Pixie, and her children Shasta and Dawn. Good's aunt noticed a strange resemblance to Eddie Lee Sexton—especially their eyes.

The mobile home on Dave Sexton's compound in Moon Lake where Sexton siblings tortured Joel Good.

The Dodge Challenger motorhome. Fourteen people lived inside when the Sextons were on the run.

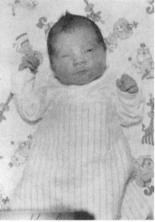

Skipper Lee Good's hospital birth photo. Eight months later, little "Ewok" was dead.

"A good snitch is a dead snitch." Ed Sexton on the run in the Dodge Challenger motorhome.

A Florida evidence tech opens the duffle bag in Hillsborough State Park to find baby Skipper Lee Good.

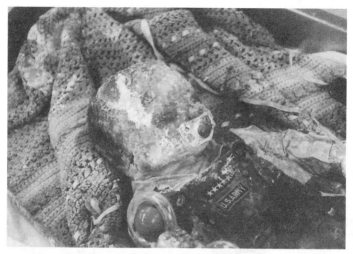

Skipper Lee Good after disinterment,
buried with his pacifier and a rattle in his hand.

Captured: Pixie Sexton, brother Willie,
and their parents in Hillsborough County Police mug shots.

Joel Good's body was found face down, buried in the wet Florida peat.

Florida detectives Linda Burton and Mike Willette.

Stark County detective Steve Ready. He chased the Sextons and their secrets after others dismissed the case.

Some questioned Otis Sexton's motives, but police say his advocacy was crucial in cracking the case.

Free at last. Social Services took custody of the Sexton children months after their parents' arrest. (*Left to right*) Christopher, James, Kimberly, Matthew, and Lana.

"On a tray," Lana said.

Tabatha Fisher called Lana's social worker. She wanted to know more details about Lana's family. My God, baby killings, Tabatha said. What the heck am I dealing with here? The social worker reminded her ritual abuse had been suspected. The stories were likely a ruse by the father to exercise control.

Near the end of June, Lana disclosed something Tabatha found more troubling. Shortly after she'd arrived that weekend, she said one of the girls in the other foster home had touched her inappropriately. Tabatha reported it to the Bair Foundation. On Sunday, as they took her back to Canton, Lana was upset. She wanted Tabatha to sit with her in the backseat.

During the ride, she leaned close to Tabatha. Her father and her brother weren't the only ones who'd done sexual things to her, she said.

"My mother touched me," she said.

"Touched you how?" Tabatha asked.

"She put things in me," Lana said.

Tabatha Fisher reported the disclosure to the foundation. On July 1, DHS worker Tracey Harlin interviewed Lana about the revelation.

The disclosures seemed to carry a price. She became bulimic, eventually losing 20 pounds. She made vague references to suicide. She became more convinced her father knew she was talking.

Soon her fears manifested in more disturbing behaviors in the Fishers' house. She withdrew deeper into her Barbies and became defiant, her personality sometimes taking on a vicious quality, profanity spitting from her mouth.

In the evening, Lana often went upstairs with her Barbies. One night, Tabatha and Ted could hear her talking to someone.

Tabatha went upstairs.

"Who you talking to?" she asked.

"I'm talking to the voices," she said.

"What voices?"

"I'm not allowed to tell."

Tabatha decided not to make a big production out of it. Maybe Lana was just clamoring for attention.

It happened the next night, and on a subsequent weekend.

One night, they heard her crying.

Tabatha snuck up the stairs this time. Lana was in a corner between the wall and dresser. She was as white as a sheet and shivering. It was a hot summer night.

"What's wrong?" Tabatha asked.

"He wants me."

"Who wants you?"

"My dad."

"Your dad's not here, honey."

"He told me he wants me. He's coming after me."

Her father was Satan. He had powers, she said.

The Fishers began to feel like a dark presence was taking over the house. They started praying regularly.

"It was even becoming difficult for my husband and I to maintain our Bible study time," she later recalled. "Our prayer time. Our personal time together. You could feel a heaviness. You walked through the door and you could feel it. And we even had other people tell us this, they felt something in the house."

It seemed as if the more they prayed, the more things happened. They'd find Lana screaming in the middle of the night, claiming there was the silhouette of a man in the hall. They'd comfort her and she'd go right back to sleep. But on subsequent nights the screams continued, and the image moved closer, from the hall into the bedroom, then from the bedroom to her bed.

Another night. More screams. Now the image was over her bed, Lana said.

"It's going to kill me," she said.

"Who is this man?" Tabatha asked.

"My dad," she said.

A few nights later, Tabatha got up in the middle of the night to go to the bathroom. She saw Lana standing by the window in her room, looking out over the neighbor's garden.

Tabatha watched for a few moments, quietly. Lana appeared completely mesmerized. Then she started whimpering, then crying.

When she began to weep, Tabatha took her into her arms. Between sobs, Lana said she'd seen her grandmother.

"Where?" Tabatha asked.

Standing outside her window in a bloody white dress, she said. "She was saying, 'Come with me.'"

The voices continued. It was her dad talking, Lana said.

During the day, the Fishers were running out of ways to maintain control of the girl. Tabatha tried rewarding her for good behavior with Barbie outfits. She remained mouthy and defiant. Tabatha was starting to feel like a failure with her very first foster child.

One day, Tabatha tried a time-out, having her sit down in a chair. Within moments, Lana was sprawling on the floor.

"Lana, the longer you're out of that chair, the longer your time-out is going to be," Tabatha said.

Lana suddenly thrust her head between her legs, covered her hair with her hands, and started screaming at the top of her lungs.

"He's killing me! He's killing me!"

It was if she were being pummeled by an unseen fist.

2

The communities had informal names: Moon Lake and Shady Hills. There were no local units of government, no town centers. These areas of Pasco County had swamp-choked lots, rusting mobile homes, and satellite dishes.

Shady Hills had a couple of adopt-a-road signs sponsored by the Knights of the Ku Klux Klan. Not even Pasco County sheriff's deputies felt comfortable venturing into some neighborhoods after dark.

This was not the Florida northerners saw on travel and real estate brochures. For years, Pasco County natives had considered the 20-mile-wide stretch of lowland between Gulf of Mexico beach towns and the ranches near Dade City to be mosquito-infested and unfit for development. Then the boiler rooms went to work. By the 1990s, the result was a continuous, car-choked 25-mile stretch of strip development along US-19 out of Clearwater to New Hudson—and inland, the haphazard development of places like Moon Lake and Shady Hills.

Dave Sexton and his wife Jean lived about 10 miles from New Hudson, on a chain-link fenced lot on a stone road in Moon Lake. Sexton had three mobile homes in his compound, one for him and his wife Jean, the other for his son's family, the third used by Sherri Sexton and her boy Christopher for a spell. The couple had moved to Florida in the 1980s from Canton, Ohio.

Dave and Jean Sexton would later detail their encounters with Eddie Lee Sexton's family in sworn depositions, court testimony, and an interview.

Jean Sexton said she was a long-time evangelist and an active volunteer in a local Pentecostal church. Dave Sexton, 56, said he'd served 23 years with the Air Force and retired on a military disability.

In fact, all the living Sexton brothers were on government relief. Eddie Sexton had his back problems. Otis received Social Security for rheumatic fever. Back in Canton, Orville Sexton was disabled in a coal mining accident after a mine caved in on him in West Virginia. Dave Sexton was asked the nature of his physical problems in a 1994 deposition.

He answered: "I have MS. I have epilepsy. I have heart trouble. I have high blood pressure. I'm—I'm neurotic." He also said he was legally blind.

The Challenger and the black Pontiac Grand Prix rolled up to Dave Sexton's compound on a stifling Sunday night in June. Though Sherri Sexton had been with his family nearly six months, Dave maintained he had no idea what kind of problems his brother faced back in Stark County with the DHS. He said his brother called him back in April of 1992 and asked if Sherri could move there "so she could start a new life for herself." That new life included a place on the Florida welfare roll for Sherri and the boy who'd been nicknamed "Little Bear." Shapely and attractive as a young teenager, at 21 her eyes had become dark and brooding, her figure heading for 200 pounds.

Dave and Jean Sexton said they were a close "religious family." Their son David Jr. and his small family rented one of the mobile homes. They'd adopted a 12-year-old boy named Tommy from their daughter in Canton. The boy suffered from emotional and developmental problems. Drinking and swearing and carousing were prohibited in the compound. As far as Dave was concerned, his brother Eddie was no threat to their way of life.

"For all the years I known them," Dave said, "I've never in my life seen Eddie take a drink of alcohol. I've never seen May."

Sherri Sexton actually had left the compound sometime in the late summer. She'd stayed with another couple, then spent some time in a battered woman's shelter. After that, she moved in with a mixed couple.

Dave Sexton said he knew what his brother thought of black people. "I knew Eddie would be very upset," he explained. "I said, this is not what you should be doing, Sherri. It's best you come back."

When the Sexton family arrived, Sherri was talking about moving back to Ohio to live with her sister Machelle. Jean

Sexton was planning to leave on June 7 to visit her daughter in Canton. She'd take Sherri and Little Bear. His second birthday was the day they were supposed to leave.

Until the Sexton caravan arrived. There was Eddie, May, Willie, Christopher, Matt, Charles, Kimberly, Pixie, Dawn, Shasta, Pixie's husband Joel, and their new baby Skipper Lee, or "Ewok." Jean said she was struck by Joel Good's appearance. His head was almost shaved clean.

"He looked like a monk," Jean said. "And he was so tiny and frail."

Now, two more would join the clan. Monday morning, Jean Sexton headed north without Sherri and her child.

"Eddie came down and told me he was going to settle down in Florida," Dave said. "And he's been telling me this for quite a few years. And he asked if he could park his motor home on our property until they found them a house. And I told them they could."

They stayed two weeks, some of the family moving into the middle trailer, others staying in the Challenger. Then, Eddie Sexton found the house he was looking for.

It was in the area everyone called Shady Hills.

3

Two hundred dollars down, 12 months to pay. New Hudson pawnshop owner Ray Santee had bought the property in 1971 on Treaty Road like a lot of other buyers. Developers were promising well-kept roads and municipal services. But not long after Santee built the four-bedroom cut-stone house with a screened-in pool, it became evident that live oaks and the Florida undergrowth were destined to rule Shady Hills.

Now Santee rented out the property, $750 plus security. Five miles out of New Hudson, the road damaged the property value more than anything. What little asphalt was left on Treaty held 10-foot long, 3-foot deep potholes that could swallow a compact car.

It was early June when the man named Ed Sexton showed up at Santee's Hudson Pawn & Music on US-19, answering a classified ad. Sexton said he'd already driven out and seen the property.

"The money's no problem," Sexton said. "We like it. We're kind of a private family."

Treaty Road certainly was private. There were few homes in the area. A couple of black families moved into the neighborhood for a few years, but soon left. Gunfire often cracked through the woods and swamps. People were free to take target practice on their own property. A KKK adopt-a-road sign was planted on nearby Ranch Road.

Santee had some bad news for Sexton. He'd just rented the stone house earlier that day.

Sexton persisted. He said he and his sons were very handy. He was on disability himself, but between them they could do repairs, fix up the property.

Santee said the lease was signed. But he also had a mobile home about a hundred yards from the house for rent. That was $275 a month.

"Well, then, we'll take that," Sexton said. "And if that home frees up, then you let us know."

Santee thought it was odd. It was as if the man had been ready to buy a Cadillac, then suddenly wanted a '67 Dodge.

But the new tenant never complained once. He'd drop by the shop after buying home-improvement supplies for the mobile home and grounds. He invited Santee out to visit to check on his progress, but Santee never found the time. He always asked when the neighbor in the stone home might be moving out.

Maybe soon, Santee said. He was having trouble collecting rent.

Santee was surprised Sexton was getting along so well, considering the size of his family.

"Oh, we like the privacy," Sexton said.

4

On July 5, four days after Lana Sexton disclosed her mother's sexual abuse to her foster mother, DHS representatives met with a standing, child sexual assault task force made up of Steve Ready, an assistant Stark County prosecutor, and other officials. The task force's role was to decide whether there was probable cause to go to a grand jury for indictments, sparing children testimony and cross-examination in a municipal court, where most Ohio felonies are first brought. The DHS had Lana's disclosures and medical exams consistent with vaginal penetration.

The task force ruled the case had probable cause to seek warrants with a grand jury. But that also meant Lana Sexton would have to take the stand. DHS workers were getting reports of Lana's behavior from the Bair Foundation. In May, North Canton psychologist Robin Tener also had submitted a report, describing the girl's fragile condition.

Tener wrote, "No amount of treatment is likely to be helpful to Lana, unless she can be assured that she is safe from her family."

It had taken seven months for Lana Sexton to disclose. They couldn't reasonably expect her to march into a room full of strangers and disclose her secrets, at least not without some time to heal.

As the Satanic details surfaced with both Lana and James, legal chief Judee Genetin also believed another factor might have come into play. Detective Glenn Goe and worker Tracey Harlin had brought sexual assault charges against Charles "Skipper" Sexton to the task force back in February and received a similar referral. But the prosecutor's juvenile division had done little with the case. Some of Genetin's own associates were beginning to question her passion for the case.

"Nobody was excited about this case from the beginning," she'd later recall. "Nobody took it seriously. People cannot believe things like this happen. We have judges on the bench who still do not believe that adults can molest children. They just can't accept it. And with the ritual factor, that comes into play even more. Part of the reason for ritual abuse is that the perpetrator knows if a child does disclose, the ritualistic disclosures will make it even more unbelievable."

Genetin knew she must have looked obsessed with the case. Later, an attorney would comment that she'd seen her arguing the Sexton matter, pacing in Family Court, her voice bellowing. "We all thought you were crazy," she said.

"I sounded like a lunatic," Genetin said. "And if you stand back and look at it, it does sound like some really bizarre stuff."

Hysterical or not, Genetin and staff attorney Edith Hough went back to the Family Court on August 4, arguing the motion for permanent custody, filed nearly three months before.

The court knew four children were still missing. Judge Edwards asked Genetin if she wanted to amend her complaint to include only Lana and James, the only children under physical custody with the DHS.

"No, your honor," she said.

Said Genetin later, "It was the strangest custody case we'd ever argued. I've never filed for permanent custody of kids that I didn't have under physical control."

Despite the public notices in local newspapers, neither the Sextons nor an attorney representing them showed up. The motion was unopposed.

Still, it would be nearly six weeks before the DHS would get a judgement from the court.

5

In Florida, Eddie Lee Sexton was preparing to take his case to a higher authority. He wanted the federal government involved.

Back in the trailer at Bushman's Lake, he'd shot a video with the family camcorder. Now, after the Sextons arrived in Florida, he wanted copies of the 3-hour-9-minute production sent to President William Jefferson Clinton and Attorney General Janet Reno.

Sexton hosted the homespun program. Well-groomed and wearing a black sweater, he sat at a table, the mobile home's wood paneling and a family portrait as a backdrop. He sat with his hands folded, a coffee mug at his right, a wedding band sparkling on his left hand. A blue tattoo poked out from his rolled-up right sleeve, a swooping American eagle, its talons bared.

"Citizens of the United States, I am coming to you in hopes that in some way that some official of the United States government can step in and find out why a family such as mine has been treated in such a manner," he began. "I feel that our constitutional rights have been violated. Our civil rights have been violated."

Sexton looked as relaxed as the host of a cable fishing show. The picture was as centered and still as a professional studio shot.

For 15 minutes, he covered the details, blaming most of the family's troubles on his daughter Machelle, his brother Otis, and the Stark County DHS, particularly Wayne Welsh and Bonita Hilson, the black social worker assigned to the family.

Sexton said Machelle had run away from home once before, in the summer before her senior year. She'd dumped urine from an upstairs window on her brothers Matt and Willie in the yard. He claimed she'd accused others of rape: a high school boyfriend; the father of a friend; her uncle Otis; and the park worker she'd dated after she left home. Sexton accused Wayne Welsh of fabricating pregnancy test results for Jackson police.

Sexton said his brother Otis was motivated by money and vengeance. He said their relationship had gone sour when Otis had falsely accused Willie of stealing his ring. Otis filed false insurance claims and a bogus disability case. He was trying to get custody of his children so he could collect their relief payments. "He is mentally ill to a great extent due to the fact that he tries to cause everybody problems," Sexton said.

Sexton claimed his own health had been deteriorating for years. He had muscular dystrophy, he claimed, and more. "I have a mass," he said. "My left eye is out and it's taken over my nervous system and I've had nine back surgeries and I have cancer in between my shoulder blades and evidently it's spreading."

He called for the Indian nations to "rise up" and support him. "My mother was Indian. My father was Indian. [My wife's] father was Indian. Her mother was Indian." He said their families didn't have tribal registration numbers because they'd left their reservations at the turn of the century, when record-keeping stopped.

On he went, in numbing minutia, covering Wayne Welsh, "a habitual liar," and Bonita Hilson, "a very arrogant person," and their contacts with his family. He said his children had been abused in the foster homes. He said he'd only staged the standoff to draw attention to his case, after becoming convinced the DHS planned to take his children away from May again. Before the standoff, his wife had just returned from a little vacation, showing his children Fort Knox, "where I did my basic training," and the General George C. Patton Museum.

He was particularly critical of Bonita Hilson, saying, "I just don't know what was wrong with her. She had no kind of inner feelings whatsoever. She's the kind of individual who is ironclad within herself. I feel that she has got a problem. I don't know what her marital status is, but I'd rest assured to state she's probably not married. I understand she has children. I don't know how many. But I figure she's had a bad time of marriage. I figure psychologically and mentally she has suffered and she has got a mental problem herself. And now anybody that has married and has children, she's going to make them suffer.''

After Sexton's soliloquy, the camera was paused, and May Sexton appeared in the same chair, cradling a Styrofoam cup. Her dark hair was short and slicked back, a bright green sweater covering her stooped shoulders. She covered a list of subjects, confirming her husband's account, her eyes rolling up to the right as if she were checking off a mental list. She mentioned nothing about being pregnant. In fact, that subject, and ostensibly the pregnancy, if there was one, had disappeared as quickly as it came.

Her children were abused in the foster homes, May claimed. She described a meeting with Lana at Harmony House, the neutral facility for DHS-supervised visits. As she described alleged foster care conditions, the details had a familiar ring.

"While we were at Harmony House, she [Lana] was showing us some bruises on her arm, ones that the foster family had put on her, 'cause she was being rebellious. And Bonita [Hilson] said she couldn't let the children be rebellious. And I wanted her out of the foster home . . . Lana told her how they were treating her. They were wanting her to do housework. She was only 12 years old, and I don't think children like that should be treated as maids. She wasn't treated that way at home. And while Kim was in foster care they tried to run away twice. They were locked in bathrooms with the lightbulbs taken out. They were even locked in closets. The boys were being worked like farm animals in the foster homes. They all were being mistreated . . . and I'd like to see them back home where they belong."

The show went on.

Eddie Sexton tried to switch from host to interviewer. One by one children took a seat next to him at the table— Kimberly, Pixie, Skipper, Christopher, Willie, and even Joel Good. But Sexton continued to carry the narrative, methodically stating the facts, the kids most of the time confirming with a single "yes" or a nod of the head.

Several themes ran through the interviews. There was no profanity or pornography in his house. There was no sexual contact. There were no beatings. The extent of punishment was grounding children to their rooms. All preferred life on the run with their parents to returning to foster care.

The children's body language often was more intriguing than the few words from their lips.

Kimberly, or "Hoggie," her long dark hair in a single, side ponytail, chuckled and swivelled in her chair like a typical 8-year-old. But her eyes frequently searched for her father's approval. She missed her sister Angel, she said.

"She's going to be coming home pretty soon," Sexton promised.

Pixie, in a smart tan, white and black sport shirt, sat next to her father, facing the camera, their body language mirroring one another. Her arms were folded across her breasts. Sometimes she smirked at someone off camera. She was attractive, and would have been more so, save the dark circles under her eyes. She looked starved for sleep.

Her father said, "I have to thank you in front of everybody that's going to hear this tape for the assistance you've given me though all this. I can't thank you enough for bringing me my medication . . . I was really supposed to be in a wheelchair . . . The doctors have informed my attorneys and so forth, my life span isn't too long right now, are you aware of that?"

Pixie nodded. She nodded for the next five minutes as Sexton rehashed details of his case.

He concluding by asking, "What was your childhood like?"

"My childhood was good," Pixie said.

When she finished, Pixie had hardly said two dozen words.

The boys took their turns, Sexton portraying them as career-minded teenagers who were planning on forming their own country band before the troubles began.

Christopher wore an army green T-shirt with a white bulldog across the chest. He had few words and showed little emotion.

Pointing out that Christopher was his last son, Sexton asked, "Which one are you?"

"Seventh," Chris said, smiling, his eyes lighting up.

"Seventh son of the seventh son," Sexton said, grinning himself. "I'm the seventh son, and my father was the seventh son, so that's pretty good."

Sexton questioned him about his goal to one day play professional football. Sexton, however, with one question seemed to indicate he himself had never attended a game.

Sexton, smoking a cigarette now, asked, "What were you trying to strive for, son, in football?"

"I just wanted you to be proud," he said.

"And I was," Sexton said, smiling.

Skipper seemed to enjoy the camera, smiling frequently. He directly contradicted later interviews, saying he'd seen no guns during the Caroline Street standoff. The kids were playing Nintendo during the ordeal, he said.

Sexton apologized to Skipper for the disruptions in his school life, then gave some fatherly advice: "The only thing I can say to you, and I've told all you children . . . there will be trials that will come into your lifetime. Take this one and cope with it. Don't hold real hard feelings for the rest of your life. It will only cause you to become nervous and create problems in your older life. Just take it one day at a time."

Joel Good looked like only a shadow of the boy in his prom photograph. He wore a black T-shirt. His hair was hardly an inch long, his face dwarfed by a pair of oversized plastic frames. His eyes were on the table through most of the appearance. He picked at his fingernails. Sexton did all the talking, Joel occasionally saying "yes" or "right."

Sexton tried to get him to disparage Machelle's character in high school.

"What was she like?" he asked.

"She was hyper," he mumbled, but went no further.

Sexton told the camera that neither Pixie nor Joel had "aided or abetted" his flight from Ohio and said they'd be going home to Canton soon.

When Willie Sexton, dressed in a black T-shirt, took Joel Good's place in the chair after a pause, the physical difference between the two young men was striking. His stature dwarfed his father's, his biceps bulging. Willie repeated the charges his father had made against Uncle Otis, saying he wanted custody of the kids for their support payments. He didn't stutter, but spoke in short bursts. Sexton talked about the confrontation with the DHS.

"That was a long trying period, but we endured it," Sexton said.

Willie nodded passively.

Sexton concluded the show alone in front of the camera. He produced family portraits of his other children, making his most passionate plea.

This was an all-American family and he was a good American, he said. He'd served in the military. He'd personally written to former President George Bush, volunteering to serve as a chaplain in Desert Storm. He wanted only his children returned to his wife, he said, the family returned to its "normal" life back in Jackson Township.

"I'm not seeking anything for myself," he said.

At one point, in conclusion, he said:

"I hope this gives you some insight or impression of the family and children and the conditions we are in at this time . . . Now, I have taken my children and placed them before you. I have placed my wife before you. I have placed myself and jeopardized myself. I know you will know I have violated the law, and I admit it.

"But I will continue to violate the law for the protection of my family and the *preservation* of my family. Just as I stated before, I would gladly give my life for my country. I would gladly give my life for my family. Because *that* is my country. *Your* family is your country. Your family is a country, the future of the United States."

Some family members would later say Sexton wrote out their parts, then rehearsed them for several nights. A bitter argument also broke out between Ed and May after her segment was shot. Sexton didn't like May's performance. But on tape, all was folksy and serene. Pixie Sexton mailed the tapes in mid August, postmarked from Hudson and New Port Richey, Florida.

They would come back to haunt the seventh-son-of-the-seventh-son one day.

6

The judgement came from Judge Julie Edwards on September 20, awarding DHS permanent custody of all the minor Sexton children. One of DHS's first acts as the official, legal parent was to contact the Stark County Sheriff's Department. DHS attorney Edith Hough wanted to file a missing persons report for Kimberly, Matthew, and Christopher Sexton.

Steve Ready received a call from his captain.

"Every large department has its top detectives," Ready would later recall. "They get the high-profile cases when they come through, and it should be that way, because they're usually good investigators. This case did not come to me that way. This was part of the slush pile. When the missing persons reports were filed, they figured, just send it over to Ready. He's already over there at human services anyway."

Steve Ready now officially had the Sexton case. Eighteen months had passed since Machelle Sexton's original disclosure, eleven months since Eddie Lee Sexton had barricaded his house.

It was no longer Jackson Township's case.

From the little he'd learned chasing the Sextons earlier in the year, Ready still was only sightly intrigued. He had 20 other cases that demanded immediate attention, cases with victims and perpetrators and witnesses and physical evidence, cases that had to be prepared for court.

He began working the phone at 7:15 a.m. Monday morning. He'd find these people, he decided. If the prosecutor could get them charged with Lana Sexton, they'd get felony warrants and get the FBI involved. Find the Sextons and their children. Get a subpoena for blood tests and prove the incest. The DHS already had custody. Take Eddie and May to trial.

Case closed.

Edith Hough had given the detective two names; one was Orville Sexton, the other Otis Sexton. He also had Eddie Sexton, Jr.'s phone number.

"This Uncle Otis," Hough said. "I think he might have a few leads."

Ready called Eddie Jr. He said maybe his mother was with her brother in Jeffersonville, Indiana. He gave Ready the number of Tuck Carson.

Moments later, he had Otis Sexton on the phone. Then he drove to the uncle's house.

The two men were mistrustful of each other at first. There was the sexual assault allegation made by Machelle at the prosecutor's office. But the prosecutor had decided not to pursue the matter, considering the fluid dynamics of the entire Sexton case. Machelle later said her parents made her file the false charge.

Otis later said, "I was so disgusted with what had happened with Jackson police and everybody else. When this Steve Ready showed up, I figured, okay, here's another disappointment standing at my door. I was very wrong."

"Look, you can't blame Glenn Goe," Ready told Otis. "This girl recanted. If you don't have a victim, you don't have a crime. His witness backed out on him. What do you expect him to do?"

Ready also began wondering, why is this guy so jazzed up? He was on disability. He had a stable of personal lawyers. He was a former preacher. It was difficult not to draw some comparisons with his brother Eddie. Ready thought, does this Otis Sexton have some kind of hidden agenda of his own?

But within weeks, phoning or visiting Otis Sexton would become a daily routine for the detective. Otis was a library of knowledge, but he seemed to loan it only a chapter at a time. Finally, the detective gave the uncle his home phone number. He'd never done that in his entire police career.

During their first meeting, Otis detailed his suspicions about incest in the family, but he didn't know his brother's whereabouts. He did have a lead, however. He said his brother was still getting his workman's compensation checks and Social Security checks for his children. He believed they were being mailed locally to his brother Orville, who passed them on to Eddie.

Ready decided not to visit Orville Sexton, concluding an interrogation would only burn the lead. If Orville was Eddie's ally, a visit would only alert Eddie Sexton that Ready was on his trail.

Instead, back at the office, he suggested the DHS make another run at the workman's comp records. Get the canceled checks. Maybe they'd show where they were being cashed, Ready said. He also asked the prosecutor's office for a subpoena. He wanted the phone records for the house on Caroline Street in the last months that Pixie Sexton was living there.

Ready also knew that Judee Genetin was working with an assistant prosecutor on the grand jury for Lana. Ready met with attorney Edith Hough again.

"We have got to get those criminal charges filed and get those warrants," he said.

Two days on the case, and something about Eddie Lee Sexton already was irritating the detective. Sexton exploiting his own children was bad enough. Ready had two daughters. But he tried not to get too emotionally involved in any case. That wasn't healthy. But Sexton running his own little sex club at the taxpayer's expense? Now maybe picking up the money on county turf?

That wouldn't sit well with any cop.

Ready called a social worker in Clark County, Indiana. She agreed to make a sweep of Jeffersonville schools for the Sexton children and eye the Carson home for the Sextons' motor home or cars. Ready called a lieutenant in the Clark County Sheriff's Department. He also agreed to check on the house for vehicles. He said while he was at it, he'd stop by and have a chat with the Carsons, too.

Ten days later, the workman's comp bureau reported back. Ed Sexton had been collecting comp payments for nearly 18 years. In 1975, the board had ruled his eligibility "permanent and total," meaning there was no way to stop the payments. Under Ohio law, he could collect in prison if it came to that. Sexton was receiving $376.70 bi-weekly. The checks were being mailed to P.O. Box 1305 in Massilon. May Sexton also received money for nursing her husband.

Ready checked the signatures and endorsements. They were being cashed at First National Bank and Citizens Saving in Massilon. They were endorsed by the Sextons.

The detective called both banks. Yes, the Sextons had an account, a First National banker said. But it hadn't been used in some time. Citizens had no record of an account.

The Sextons were probably driving in for their checks, Ready reasoned.

But from where?

When the Ohio Bell records arrived, Ready found numerous calls charged to their number on Caroline Street from Afton, Oklahoma, to Jeffersonville, Indiana. He called the Oklahoma number and reached a motel called the Grand Lake Country Inn. He described the Sexton vehicles to the clerk. Asked if anybody had registered under the name of Sexton or Good.

No luck.

Ready also saw calls to Hudson, Florida, Dave Sexton's number. He'd already been calling Dave Sexton for months and still was getting the same results.

"No, Sherri's not here."

Indiana, Ready thought. They had to be in Indiana.

Ready called up the Bureau of Motor Vehicles for the state. Soon he had a fax of an accident report. On January 16, a vehicle driven by Ed Sexton, but registered to Tuck Carson, had been in an accident in Jefferson Township, Clark County. He saw Estella "Pixie" Good's name as a passenger.

Ready called the ambulance company that transported Pixie and Ed Sexton to an Indiana hospital. Sexton had given Caroline Street as his address, Pixie her old apartment in Bolivar.

No luck.

Ready found a police report in Canton filed by Patrick Sexton early in the year against his father. In January, his father "swung at him" in Monument Park and issued verbal threats, the report stated. Patrick Sexton told Canton Police his father could be found in Charleston, Indiana.

Ready called the Clark County Sheriff's Department again.

No, his contact said, he hadn't seen any vehicles, and they were checking. He'd talked to the Carsons. They claimed they hadn't seen Eddie Lee Sexton.

They had to be in Indiana.

Steve Ready was four months behind the Sextons, he'd later learn, but closing.

7

Eddie Sexton had found a new dream house. It wasn't Skytop Ranch in Montana anymore. It was the stone home with the pool only a hundred yards from the small trailer on Treaty Lane.

The patriarch began spinning big plans for the property. They'd buy the house and all get four-wheelers. They could hunt and fish and shoot and put an off-road track on the back property. If only the renter would move out.

"We were going to stay for eternity," Skipper later recalled.

Running concurrently with plans to settle down was Sexton's obsession with the family's capture. The patriarch stepped up the drills. They could practice shooting their weapons in Shady Hills. Sexton carried a pistol in his belt. He drew red hearts on trees and the boys fired away at the targets. He taught them to make head shots, and neck shots. When the FBI came, he predicted, they'd be wearing bullet-proof vests. On his trips to Ohio with Willie and Pixie, sometimes Skipper, Sexton took shotguns. They made the drive every two weeks, coinciding with the government pay periods. They were grueling, 2,000-mile round trips up and down I-75.

He appeared to envision himself as public enemy number one. He eased the tension by mixing beer and pain pills, but became more paranoid at night. He was convinced the FBI assault would come after dark.

Sexton came up with a night plan. Eddie, Willie, and Skipper wore dark clothes. If the law came, Chris and Matt were to flee with their mother to Dave's house. The boys were to stay low in the weeds, take the cops out with sniper fire. Night after night, Eddie and Willie sat on the porch, watching the rural darkness with their guns.

"No one was supposed to get in; no one was supposed to get out," May Sexton would later say. "He swore he'd never be taken in alive."

Sexton still excluded Joel Good from the drills. He was a "female," the patriarch said, spending too much of his time around the women, caring for his kids. Skipper was spared such remarks, though he liked to hold and play with the little baby, Skipper Lee, his godson and namesake.

Joel and Willie seemed to get along well, their relationship cemented, perhaps, by their fear of the patriarch and their low IQs. Willie remained the one son still regularly beaten. A hesitation in following an order was all it took to "get the fist." Some siblings would later say Joel and his father-in-law seemed to like one another, Joel calling the patriarch "Mr. Sexton" and "Dad."

"Well, Joel would do anything for my dad," Christopher would later say. "He was scared of him."

Matt, describing his father's relationship with Joel as "excellent," would add, "Yes, he'd treat him good. He didn't actually like him, but he'd treat him good when he was with him."

Sexton had brought on the road the photograph taken of Joel Good after he'd been beaten back in Canton. Some of the boys would later say their father ordered the beating and photo as a way to keep Joel in line. If his son-in-law began thinking too independently, the father would have one of his sons show Joel the picture.

"You see that? See what you look like?" one of the young henchmen would tell him. "You're going to look twice as bad next time."

Joel fared no better with Pixie. He complained to her siblings she refused to have sex with him. Pixie carried all his personal ID. They argued frequently. Later, none of the siblings seemed capable of detailing other subjects that fueled the arguments.

Alcohol and drugs were added to the mix. The older siblings started scoring pot in the neighborhood. Joel and Pixie bought six-packs. They partied when the patriarch was away. Joel, already ridiculed by Ed Sexton to his kids, found himself the butt of jokes and pranks. Sometimes the booze and pot escalated his role to that of a punching bag. Skipper attacked him one night. Another night, he was jumped by several brothers. Good would lie motionless, badly outnumbered. One time, Pixie came to his aid.

Then, Pixie turned on him completely, other Sextons would later recall. She began telling siblings he'd had sex with her two children, Dawn and Shasta. Even little Kimberly heard the accusations. Her only evidence: Shasta walking out of a bedroom, blood dripping from her rectum, with Joel standing nearby.

The talk of a deadly insurance fraud began again. Sherri Sexton would later say in a sworn deposition that she watched Pixie call various insurance agents, getting quotes on policies for Joel Good. Matthew noticed that Willie and Pixie were spending a lot of time together, talking secretly. After one such conversation, Matt pestered Willie to reveal their secret.

"I swore I wouldn't say anything," Matt later said. "He told me that him and Joel were supposed to be fixing the brakes on the Grand Prix, and he was supposed to rig it up so Willie was supposed to bump the car and the car would fall on Joel."

Willie and Skipper also were drawn to the occult. They found a cassette tape of Satanic chants under the trailer. Their father showed them how to draw a pentacle in the earth, the five-pointed, circled star. Perhaps not coincidently, the Satanic symbol was very similar to the Fraternal Order of Police badge logo on the bumper stickers of the Sextons' cars.

One night Skipper and Willie ventured out to a nearby

sand pit, drew the pentagram, and placed a cat in the center.

"We stabbed the cat," Skipper later recalled. "It died. Then we played the tape."

They tried to burn the cat with a cigarette lighter, but it wouldn't light. They went back to the trailer, covered it with paint solvent, then lit it.

"Caught that bitch on fire," Skipper would recall. "It went up. I'll tell you, that was scary."

Christopher later confirmed similar accounts. He said Willie frequently drew pentacles. Chris said Willie had been taken by his father once to West Virginia where they'd been presented with a Satanic book by an old woman. Other Sexton children would later talk of a "Satanic Bible." One description had it with a pentagram, another with a serpent wrapped around a cross.

The black magic did nothing to ease a persistent problem for the clan. With Sherri and her child now part of the brood, money was running low. Sexton started pawning valuables, including some of his arsenal, siblings later said.

Within weeks after they moved in at Treaty Road, the Sextons' neighbors began reporting problems. Robert Wilson, a cooling contractor who'd rented Sexton's stone dream house, and another nearby neighbor, Angie Danser, would later maintain they called Pasco County sheriff's deputies a half dozen times to report suspicious behavior. Danser said family members tramped around in her woods almost every night. They kept their front gate locked with a thick metal chain and padlock. Oddly, Wilson later reported a boy he'd been told was Joel Good—"the cocky one"—told him to stay away. Buried spikes were waiting for anyone who came into their yard, Good said. Wilson also would say he heard a baby's high-pitched screams one night.

The only police report on file with Pasco County would be dated August 13, when Robert Wilson called deputies to his house to file a formal complaint. The family wanted to rent his house the same time he did, he told a patrolman. The neighbor seemed to resent him living in the house.

The night before, the report stated, someone had broken the windows in Wilson's Ford Escort and Dodge van, and taken a cassette deck and a necklace from the car. The plates on the cars were also gone. Now his daughters said they'd seen a juvenile at the trailer wearing the jewelry. Nobody in the family seemed to have jobs, Wilson added, but they were always bringing new tools and home improvement items to the trailer.

Police dusted the cars and found a partial print. They noted on their report that distinctive boot prints were all around the cars. They found the same prints around the Sexton trailer when they approached the residence, but no one was home. It was not a high priority crime. The stolen goods were valued at less than $50.

But later that week, a detective named William Shallwood returned to Treaty Road to investigate again. He found Estella "Pixie" Good at home. She said her father was out of town, but would be back in early September. She allowed him to search the house. He noted serial numbers on new tools. But he didn't find any stolen property at the trailer or the pawnshops he later checked.

Ed Sexton stepped up the patrols, warning his young sentries he was convinced cops were watching the house. Then, frustrated that Wilson had not moved out, he was trying to convince another neighbor to sell him some land. When he didn't, he ordered Willie, Skipper, and Matt to torch the abandoned trailer on the property.

Soon, a fire marshall showed up, interviewing the Sextons and other neighbors. Matt would later say the arson investigation put a stop to all plans for Joel Good's accident for the life insurance. Later, police never were able to determine whether a policy had actually been taken out on Good.

On September 20, the Pasco department marked the

original burglary file "inactive." The Sexton family hadn't hung around to find out they'd been cleared.

By then, they had already moved from Treaty Road.

8

Colleen Carson had bought the silver '93 Nissan just about the time the Sexton family came to stay in Indiana. Her brother-in-law had noticed the Sentra, complimented her on it. But she'd wondered out loud if they really needed it. They already had four vehicles in the driveway as it was.

She later explained what happened.

In the summer, Eddie Sexton called from Florida. He was coming back to the Midwest for business, he told her. The Canton house was sold now, he said. He had to go to Ohio for the closing. But they were having car trouble.

"May really likes that car of yours," he said.

After he offered to take over her payments at the bank, she talked it over with Tuck. Colleen felt sorry for them, she said.

"We try to help anybody," she'd later recall. "Anybody that needs help, we help them. That's the way we were brought up."

Tuck said fine, but he didn't want to transfer the title until they paid the loan off. He also wanted some assurance they would be responsible for the car.

When Eddie and May showed up back in Indiana, they had a typed sales agreement, promising to take over payments and cover the insurance. It was witnessed by his nephew, David L. Sexton, Jr., and dated August 25, 1993. Dave Jr. apparently had driven them up from Florida.

Eddie asked for the payment book. There was nearly a $10,000 balance.

"I'm going to make the first payment, and after that I'm going to pay it off entirely," he said.

Colleen said, "Maybe you should go to the bank and have the loan put in your name. Make it legal."

Sexton smiled, saying, "We'll be paying it off next week anyway. They sold my house in Ohio. The only thing I have to do is sign the paperwork and get my money."

She gave him the keys. But sometime later, Eddie called her again from the road. He wanted Colleen to meet him at the local license bureau and transfer title. Not until he paid for it, Tuck said. Then, after Tuck left for the road, May Sexton called.

"These tags have run out and we can't go anywhere with these tags expired," May said.

Colleen held her ground, saying, "Well, if you're getting money for the house, you'll have plenty of money to get those plates."

9

Jean Sexton later said she drew up a contract when Pixie, Joel, Willie, and Sherri said they wanted to rent the middle mobile home. No fighting. No alcohol. No dope. No cursing. No arguing. The price, $275 a month.

The Challenger motor home, the Pontiac, and soon a Nissan were parked at the Dave Sexton compound, Eddie saying that he'd had to move from Shady Hills because of trouble with a neighbor. Eddie and May went back to Ohio, presumably to pick up their checks.

The parents gone, all the siblings ignored the rules, scoring more reefer and more booze. They'd also discovered the brain-twisting high of sniffing gasoline. The results were later revealed independently by several Sexton teens.

During one party, Joel Good was fed a live goldfish. Matt held his mouth open. Skipper dropped the fish in. Another time Joel was stripped, a funnel inserted into his rectum and hot sauce poured into his bowel. Another time, Skipper tried to force a broomstick up Joel's backside. Pixie didn't try to stop him that time, Matthew later said.

Sherri, who refused to take part in the sessions, would say Pixie was the ringleader. Matt would say it was Skipper who usually instigated. Plus, Joel wasn't a Sexton. He was an easy target. He never fought back.

"Because he loved Pixie," Sherri later said.

Most agreed Skipper Lee, little "Ewok," also suffered. When the baby cried for food or attention, Pixie slapped it in the face a couple of times, stunning it into silence, both Sherri and Matthew later said.

The parties sometimes turned sexual. Later, some siblings said Pixie had sex with Willie, and another time with a cousin, emerging from the bedroom with rug burns on her backside. But Sherri also would later admit she'd had sex with Skipper.

"You're father encouraged that as normal among family members, correct?" an attorney would later ask Sherri.

"He didn't know we was doing it," she'd answer.

Neither did landlord Jean Sexton, not to mention the rest of the gas-driven mayhem.

Jean Sexton was running an errand when Joel Good staggered up shirtless to Dave Sexton's trailer about 10 a.m. one hot September day. Dave let him into the house. He had lash marks all over his torso and burn marks on his back.

"Don't let them get me," Joel said, whimpering. "Don't let them get me. Until Dad gets home."

Dave asked Joel what happened. He'd been held down and whipped with a belt and a sweeper electrical cord and burned with cigarettes. He'd been hit in the head with a frying pan.

Dave asked, by who?

"Pixie and the rest of them," Joel said.

The rest of them were Skipper, Matthew, and Willie. They held him down, he said. Pixie did the whipping and burning. Little Dawn and Shasta also joined in, as well as one of Dave's granddaughters from the other trailer.

Dave went to the middle trailer, demanding an answer. Only Pixie would admit to the beating. She didn't mention they'd been sniffing gasoline all morning. She said Joel had sodomized her two daughters, apparently weeks earlier, on Treaty Road.

"That's something you need to take up with the law," Dave later told them. "You shouldn't take things into your own hands—especially not on my property."

Dave warned her that their father was going to hear about it. Pixie begged him not to tell. Some of the Sexton children asked their uncle to send Joel back over to their trailer.

"No, you're not getting that boy," Dave Sexton said.

When Dave returned to his home, he sat Joel Good down. "I offered to put him on a bus so he could go back to Ohio," Dave later recalled. "I said, you don't have to put up with this."

But Joel Good wanted to stay. "Dad will take care of it," he said. "He'll take care of it when he gets back."

When Jean Sexton arrived home and saw Joel she was furious, particularly after she found out her granddaughter had been encouraged to beat Good as the older boys held them down. So had Sherri's little boy, Christopher Lee, only 3 years old. She stomped over to the middle trailer, found them all sitting around inside.

Jean asked Sherri, "Why in the world would you stand by and let this happen?"

"He's not my husband," Sherri said, shrugging. "Why should I care?"

Jean turned to Pixie, demanding answers.

Pixie said she'd once found blood coming from Shasta's rectum, believed it was Joel's doing; he had to be punished.

"If that's the case, you should have taken the child to the hospital and called the law," Jean said. "But don't you ever use any of my grandkids to do your dirty deeds," Jean said. "Furthermore, you get your stuff and all of you get out of this trailer!"

When she left the trailer, she noticed a pentagram drawn in the dirt in her backyard. Some fundamentalists believe in a specific prayer when faced with overwhelming evil. It is called a "Jericho March," named after the story of Israelites circling Jericho seven times and bringing down its walls.

"I felt the Lord telling me to put on my shoes and go do a Jericho March," Jean later recalled. "I went around that trailer seven times, praying in the spirit [tongues]. I'm going to tell you, people don't believe this, but when I finished, all the doors and windows in that trailer were open and they were gone."

They moved back into the Challenger. They'd lasted only two weeks on their own. They were banned not only from the middle trailer, but Dave Sexton's mobile home as well.

Dave Sexton later recalled the tongue-lashing his brother Eddie gave the children when he returned from Ohio. He called Joel, Pixie, Willie, and Sherri into Dave's mobile home, where they admitted to the beating.

"Eddie said, 'This boy did nothing to you at all. Keep your hands off him.' He said to Pixie, 'This is your husband. You're supposed to love him and honor him.'"

Other siblings would say their father told them privately the abuse of Joel Good had to stop for another reason. As Matt later recalled, his father said: "We don't need him running off and telling people that he was getting beat."

From now on, the patriarch said, anybody who beat Joel would have to answer to him.

Dave Sexton later told his younger brother he noticed a pattern during their stays at his compound. "When you were gone your kids were very disobedient," Dave said.

"I have warned my kids not to be disobedient to their Aunt Jean and Uncle Dave," Eddie said. "You know I expect my kids to be obedient."

"I know that," Dave said. "But I just can't understand it. When you're home, they're obedient. When you're gone, it's like a prison yard."

Eddie Sexton began talking about moving on. Dave later recalled he counseled his youngest brother.

"I said, 'Eddie, for heaven's sake. Get rid of those kids. Grown kids. With the trouble they're causing you, you're going to end up in jail.'"

Eddie Sexton said, "I took care of them all my life.'"

"I said, 'Well, it's time to separate from them. The time has come to let them go on their own.'"

As the Sexton caravan left Moon Lake and Pasco County in late September, it was clear Eddie Sexton had no intention of taking his advice.

10

The state park sprawled along the Hillsborough River, 15 miles northeast of Tampa, 2,994 acres of hardwood hammock, flood plain forests and pine flatwoods. Cypress swamps hugged the river and Spanish moss hung from the trees. Some 200 species of birds perched in the park through the seasons. In fall and winter, the most common large birds were the vultures and ravens that swooped to pick at roadkill and scraps left in vacant campsites.

Hillsborough River State Park had 114 campsites, a pool, a snack bar, and a canoe launch. But in the cooler fall months, the pool closed and only a third of the campsites were occupied, where campers with water and electrical hookups paid $16.50 a day.

The Dodge Challenger rolled into Hillsborough and registered on October 5. The Sextons parked the motor home in Campsite Number 89, one of 32 spots in a large traffic circle surrounded by pines and palmetto trees. Campsite Number 89 was on the woodsy side.

Estella Good registered. The title to the Challenger now

was in the name of William L. Sexton, the transfer apparently forged sometime on the road.

The patriarch announced new rules. The park limited each campsite to eight people, excluding children under five. Fourteen people were making their home in a 24-foot vehicle built to sleep eight. Eddie, May, and Kimberly slept in the double fold-out bed in the front. Pixie, Sherri, and the little children doubled in the bunks in the back. Joel, Willie, Christopher, Matt, and Skipper took turns sleeping in the remaining bunk and the two cars, and on the green shag carpeting that covered the camper's floor.

By day, no one left the mobile home without permission, not even for a trip to the bathroom. The youngest children were not allowed to play outside. Older children were allowed to walk only a couple at a time. Sexton relieved the pressure with two small televisions, one in the camper, one just outside. They had "picnics." Eddie and May packed lunches or dinners and took some of the children to eat at distant picnic areas, so as not to associate everyone with the campsite. They always had picnics when Sexton returned from the Ohio road trips. At night, they had campfires. If rangers asked questions, some of the Sextons would say they were visiting.

The strategy largely worked. One ranger would later say he never saw Eddie or May Sexton on his routine patrols, only Pixie and her kids. Another noticed more people, noting the group always seemed to casually walk to the back of the motor home every time he drove past. There were no complaints about the family or violations of a noise curfew called "quiet time." "All noises," the camp brochure stated, had to be held to a minimum after 11 p.m.

October in south Hillsborough County would be one of the wettest on record. Seven inches of rain would fall that month, four inches above normal. On a Saturday 11 days after the Sextons arrived, nearly three inches poured from the clouds in one day.

On clear days, Sexton drilled the boys at distant locations. On others, the TV was perpetually on, the motor
home hazy with smoke. Cigarettes burned between the
fingers of Eddie, Pixie, Skipper, Willie, Sherri, and Joel.
At night, the boys listened to the radio in the Nissan. Ed
Sexton continued nightly Bible readings, then groused
about the "sonsabitches" in Ohio and brainstormed ways
to defend against an FBI assault. Though Sexton had been
talking about the FBI as far back as Indiana, the bureau
was *not* chasing him. In Ohio, there wasn't even a warrant
for Eddie Lee Sexton's arrest. And the Sextons were no
longer the same spit-shined military crew that had first left
for Oklahoma. Eddie Sexton wore an old army jacket. The
boys still wore camouflage, but the uniforms were fading,
their hair home cut and disheveled, their boots dull with
Florida dirt.

The siblings' accounts of what happened two weeks into
the Sextons' stay in Hillsborough River State Park would
vary somewhat with each witness. But certain facts would
remain undisputed.

It started with little Skipper Lee Sexton, Joel and Pixie's
"Ewok"—by most accounts, the only child who carried
genes from outside the immediate Sexton clan. Or maybe
it started with Eddie Lee Sexton's growing paranoia. Or
Pixie's penchant toward child abuse.

Little Skipper Lee was "sick," everyone would later say.
For two weeks the baby hadn't been able to hold down
solids. Awake, he was either listless or fussing, sometimes
having cold sweats. A later examination would reveal the
infant was teething. Pixie gave the baby Tylenol and rubbed
crushed aspirin on his gums. Aspirin has no topical analge-
sic value, but could become toxic in infants.

The baby's other symptoms were likely related to
another Sexton solution. For at least two weeks, Skipper
Lee's mother and grandfather were pouring at least a cap-
ful of adult-strength Nyquil into Ewok every day. The green
mix of alcohol, decongestants, and antihistamines not only

would make the child listless and nauseous, but produce cold sweats, one physician later said, calling it "a gross overdose" of the intended use of the cold remedy.

Pixie would later say she wanted to take the child to the hospital. Her father said that was impossible. They were fugitives.

"We'll all be busted," he said.

Skipper took Pixie aside about the Nyquil, he later recalled. "It says adult Nyquil on there. It doesn't say child Nyquil. It doesn't say teething medicine. I says, you're gonna overdose it. I said, look, the kid is sleeping 17 hours a day. No baby sleeps 17 hours a day. You're gonna kill it, then what are we gonna do? And she says, 'Oh no it won't. Dad says it's okay.' "

On a cool Saturday night in mid October, Pixie prepared Ewok for bed. A half cap of Nyquil, then mother and child curled up in a back bunk. Willie was on a bunk across the aisle, Sherri in another with Little Bear, Joel Good further to the front of the camper on the floor. Ed, May, and Kimberly up front. Skipper, Christopher, and Matt in the cars outside.

The only witnesses to state what happened at about 4 a.m. the next morning would be Pixie and Willie Sexton.

The baby woke up crying—and wouldn't stop. Pixie would say she tried to cradle Ewok, feed the baby a bottle, but the child pushed it away.

Willie woke up, turned his head, and watched. Pixie gave Skipper Lee another half cap of Nyquil, he'd say, but the crying continued.

Pixie would say the crying lasted a half hour. But neither Sherri, May, or the boys outside, sleeping with open windows, would say they heard anything that night.

Pixie would say her father's voice boomed from the front of the Challenger. "He told me to get that baby quiet or he would come back and do it," she'd say.

Willie would recall, "Then I seen my sister jap slap the

baby.'' Slap it back and forth using both sides of her hand. Maybe 10 times, he later said.

Then, Pixie Sexton took her hand and covered the child's mouth.

Holding it there.

When she removed her hand there was silence. She placed little Skipper next to her in the bed.

And went to sleep.

11

Skipper heard his sister Pixie screaming, ''Dad!'' at twilight. Christopher and Willie, who were outside tidying up the campsite, heard it, too.

Skipper was waking in the Nissan, the windows open. He pulled a knife from his boot and ran inside the motor home. He thought a ranger was busting his father inside.

Inside, the baby was lying on his parent's bed. Pixie, his father, and his mother were standing over the child.

The baby's face was grey, its eyes open and vacant.

Skipper turned to Pixie, saying, ''What happened?''

''It just died,'' his sister said.

His father turned to his mother and said, ''It's crib death.''

''He just can't breathe,'' Skipper said.

It was his namesake, his godson.

''No baby's going to die,'' he said.

Skipper pushed a finger into his mouth, clearing the mucous. He pushed on the baby's chest, then breathed into its mouth, attempting a crude version of CPR. He would remember trying for a minute, maybe two. Sherri was up now, other family members coming into the camper.

When Skipper stopped, when Ewok wouldn't come back, he looked up and saw mostly stares. Pixie was crying. His father, he would later say, was ''calm as all fuck.''

Strangely, in later statements, Joel Good, the baby's father, was never mentioned as being a participant in the scene.

Skipper looked at the baby.

"A tear came out of its eye," he later said. "And that really ticked me off."

It was the morning of October 19, Estella "Pixie" Good would later recall. She'd be the only Sexton sure of the date. After all, she was the baby's mother.

Somebody said, "Now what are we going to do?"

12

On a sunny Sunday 1,200 miles away in East Liverpool, Ohio, Lana Sexton and her foster mother Tabatha Fisher began what looked like a very good day. The foster family went to an apple orchard. They sipped cider and bumped along on a hayride. The orchard had a face painting artist. He painted a fluffy grey cat on Lana's cheek, not black. As fundamentalists, the Fishers didn't celebrate Halloween, less than two weeks away.

That night, the family got ready to go to a home Bible study. Lana liked attending them.

This night she said, "No, I don't want to go."

"Well, you can stay with somebody," Tabatha said.

She changed her mind, but at the group, she was not herself. She lay on the floor, scrawling in coloring books, frequently interrupting.

"She had absolutely no manners," Tabatha would recall. "It was as if everything we'd taught her was suddenly gone."

When they returned home, Lana had her bath, but Tabatha sent her to bed one hour early, at eight o'clock, for being so disruptive. As Lana slipped under the covers, she wanted to hear a music box the Fishers kept in her room.

Tabatha wound it up and put it on her small TV, turning off the light.

The music box played the Carpenters' classic, "Close to You."

Downstairs, Tabatha heard the music stop, then Lana tiptoe across the room to wind it, "Close to You" playing again.

Then, both Tabatha and Ted heard a strange sound.

Tabatha climbed the stairs. Lana was cradling the music box in her bed. Tabatha reached for the box, reminding Lana it was time to go to sleep.

"Suddenly she began this whining, a whine I've never heard before," Tabatha later recalled. "A whining like an infant, or a toddler."

Tabatha put the music box back on the TV.

Then it began.

Lana Sexton was jumping on the bed, screaming. Tabatha scurried over, but Lana swung at her. Ted came running up the stairs. Lana had thrown tantrums before. When they hugged her, she usually calmed.

But not this time.

"She went absolutely beserk," Tabatha later recalled.

They wrestled her to the bed, where her body suddenly went strangely limp. They laid her head down on the pillow. Then she sat up abruptly, her eyelids wide open, only the whites showing. Her body posture changed, as if another personality had crawled inside her skin.

A deep, menacing voice came from her throat. "You're not getting her," the voice said. "You're not taking her. She's mine."

Ted Fisher began praying.

Tabatha tried to talk to Lana. "I want to talk to Lana," she kept saying. "Lana, are you all right?"

"Do you want to talk to Lana?" the voice asked back.

"Yeah, I want to talk to Lana," Tabatha demanded.

Lana passed out again, her body limp. In seconds she

opened her eyes again. Now she was crying, bawling. With terror.

"Everything's okay, honey," Tabatha kept saying.

When Lana stilled, Tabatha asked, "What's wrong, honey?"

"Help me, Mommy," she said. "Help me."

"I'm here," Tabatha said.

Lana began rubbing her own throat, then her arms.

Saying, "I gotta go, Mommy. He's got my throat. I gotta go. He wants me. I gotta go."

She passed out again.

"And then this thing came back again," Tabatha later recalled.

Ted started praying out loud, asking Christ for help.

"Fuck Jesus!" the voice shouted. "Fuck Jesus!"

Lana began spitting on him defiantly. The voice went into a tirade of more obscenities. Within a few minutes, Ted's shirt and face were covered with her saliva.

Then, she passed out again.

In a calm period, Lana said, whimpering, "I love you, but—" She hesitated, then continued, "*You* know too much."

The 12-year-old looked at them both and added, "I'm going to have to kill you. You know too much. It's time to kill you now."

Then, she had to kill herself, she said.

Lana attacked them again. They wrestled her to the bed. She weighed only 90 pounds, but it took both adults lying directly on top of her to hold her down.

She passed out again.

This time, she didn't get back up.

Tabatha tried shaking her shoulders, then took her pulse. It was very slow, though only moments later she was tossing their sprawled bodies up and down like a white-water ride.

Ted scooped her up in his arms and carried her downstairs to the car. They arrived at the local emergency room at midnight. Lana was still unconscious as a doctor tested her reflexes.

"She's faking," the physician said.

"This girl is not faking," Tabatha said. "You have no idea what we've been through."

A few minutes later, Lana opened her eyes, as a nurse put cool compresses on her head.

The next morning, an ambulance took Lana Sexton to the psychiatric ward at Akron Children's Hospital, the Fishers not far behind.

It was October 18.

The Fishers, social workers, and others working the Sexton case might have written the episode off to hysteria, or acting out, or a viewing of *The Exorcist*, though there was no evidence Lana Sexton ever saw the film. A psychiatrist said it was post traumatic stress disorder, or PTSD. The manifestations were flashbacks, the occult manifestations perhaps triggered by the upcoming Halloween.

They might have been.

Then the next day, October 19, another Sexton showed up at Akron Children's Hospital, a sibling Lana hadn't seen for months, a sibling living in a foster home some 70 miles away. Social workers had received the news the day before. James Sexton was having psychotic episodes. He'd dreamt his father was telling him to kill himself, the same night of Lana's episode.

Three days later, Machelle Sexton would report to DHS social workers the same dream on the same night as her siblings. Dad, and other voices, she said, were telling her to kill herself and her new husband, Dave Croto.

Everyone might have written it all off to PTSD, coincidence, and Halloween. But it wouldn't be until years later that someone would come up with one more *coincidence* by computerizing all the significant dates in the Sexton case.

As Lana and James were reunited in the psychiatric ward,

little Skipper Lee Good was being murdered in the Challenger at Hillsborough River State Park.

Four months later, James Sexton would tell police a haunting anecdote. The day before the children were first removed from the house on Caroline Street by the DHS, he said, his father sat the entire family down at the kitchen table.

"He told us if we talked," James said, "he would see us in our dreams."

ix

Campsite Number 18

1

Detective Steve Ready always parked the department Chevy on South Erie, across the street from the Massilon Post Office. He always walked inside and eyeballed P.O. Box 1305. When it was empty, he moved on to other business. When it was full, he went back to the car and sat.

He had a pair of binoculars and a clean line of sight through the building window at Eddie Lee Sexton's postal box. Ready would sit for a couple of hours in the mornings or late afternoons during the workman's comp pay periods at the beginning and middle of the month. He thought, these people can't be very smart. They'll screw up.

It was just a matter of time.

One day, after a half day of watching postal patrons, he asked himself, what am I doing here? This is bullshit

But he sat anyway.

Back at the Renkert Building, the Sexton case was taking on trappings more suitable to a serial killer hunt than a

DHS child custody matter. Workers and attorneys had put up poster boards of the children with family pictures, identifying them with their dates of birth and nicknames. It helped keep track of who was who.

The news of James's and Lana's psychotic episodes hit the DHS hard. Both siblings were scheduled for the Stark County grand jury the week of the hospitalization. The DHS asked for an independent psychological evaluation. Everyone wondered, would they be in any shape to testify? No testimony, no indictment. No warrant, no help from the FBI.

"The whole thing was going down the tubes," Genetin would later say.

Steve Ready couldn't get his hands on the Sextons, but his knowledge base was growing. He'd gotten an earful not only from Otis, but from Anne Greene, who'd filled him in on Machelle's saga since she'd left home. She'd lived in a dozen homes, gotten pregnant, and now was married. She'd miscarried the baby she was carrying. Now she was three months pregnant with her husband Dave Croto's child.

Ready decided to talk with Wayne Welsh, the original social worker on the case. Nearly 14 months had passed since Machelle Sexton had recanted.

He asked, has anybody bothered to talk to her lately?

"Let me give her a call," Welsh said.

The next morning, Ready and Welsh drove to Bolivar. The small trailer where Machelle and David Croto were living was in a little mobile home park on the edge of town, on a road called Lover's Lane.

Shelly Croto was happy to see Welsh. So happy that by 9:30 a.m., Steve Ready had a tape recorder running.

She gave Ready the most complete statement in the case to date. Not only had her father raped her behind Wales Square, he'd tried to have sex with her at 15, but found her too small. He'd also tried to make her give him oral sex, but she'd refused. He knocked her against a coffee table, chipping her tooth.

Ready was already counting to himself. That was three felony counts, and they'd just begun.

For the first time, Shelly revealed in detail what seemed to have precipitated her rape. Again, she recalled the day before the assault, seeing the bloody body in the trunk. The argument in the van behind Wales Square was over what she'd seen, she said. She believed the body was somebody named "Uncle Toehead." She didn't have a last name. Supposedly, Uncle Toehead had been beaten for showing pornographic pictures to Pixie.

Ready moved on to possible assaults on other siblings. She told about seeing Pixie having sex with her father on the couch. She detailed how she and Matt saw their father have sex with Sherri while hiding in the family van.

That's five counts, Ready thought.

"Did Sherri tell your mom that your dad was doing this?" Ready asked.

"No, Stella did," Shelly said.

"Estella told her, and you told her too, right?"

"Yes."

Their mother didn't believe them, she said.

Ready moved onto areas of ritual abuse. He'd been reading the disclosures coming from Lana and James. Shelly said her father, dressed in black, once gathered them around a dead cat on the table, having them hold hands.

"He said he needed a sacrifice, or whatever, to make spirits come," she said.

Once he made them drink deer's blood out of his cupped hands on a hunting trip.

Ready wondered if she knew anything about dead babies in the household. James and Lana had disclosed that to social workers.

Sherri had a miscarriage at the house, Shelly said.

"And there was a baby?" Ready asked.

"It wasn't formed." She was five or six months along, she said.

Ready wondered what happened to the fetus. Shelly didn't know. She hinted at some kind of ceremony, but had no details.

"My dad said they had to save its soul or something like that. I don't know. I didn't stay and get involved in it. I couldn't. It was gross."

Ready wondered if she'd seen any other rituals.

"He married Angel," Shelly said.

"He married Angel?"

"And Kim, too."

To himself. They had white gowns and veils, she said. He was in a suit. Then he took his young brides away one by one.

"Where?"

"He'd always say it was their honeymoon, or whatever."

He took them to the bedroom, she said, adding that her mother went into the bedroom, too.

After the tape was turned off, Ready and Welsh talked to her for at least another hour. They needed her to testify before a grand jury, they said. She was reluctant. Nothing happened the first time she'd gone to police, she said. Why should it now?

Besides, she'd recanted, she said. Nobody would believe her.

"Shelly," Ready said. "You're really not that unusual. In these kind of cases, people often recant for one reason or another. It kind of goes with the territory."

It seemed to make her feel better.

"You know, this is the time to tell it," Ready said. "You have other brothers and sisters with them. They're in danger."

"When would I have to go do this?" Shelly asked.

It was October 21.

Ready asked, how about this afternoon?

2

The body of Skipper Lee Good had remained in the Challenger most of the entire day before, October 20, the corpse still in its night clothes.

Numerous hazy stories later were told by the Sexton siblings about what went on that day. Skipper saw the baby's body turn colors, marbling. The likely cause was livor mortis, producing red and purple streaks under the child's skin. Family members came and went from the Challenger, and the campsite. There were stories of the baby being taken away in the car by Willie, Pixie, and Joel. There were stories of Sherri and Joel being forced to stay in the motor home with the dead child, watching that it wasn't discovered by outsiders who might wander into the camp.

They were to say nothing to anybody, Ed Sexton warned.

Few details of Joel Good's whereabouts, his feelings about his dead son, or his role in the aftermath would be revealed in later accounts, as if he were little more than a transparency in the drama.

Most would remember the patriarch's wishes. Contacting the authorities and arranging a proper funeral was out of the question, he said. What's done is done. But they were still fugitives. The FBI was on their tail. A decision was made to bury the baby in the park. Some said the decision was Eddie Lee Sexton's. Some said it was Pixie's. Some said it was both.

Late that afternoon, Pixie took off the child's pajamas and fitted the corpse with burial clothes, its joints cracking with rigor mortis. She put a white shirt and blue overalls on Skipper Lee, patches with five stars and "U.S. Army" on the bib. She placed a pacifier in the baby's mouth and a blue, red and yellow dumbbell rattle in its right hand.

That night, in the dim motor home, Eddie Lee Sexton

held what his family members described as a "service."
They would offer no details as to exactly what that entailed.

Pixie Sexton slept with the dead baby that night. Some
siblings later said she was hoping it would return to life.

The next morning, Pixie wrapped the corpse in a blue
and white afghan. It was placed in a blue duffel bag, zip-
pered across the top. The bag was placed in two black
garbage bags. Joel carried the bag, Willie, a collapsible
army shovel. They walked into the mossy hardwoods
behind Campsite Number 89.

Fifty yards in, they stopped.

Skipper would later recall the spot, but give two versions
of how he knew where the grave site was. At first he said
he was taken there by Joel after the burial. In a later version,
he said he joined the burial party. He'd say:

Joel dug the hole. Joel was crying and scared.

He kept repeating, "Why me? Why does it have to be
my son."

The hole in the black Florida peat was knee-deep when
they hit water. They placed the bag in, then started filling.
Skipper brought some broken fire bricks from the campsite
to weight down the gym bag.

As Joel and Willie filled, Skipper took one of the bricks
and made a gash on a large oak nearby.

"What you doin'?" Willie asked.

Said Skipper, "I just want something to remember him
by."

They covered the fresh earth with fallen leaves. Later,
Pixie would be shown the spot. She'd bought a silk rose
in a plastic tube, the kind sold at convenience stores. She
placed it on the grave, hiding it under a couple inches of
peat.

The subject of the baby apparently dominated conversation all that day. Most of the siblings later said they first
thought it had died from crib death. Pixie broke down
crying as Ed, May, Willie, Pixie, and Skipper sat around
the picnic table. Joel was complaining, saying it wasn't

right. The authorities should be contacted. A proper funeral should be held.

Pixie later said her father pulled her aside and told her she'd go to prison for murder if they went to the police. That day, others heard the patriarch talking about the fuss Joel Good was making.

"If he keeps this up," the patriarch reportedly said, "we're going to have to take him out."

3

They spent hours talking, Otis telling stories, making observations. Otis had a habit of saying the same things over and over again in different ways, but keeping the facts the same.

Steve Ready had been listening—on his home phone, at coffee shops, over Jackie Sexton's instant coffee in Otis Sexton's living room.

Eddie had mistreated those kids for years, Otis said. He told Ready about his daughters baby-sitting at Caroline Street. He told more subtle, but telling anecdotes, as well. Eddie and May savored steaks and Cornish hens, Otis said. The kids munched on hot dogs and macaroni and cheese. Eddie and May had eggs, sausage, and potatoes for breakfast. The kids got an egg sandwich or oatmeal.

When Machelle was staying with him, Otis said, she wouldn't touch the milk. His wife Jackie asked her why.

"Milk is only for the little kids," she said.

See, something must have happened to Eddie in prison back in West Virginia, Otis said. Something must have made him this way. The family they grew up in, Otis said, was dirt poor, but not twisted. There was no drinking or swearing or carousing. They got their whippin's, usually with their father's miner's belt. "But Dad knew the limits," Otis said. And they *deserved* it when they got it, punished for neighborhood pranks, stealing a neighbor's toy.

Then their father "backslid," a fundamentalist term for falling away from a religious life, Otis said. When they were all living in Ironton, Ohio, he moved in for a year with a woman in Ashland, Kentucky. William Dewey Sexton stopped preaching. Otis, only 12, cursed him when he found out. His mother Lana ran out the door, saying, "Billy, you whip that boy."

"No, I'm not going to whip him," his father said.

"Why?" she asked.

"I'm not worthy of whipping that boy."

Otis said, "He said he'd much rather go to hell as a sinner than a hypocrite."

But, with Eddie, you never knew what you were getting. Take that Futuretron nonsense, Otis said. He told Ready about the Futuretrons and the supposed Burger King deal. Eddie had been talking about it for years. He had grand plans. Eddie predicted Futuretron images would be put on burger wrappers and french fry boxes. People would flock to see Eddie "the warlock," and Lana "the witch."

"What the hell is Futuretron, Otis?" Ready asked.

It wouldn't be long before Ready would see mock-ups Eddie Sexton ordered Machelle to paint. One well-done color drawing showed Eddie and Lana in space-age uniforms, red capes flowing from their shoulders, lightning bolts flashing across their chests. Eddie was holding little Lana's hand. They stood on a cosmic vista, a jet car in the back, the planet Saturn sinking in sky, the Burger King logo above. Just above their genitals, a left hand appeared to emerge.

Otis said Eddie had it all worked out. He'd have this big semi rig that would roll up to a franchise. The side would open up. A ramp would drop. And Eddie would come roaring out on a Honda Gold Wing in the Futuretron outfit, Lana behind on a bike. There would be a contest in the days before the appearance. The person who guessed the exact time the Futuretrons would appear would win a prize.

And, man, Otis said, could Eddie sell it to the naive. He'd convinced a couple of Eddie Jr. and Patrick's neighbors to go with him on the road when it happened. Otis watched him do it one day, while the neighbors dug up a broken sewer line. One guy even quit his job. A nephew was ready to take his country and western band on the road with Eddie. But first, Eddie asked him for $2,000. He was raising money for the venture, Eddie said.

Otis pulled the nephew aside. "Think about it," Otis said. "If he's getting a million dollars from Burger King, why does he need two thousand dollars from you?"

Eddie was a con man, Otis said. He burned houses for profit and filed false police reports for insurance claims. He plastered the FOP stickers on his car to avoid police scrutiny. He also had a Masonic ring he'd bought at a pawnshop. He wore it camping and on other outings, using it to break the ice or curry favors from other Shriners.

"Eddie had a way," Otis said. "If you really knew him, he couldn't pull this stuff. But if you did not know Eddie, he could sell a snowball in Alaska. And if you didn't *really* know him, he came across as the nicest guy in the world."

4

The day after Shelly Croto testified to the grand jury, Steve Ready's patient ear with Otis Sexton paid off. On October 22, Otis called him. Eddie Jr. was at his house, Otis said. He had something to say about his father.

Ready drove to Otis's house on 15th Street. They sat down at the dining room table, but Eddie Jr. kept glancing at Otis's wife Jackie, sitting in the living room.

"Why don't we take a little ride," Ready said.

They drove only one block, parking at a power station,

its transformers humming outside. They talked for a while in the idling department Chevy. Then Ready turned on his tape recorder, putting the story on the record. Otis sat in the backseat.

"Eddie, you came to me with your uncle, Otis Sexton, and wanted to talk about things that had happened to you while you were growing up in your family's household," the detective said. "Is that correct?"

"Yeah," Eddie Jr. said, barely audible.

The detective told him he'd have to speak up, then asked, "Were you ever sexually abused by your parents?"

"By my father," Eddie Jr. said.

It was a brutal, disturbing story. His father had raped him "from the backside" when he was 13 or 14. He'd done it twice in puberty, then another time when he was 17. It was why he'd run away once in high school.

Ready wondered if that had happened to any other Sexton boys.

"Probably Willie," Eddie Jr. said. He added that his father had told him when he assaulted him that he'd also had sex with his other brothers as well.

Ready questioned him about his sisters. Eddie Jr. had seen his father having sex with Pixie. He'd seen the act by hiding under a bed in the family van on a trip to Wales Square.

Another assault at the shopping area, Ready thought. Later he'd learn it was also the location where Eddie Sexton taught his kids how to drive.

Ready asked about rituals.

"There was weird stuff that went on there," Eddie Jr. said. But he hadn't seen any animal sacrifices, only seances. Ready couldn't get any more specifics than that.

Ready wanted to know about this "Uncle Toehead," the body Shelly had supposedly seen in the trunk of the car. Otis and Eddie Jr. had given Ready a full name to work with.

Yeah, his father had beaten up Toehead, Eddie Jr. said,

for showing dirty pictures to Pixie. But he didn't know anything about a body. Unlike Machelle's early accounts, he maintained he wasn't there.

Ready thought, it's okay for the old man to do his daughter, but God help anybody else who makes a move. Rape. Incest. Fraud. Possible murder. Disappearing bodies. Sodomy. He'd talked to only three Sextons, and already he could see a half dozen potential crimes or leads.

Ready wondered if Eddie Jr. would testify before a grand jury.

"Yeah," Eddie Jr. said.

On October 25, three days later, the grand jury handed down indictments. Besides Eddie Jr. and Machelle, Lana and James had managed to testify. Ed Sexton was faced with four counts of rape and four counts of sexual imposition. May was indicted on gross sexual imposition and child endangering, based on a disclosure by Lana that her mom had fondled her. On November 5, Steve Ready would have a long talk with special agent Randy Howell in the Canton office of the FBI.

In between, he was back at the post office. His eyes watched the brass boxes through the binoculars. But too often his mind flashed with disturbing snapshots. They appeared without warning from his imagination. Pictures of Eddie Lee Sexton alone with his daughters and boys. Family portraits no one would dare put up on the shelves.

One day he sat five hours.

He'd been thinking it the day Eddie Jr. told him he was sodomized, getting angrier, getting emotionally involved.

He was thinking, *How dare that motherfucker do that to those kids?*

5

The names of Eddie Lee and Estella May Sexton of Ohio produced an immediate hit in the FBI network. Special agent Randy Howell received a call from Washington. FBI headquarters knew about the couple. Attorney General Janet Reno's office had received a videotape, the return address P.O. Box 1305, Massilon, Ohio. May Sexton had been making follow-up calls to the Justice Department, asking for a meeting.

Three days later, on November 8, an agent in the FBI's Correspondence Unit called Howell. Actually two tapes had been sent in August, she reported, postmarked in New Hudson and Port Richey, Florida. There was one more thing. May Sexton had called again. She'd been told to contact Agent Howell.

May Sexton called at 5 p.m. that day. Howell told her there were outstanding warrants against her and her husband. May Sexton claimed they'd committed no crimes against their children. Well, Howell said, the best way to straighten that all out, was to first turn themselves in so the entire matter could be resolved.

He asked her where she was.

"Down south," she said.

Howell could hear her pumping coins into the telephone.

"Is your husband with you?" he asked.

"Off and on," she said.

He asked her again if they would surrender.

May told the agent she'd check with her husband and call back at 1:30 p.m. the next day. He told her if she didn't call back, he'd take that to mean they were not coming in, and a federal warrant would be issued for their arrest.

The call did not come. But a copy of the video from bureau headquarters did. Agents were struck by Sexton's statements in the tape, the segment where he said that if the children were taken from him, "God help us all."

Howell began with the phone records provided by Steve Ready. The agent began notifying bureau offices in Indianapolis, Oklahoma, Knoxville, Louisville, Minneapolis,

Newark, and Tampa. Agents would be assigned to interview every person the Sextons had called.

In his bureau memo, Howell warned agents to proceed cautiously. Sexton had been in a barricaded situation before. Howell's memo ended with an underlined warning:

EDDIE L. SEXTON IS TO BE CONSIDERED ARMED AND
DANGEROUS WITH SUICIDAL TENDENCIES . . .

6

May Sexton later recalled that she, too, had her hands full with Eddie Lee.

"I didn't hear the baby [Skipper] crying, because every night I was getting knocked out with something. I didn't really know what was going on that night. Eddie wanted to be the doting husband and always wanted to fix my plate. And he didn't want anybody to eat what I was eating. And it seemed like about a half hour or so after I'd eaten, I'd be out. I'd wake up in the morning half here and half there. He was drugging me.

"Oh, he was real hateful. He was going every two weeks for the checks. And it seemed like every time he would come back from Canton it would be worse than when he left. He was in a good mood when he left, and he'd say he'd be back the following day. Real fast. But when he came back he'd always find something wrong, like I did something wrong, or the kids did something wrong.

"His look always scared me. I mean his eyes were always real bloodshot. I didn't know if it was from the lack of sleep or the medication or if he'd been drinking, or what it was. Sometimes I'd get smacked, sometimes I wouldn't. Then I'd just get tired of it and smack him back. I'd take a walk. I just wanted to do anything to get out of there.

"Now, I called the FBI because I wanted Eddie to turn himself in. I talked to the FBI man. He was trying to make arrangements to set up a court date. Eddie was supposed to turn himself in, and they were supposed to drop the charges against me. I didn't know what kind of charges they were. And [the FBI man] said they would drop the charges against me and I could go to court and get my children. I said, all right. I told Eddie.

"The next thing I know, he's saying, 'Oh, they're just tricking us.' I said, 'Why do you have me call and set these dates up, if you're just going to make an ass out of me and get the authorities mad?'

"It was my idea to start with. Because I wanted to get out of this situation because it was getting so hot and heated I thought, something is going to happen to one of these kids."

7

The park was halfway between Tampa and Sarasota, not far from Highway 301. The Little Manatee River State Recreation Area billed itself as "More of the *real* Florida." The park featured 1,600 acres of slash pine, swamp, and palmetto, 40 miles upstream from Tampa Bay on a river that rose and fell with the ocean tides.

Little Manatee also had seniors, lots of them. They started arriving in late fall with expensive campers and motor homes, usually towing cars behind. They came from Michigan and Ohio and Canada and New York. A few miles up the highway was Sun City, a large retirement community where personal golf carts were legal transportation for seniors buzzing up and down its blocks.

Little Manatee catered to the northern retirees on bigger wheels. Many spent the entire winter moving from one Florida campground to another. Little Manatee had only 30 campsites with electrical and water hookups. Fourteen dollars a night. Eight-person limit. If the park wasn't full, rangers routinely granted extensions to the 14-day limit.

There was no pool, not even a playground. There were picnic tables and a nature trail through the swampy riverbed.

As one local ranger would put it: "Most of our campers' idea of excitement is the toddy hour after supper where everyone sits around and talks about the good old times."

A uniformed ranger named Yale Hubbard noticed the Dodge Challenger the day after it rolled into Little Manatee on November 17. Hubbard had been on the job 12 years. He'd learned to read the subtle signs of problem campers, though in Little Manatee, about the worst that ever happened was illegal dumping or an occasional vehicle B&E.

The way the Challenger was parked in Campsite Number 18 immediately caught his eye. Most campers faced their motor homes and trailers toward the paved traffic circle, or toward the fire pit, putting up awnings and mosquito netting out front. The front of the Challenger faced the woods, revealing only the side without awnings or doors. In the days that followed, Hubbard watched for illegal fires and digging. He'd seen campers dump their trash and waste tanks in holes near campsites.

But Campsite Number 18 remained still and silent. He saw only a handful of adults and children there on his daily tours. That raised another flag with Hubbard. You didn't see families *that* quiet.

Hell, even the old-timers made *some* noise.

8

The survival strategies developed with each new location. Eddie Lee Sexton had designed a state park defense plan for "those stupid sonsabitches" in the FBI. If the law arrived, Eddie would start shooting to pin down the agents. Willie would start the camper and bulldoze through the police line. Christopher would return fire from the back window. If that wasn't possible, they'd flee into the woods. They spent time in Little Manatee practicing escape routes and places to hide in trees.

For 10 months now, the patriarch had drilled the boys on firearms, knife throwing, and a variety of hand moves. In Florida, he'd added another maneuver—strangulation by garotte. You made a garrote by attaching both ends of a rope to wooden handles, he said. You wrapped it around a cop or agent's neck from behind, then you twisted. Even a couple of sticks would do.

The handles gave you leverage; that was the key.

In Florida, siblings would later say, Willie Sexton began carrying one in his pants.

The patriarch seemed to take more interest in his daughter's marriage. The couple's bickering only continued. The make-shift burial of the baby was a new dispute.

Sexton took Pixie on walks, counseling her.

"Treat him like a husband," he told her. "Have relations with him."

Other siblings saw him encourage the couple to hold hands. He told Pixie and Joel to go on walks together. Find some privacy up the road.

"Sometimes he would tell them to take a blanket with them," Sherri later said.

9

In 1993, Teresa Boron had made every effort she could think of to find her missing nephew. She kept checking the house on Caroline and his old apartment in Bolivar. She called her lawyer, who suggested she contact Jackson Township police and file a missing person report. She called the department, telling someone on the phone everything she could think of about her nephew and the Sextons. A police officer told her she couldn't file such a report. He was over 21. He was married. She couldn't file it unless she was his legal guardian or his wife.

She tried again with the Canton PD.

"It was basically the same thing," she later recalled. "They said I was overreacting. They said you might be missing your nephew, but he may not be missing his aunt."

She went to the post office and found Joey had filed a change of address to the Sextons' post office in Massilon. She wrote him a letter there. If he didn't want anything to do with the family, she wrote, that's fine. Just let us know where you are.

She never received an answer.

Teresa wrote again in September, making the same case, but adding this time that his grandfather was very ill from emphysema. Grandpa was asking for him. His condition was day to day. She included family home numbers and the 800 number for the shop.

Still, no answer came.

On Thanksgiving, November 25, Teresa had the entire family over for the holiday.

Gladys and Lewis Barrick. Brother Sam and Sue. Sister Velva.

They were all talking in the kitchen, the turkey roasting.

"Everybody's here but Joey," Teresa said.

"Aunt Tee Tee." That's what he used to call her.

A feeling overwhelmed her.

She found herself saying, "I think Joey's not with us anymore."

10

It was a perfect fall day for studying. The morning temperature was climbing out of the 40s. Cloudbursts sprayed the campus of the University of South Florida at Sarasota as students crammed for finals or finished papers for the end of the term.

A 43-year-old reference librarian named Gail Novak had her hands full in the J.B. Cook Library, a modern, light-filled facility in pink, blue and walnut motif. She was the only librarian working reference. Another staffer checked out books. The public copying machine was on the fritz. Novak was shuttling student copy requests to a machine in the back office. Every minute or two, students leaned against her desk with a reference question or request.

Gail Novak had a masters in library science, taught a library class at the university and, with six years at J.B. Cook, knew the collection well. She looked as if she'd been sent over from central casting. Oversized glasses. Blousy dresses and sandals with socks. Timid, but quietly diligent and eager to shepherd young patrons through the world of books.

She saw the young man walk through the glass doors in late morning, then wander across the sandstone carpet to her desk. He seemed hardly able to talk. His voice was slurred and he accented some of his vowels, as if his tongue were too long for his mouth. He told her his name, but she could hardly understand him. Soon a young woman with raccoon eyes appeared at his side.

Gail Novak later would remember the day as being November 30, the Tuesday after Thanksgiving. She was sure of it. She'd marked down in her date book a lecture she had to give in the mid afternoon. The new candidate for university president also visited that day.

The boy's name was Joel, she learned at the desk. The woman's name was Pixie. Pixie's shoulders were hunched, collapsed in. Her hair was a mess. And those eyes. The circles were so dark, they looked like bruises.

Joel and Pixie wanted information about Sudden Infant Death Syndrome, or SIDS.

"How does a baby's head and arms look when a baby dies of crib death?" Pixie asked. She wanted books. She wanted to see a picture.

Then another young man wandered into the library,

joining them. She'd later remember his name as "Billy," but maybe it was Willie. Later, she would identify Billy as William Sexton.

"Willie drove us down Highway 301," Joel said, introducing him.

Highway 301 ran north to Tampa. But the group, she later learned from their conversation, was staying in a nearby state park, somewhere off Highway 301.

They followed Novak over to a patron reference computer, where she started pulling references. But the girl Pixie seemed disinterested, lost in her own thoughts. She was half talking to Novak, half talking to herself, repeating a story over and over, as if she was trying to memorize it. She said they were camping and she'd had a baby. Now it was dead. It was the second baby she'd lost in quick succession that fall.

"The old man is the father," she told Novak. She didn't even have time to name it, she said.

All morning, Pixie added, they'd been looking for a migrant clinic, a place to take it. Willie got lost on Highway 301, saw the campus. The library building. And that's why they were there.

They said they had the baby in the car.

Novak kept her eyes on the computer screen, but thought are these people serious? Or were they really students, playing some kind of gag?

Months later, when Novak was told that Skipper Lee Good had been killed six weeks earlier, and there was no evidence Pixie was pregnant, she stuck to her story and her November date. "No, Pixie said there was a *second* baby," she said. "I'm sure of it."

Joel shuffled to the vestibule outside and lit a cigarette. All three would do that for the next few hours, spend time in the library, then go outside to smoke. Novak saw Joel making a call on the pay phone.

Novak had turned up a couple of books for Pixie, but didn't have time to thoroughly research more reference hits. When Joel came back Novak offered to take his name, telling him that she could call him later with more research.

"I'm not going to be here. I am going to be in Ohio, but maybe you could get in contact with Pixie."

Pixie said she had no phone.

"I'm going on an airline to Ohio," Joel said. He said he'd just made a reservation on the phone.

Then Joel said, "They told us we should have a funeral for the baby." But as he rambled on, it sounded as if the young man really didn't know the details a funeral entailed.

Then Pixie grabbed Novak's arm. She wanted the librarian to come out to their car, to look at the dead child. Pixie began pleading.

"I'm very busy," Novak said, thinking, she wasn't leaving the library, certainly not with them, certainly not for *that*.

Willie wondered if he could use the library's phone. Novak took them to another desk. Willie dialed, then sounded as if he were asking a park ranger to get someone to come to the phone. After a few minutes, he spoke to someone.

Afterwards Novak pulled out a Yellow Pages, opening it up to funeral homes and handing it to the boy named Joel. She dialed the number of one for him, and handed him the receiver. She heard him ask someone on the other end of the line about a grave marker.

My God, she thought, there is a dead baby. These people do need help. She called the library director upstairs, but there was no answer. She called the campus emergency number. It was staffed by students at the campus police department.

"This is Gail Novak at the library," she said . "There's people with a dead baby over here."

"Is it a baby belonging to a student?" a female voice said, snickering.

"No, it's people that have walked into the library."

She put Joel on the phone, who slurred words into the

mouthpiece. He's either retarded, or on drugs of some sort, Gail thought.

Novak got back on the phone. "Quit playing pranks," the emergency staffer snapped. She threatened to fine the librarian.

Then she hung up.

They don't believe me, Novak thought. It was finals time. It wouldn't be the first practical joke played on police.

"Will you let me call a hospital or go to the emergency room?" Gail asked Pixie.

"We don't have money for an emergency room," Pixie said. "The baby's already dead."

Novak thought, what in the world is going on with these people?

The librarian walked away. Students were waiting at the reference desk.

Thirty minutes after the threesome arrived, Gail Novak noticed someone she'd later call "the old man." He was tall, bearded, and had angular features. He looked angry, his fists clenched. Within minutes he was at her desk. He wanted to see books on names for American Indians. He wanted to see books or maps that identified local campgrounds.

Novak walked him over to a shelf of Native American reference books. He stood so close they almost touched, staying that way as she moved down the shelf of volumes. Invading her space.

Novak pointed out the *Encyclopedia of the American Indian*. "That's not the kind of Indian names I wanted," he snapped.

His face was red with agitation. He said he wanted names like the Boy Scouts used, names with "running" or "jumping" in them.

Then, Willie approached. The old man seemed to turn his frustration toward the younger man.

"You left me with that back-breaking work," he told Willie. "I expected you to help me. Anyway, the grave is ready for tonight.'' The old man added he'd dug a hole big enough to bury a truck.

Novak went about her business, but listened. The old man was mad that Willie had burned up gas in the car. ''Why did you drive all the way down here?'' he asked.

''There was no funeral parlor on the road,'' Willie said. ''That's why we drove so far.'' He'd gotten lost, made a wrong turn. Was looking for a large building and a phone.

The old man's move was instant, ''cat-like,'' Novak would later recall. He dug his nails into Willie's collarbone, then pushed the knuckles on his other hand into Willie's Adam's apple. Discreetly, he slammed the young man into a bookshelf, then into a computer table. Then, he marched him across the library, bouncing him one more time off the edge of the alcove at the men's bathroom. He took him inside, then returned alone.

The old man wanted a map now. Novak could see Joel and Pixie outside, smoking cigarettes just outside the doors.

The librarian was moving quickly now. She wanted to be away from this man. She spread out a Florida map, started to leave him with it.

He didn't like that map.

''Where is a park near here?'' he demanded.

She pointed to a state park south of Sarasota.

No, he said. He didn't want to go south. ''Where is one north of Tampa near the Interstate?'' he asked.

She showed him Hillsborough River State Park.

No, he said, standing close to her again. He'd camped there before. Too many campers. Too many mosquitos and fleas.

Plus, they took down license plates there, he said. She listened passively, blinking, as the old man went into some story about abuse charges made against him by one of his kids.

''The welfare people believe whatever kids tell them,'' he said. His girls would do what he told them to do, he added. "The welfare workers would believe them if I told them to tell them that we stick pins in dolls, kill cats, and things like that."

She'd had enough.

"Look, I'm sick of hearing this," she said.

It was time for her lunch break. Moments later, she was out the door.

Gail Novak drove over to a nearby McDonald's, then back to the campus, parking her car in an empty lot behind a business on Tamiami Trail. She had a frozen yogurt she wanted to finish. She could see the library across a vacant field.

Then she saw him, the old man, a hundred yards away near a line of palmetto trees. He'd pulled a silver pickup truck there. He was making a motion like he was digging with a shovel handle, but she couldn't see the ground. An old foundation in the field blocked her line of sight. After he was done with the shovel, she watched him get a machete from the truck. He hacked off a couple limbs from a palmetto tree.

Novak finished the yogurt and drove slowly back to the library, watching. She watched the old man put the shovel in the back of the pickup, then cover it with the palmetto leaves.

At the library, she bought an ice tea from a machine and stood under the building's portal. It was drizzling now. The old man wheeled the pickup into a spot in front of the library. Novak turned sideways, looking disinterested.

She found herself frozen with both curiosity and fear.

Willie backed a large, black car up to the pickup. Joel and Pixie came out. The old man kept asking Joel to transfer the shovel from the pickup to the car, but he didn't want to do it, and went back inside.

Novak tried to finish her drink quickly. But before she could, the group wandered toward the entrance. The old man was sweaty. He had wet clay on his left shoe and wet sand up the side of his leg, a Big Gulp cup from a 7-Eleven in his hand. She heard him tell Pixie and Willie that he'd drunk a couple of cordials of liquor. It sounded as if he also had some in the cup.

When they reached the sidewalk, the old man, Willie, and Pixie were arguing, oblivious to her, lost in their own world. She heard Pixie and Willie say they wanted to have a little cross for the baby's grave. They must be talking about that funeral, Novak thought.

"We can't afford a marker," Sexton said.

"How we gonna find it?" Willie asked.

Sexton pointed out nearby landmarks. A wrought iron fence, a nearby flagpole. He handed the Big Gulp to Pixie and said, "Make sure Joel drinks this."

Then the old man headed through the door, stamping the mud from his feet.

Novak waited, then went back inside.

He was just inside the entrance, doing what looked like an Indian dance. He stamped his foot and slapped his hands against his legs, turning east, then west, then north, then south. He almost touched her with one move as she passed.

She ignored him.

The invasion of these strange people only continued. They browsed around the library, the old man in the books, Pixie near the computer, reading the medical texts she'd pulled. The old man asked Novak if he could cash some checks, pulling out a handful. The boy named Joel kept talking about his airline reservation. The Sarasota-Bradenton Airport bordered the campus. Joel kept telling Pixie and Willie he had to be dropped off there. His plane was leaving at three o'clock.

Then Joel would go back outside, smoke another cigarette, and drink from the Big Gulp. Soon the young man seemed to be slurring his words more, losing coordination. At one point, Willie and Pixie had to support him by the arms.

Novak studied Pixie at the computer. Those dark eyes.

Maybe she was beaten up. Maybe she was an abused woman. She found a brochure for a battered women's shelter and walked over, discreetly handing it to her.

But Pixie was lost in her own baby story again. She'd had to leave the baby in the camper to go to another campsite, she was saying. She said she had to have sex with a man there so he would feel guilty and wouldn't call the police when she took his wallet. When she returned she found the baby dead.

Suddenly the old man was there. Right next to them.

"You ain't going to no funeral," he said to Pixie. "You can't get your story straight."

His bony fingers grabbed Pixie by the collarbone, lifting her up like a magician doing an elevation. Then the old man pushed her hard into the edge of the computer table, her tummy hitting the edge.

"Remember last time," he said. "You better get your story straight."

Novak returned to her reference desk, still watching, still listening. She thought of calling the emergency number again, but they'd already humiliated her one time. She didn't want to get into it with them again.

Novak eavesdropped on a conversation between the old man and Willie. Pixie and Joel were outside, smoking. Willie was saying Joel wanted to get back to Ohio. Joel wanted to go back and "testify," Willie said.

"If Joel testifies, he is going to get on the stand," the old man said. "That retarded boy is going to start telling stories. And get everything all mixed up."

That was the reason they brought him to Florida, the old man said. His face was red, his fists clenched again.

"The only way he is going back to Ohio is in a body locker," the old man said.

"A body locker?" Willie asked.

"Like Vietnam. When they send the dead home on the plane in a silver locked chest."

Minutes later, Joel came back inside, staggering. He told

the old man he had to go to the airport. His plane was leaving.

"You don't have enough money for a bus, let alone a plane ticket," the old man said.

"Yes, I have a hundred dollars," he said.

The old man told Joel he didn't have $100 earlier. Where did he get it?

Joel said people in Ohio had wired it to him. He seemed to be trying to stand up to the old man. The old man frisked his pockets, finding nothing.

"Where's that hundred?" he demanded.

When Joel didn't answer, the old man clamped one hand around his nose, slapped his other hand under his chin, pushing his head back. Again, cat-like. Discreet. Then his fingertips grabbed Joel by the esophagus, squeezing.

"Where's the money?" he demanded again.

"In a bag in the car," the young man named Joel finally said.

The old man, who Gail Novak later identified as Eddie Lee Sexton, marched Joel out of the library toward the parking lot.

And just like that, they all were gone.

11

It was a Tuesday, one of the Sextons later would remember, the day after Pixie, Willie, and their father had returned from yet another Ohio trip. In the morning, Ed Sexton had cooked everyone breakfast. Egg sandwiches. Later that morning, Sexton and his son Willie went for a walk.

By the time they got back, May Sexton was preparing for a picnic. The patriarch had brought a couple of buckets of Kentucky Fried Chicken back from Ohio, and the side fixings from the Colonel. Pixie and Sherri helped their mother pack the car. Half the family was having a picnic.

May, Ed, Skipper, Matthew, Chris, Kim, and Dawn would go. Pixie, Willie, Sherri, Joel, and Shasta remained behind.

What happened in the couple of hours between the time the group left and returned to the campsite would constitute a new chest of secrets within the Sexton family.

Safe to say, by dark Campsite Number 18 looked as if it could have been any typical family at any Florida campground. The boys sat in the Nissan for a while, listening to rock music, the windows rolled up, out of earshot from other campers and their dad. A barbecue was lit. Dinner cooked. Dishes washed. The young ones were put to bed.

Later, somebody built a campfire. The Sextons all sat around, listening to the flames crackle and the occasional rustle of an animal back in the brush.

The chill of the Florida night pushed everyone closer to the fire circle, their silhouettes dancing in the dark treetops.

They were all Sextons.

Little Skipper Lee, and now Joel Good, were no longer among them. Even Joel's clothes were gone.

"A good snitch is a dead snitch," the patriarch said, the flames leaping like puppets in his eyes.

12

Ranger Yale Hubbard had seen some of them at the park office, or on his daily tours through Little Manatee.

The girl named Pixie always came up and paid for the registration, the husband she called Joe usually in tow. She told Hubbard her father was an author, working on a book on Indians. He had to make frequent trips to Ohio to meet with his publisher and pick up advance checks, she said. Hubbard had seen the cars come and go.

She was a pretty girl with a big problem, other rangers joked after she left. It wafted in through the open window when they took her registration money. The girl had the worst body odor anyone had ever smelled.

Hubbard met Eddie Sexton. The ranger kept the meetings to brief chats. You linger too long with some of those older campers, you could easily lose a half a day.

"He could have been a writer," Hubbard later recalled. "There's some pretty strange writers out there. And he didn't appear to be a dummy. He looked like he was thinking all the time. He always knew exactly what he was saying. He planned ahead before he spoke."

When Hubbard began noticing three teenage boys roaming the campground, he sharpened his observations again. It struck him a little odd that they all dressed in military fatigues. He scanned them for weapons, but saw none. He was a little concerned about break-ins or maybe hunting in the park. But they never gave him a reason to question them during their entire stay in the park.

Hubbard chatted with Willie Sexton the most often. He asked about the wildlife. There were foxes and bobcats and snakes, Hubbard said. They talked about the manatee, the giant, gentle water mammal, the state animal that swam up the rivers in the coldest months.

Willie seemed like a rather innocent, vulnerable kid. "I wouldn't call him retarded or anything like that," Hubbard would later recall. "I would just say he was slow."

On Thanksgiving, the park all but emptied, but the Sextons stayed. After the holiday, Little Manatee began to fill again, the girl named Pixie returning to the office to re-register, never paying for more than three days at a time. The family would stay nearly two months.

It was only much later that Yale Hubbard would realize that the husband named Joel wasn't coming with her to the office anymore. It didn't raise a flag. They always had cars coming and going. They had relatives nearby in the county, they said.

Old man Sexton usually kept to himself. He'd see him disposing of trash at the Dumpster, or walking down the camp road with his wife. Only once did he show any sense of humor.

Sexton was walking down the middle of the road.

Hubbard approached behind him in the park truck.

Sexton lingered on the pavement, waiting until the bumper got close. Then the old man wiggled his butt, like a startled game bird.

As if to say: *Go ahead. Here I am. Get me if you can.*

X

Wise and Friendly

1

Tuesday, December 7. Steve Ready tossed his pen on a pile of reports and picked up the ringing telephone. It was the secretary at the sheriff's department's detective bureau.

"We just got an anonymous tip that Eddie Sexton is at his brother's house at a Third Street address," she said. "He's supposedly leaving in ten minutes."

Moments later, Ready was behind the wheel of the Celebrity, another detective and a K-9 unit on their way in separate cars. The address was Orville Sexton's, Eddie's older brother, whom Ready had avoided interrogating while he staked out the Massilon postal box. The house wasn't a half mile away. Eddie Lee runs into the neighborhood, Ready figured, the dog will hunt him down.

Ready didn't linger for pleasantries when Orville Sexton opened the door to his ramshackle two-story. He walked right past him into the living room, the other officers scrambling up the stairs, searching room to room.

"Your brother here?" Ready demanded.

"No, he ain't here," Orville Sexton said in a nearly unintelligible mountain drawl.

"Was he here?"

"Yeah, about four hours ago."

"Did you know he's wanted?"

"I didn't know that, Mr. Ready."

"Did you give him money?"

"I didn't give him nothin', Mr. Ready."

Ready's eyes darted from Orville Sexton to his wife Sarah, also in the living room. The 68-year-old former coal miner looked like he'd stepped off Tobacco Road. He and his wife were in their bare feet, their soles black with dirt. Orville was missing a toe. A small child was standing in the room now, apparently a grandchild. The house was a mess. A decaying couch squatted across from a large projection TV.

"Call me Steve," Ready snapped. The detective's patience was running out, not only with Orville Sexton, but the entire family, the entire Sexton case.

Ready walked over to a telephone.

"This place is a sty," he said. "I'm going to pick up the phone. And I'm going to have human services here. You'll be lucky if they don't take this child."

Sarah Sexton complained she had a bad heart.

"Damn right you're going to be sick, lady," Ready said. "I want to know where the hell Eddie is at."

She asked, "Who'd you say you worked for?"

He told her the Stark County Sheriff's Department.

"I'm going to call the sheriff," she said.

Ready picked up the phone himself and handed it to her, saying, "You go right ahead and do that."

He thought, who was she kidding?

Ready turned back to Orville. Where was Eddie? Where had the entire family been all these months? He could hear Sarah Sexton leaving a message on the phone.

Eddie had been there with Willie and Pixie, Orville said. Beyond that, he didn't know a thing, he said.

The phone rang.

Sarah Sexton answered, saying, "Yes, Officer Ready is here. He's just yelling and cussing and screaming at me."

She handed Ready the phone.

"Hello," Ready snapped.

It was Sheriff Bruce Umpleby. "Steve, what is going on there?" he asked.

"I'm looking for Eddie Sexton."

The sheriff said the woman was complaining.

"I'm just doing my job, Sheriff."

"I know you'll do it in a professional manner, Steve," he said.

"Yes sir, I will," he said.

The two other policeman gathered in the living room. They'd found nobody. As Ready worked his way to the door, he asked, "Did Eddie make any phone calls here?"

No, Eddie made no calls, Orville said.

They looked at him blankly.

"I'll be back," Ready said.

The detective stopped at the door, turned around and pointed.

Adding, "And next time, I'm bringing the DHS."

2

If anybody asked, the official story in Campsite Number 18 was that Joel Good had been picked up by a woman in a red Nissan. He'd received a letter from his aunt Teresa, Pixie later told a brother, reporting that his grandfather was deathly ill.

Nobody had seen him since.

Eddie Lee Sexton's mind continued to churn between his nightly Bible readings. One night in the smoke-choked camper, he hatched a plan to rob a bank in Tampa. Pixie would do surveillance. Willie would get the money with a gun. Eddie would be the wheel man. But like so many of Sexton's schemes, the plan never got farther than the talking stage.

They did rob a convenience store one night, Skipper would later claim. Three of them wore camo and ski masks. The old man had a 9mm semi-automatic. He and Willie hit the store, while Skipper waited outside in the car.

Another night, Skipper was convinced his father killed someone. The patriarch came back from a trip to town shaking and chain-smoking cigarettes. He'd never seen his father rattled. "He didn't talk for a while," Skipper would later recall. "And what you gonna think? He's done something really bad."

Locally, there were no reports filed on felonies that matched the Sextons' descriptions. Later, none of the siblings could remember names of towns or roads, let alone the names of banks and stores involved.

The same would not be true of other marks. There were more trips back to Ohio. In a little over four months, the Sextons put nearly 50,000 miles on the new Sentra. One day, Eddie Sexton took Skipper and Willie aside. He talked about "erasing" Eddie Jr. and Otis Sexton in Ohio. After they killed Otis, they would "take out" Eddie Jr., his wife, and his children, save one. Eddie Jr. had a new son, born in 1993. He proposed using the child as a replacement for the buried Skipper Lee.

On a frigid Canton evening in early December, Otis Sexton received a call from a neighbor, saying, "There's a car full of people watching your house."

Otis turned off all the lights in the house, then went upstairs and looked out a bedroom window. He could see a light-colored car parked on the street out front, the glow of cigarettes inside. He found his .357 Taurus and watched for an hour. They'd had problems with a drug house in the neighborhood.

When he pushed the curtain aside, the car drove away.

Skipper Sexton later recalled that he, Willie, and his father were in the car. "We were just going to wait until he came out and blow his ass away. Then torch the house. We sat there for about two and a half hours, and we seen the curtain come open in the top window and I think it was him that looked out. We jetted."

Then they went to Eddie Jr.'s house.

"My old man had me against Eddie Bug so bad. I walked up with the nine millimeter stuffed in my pants, knocking on his door, my hand behind my back. And if he would have come to the door I would have just blown him away. I'm glad he wasn't there. My dad had me against my own blood."

Christmas came in Little Manatee Park, Pixie Good continuing to renew the camp permit. Packed away in the camper were family snapshots of holidays past, Christmas trees, and gifts being handed out to the youngest kids. When a child turned 13 in the Sexton family, he was taken off Santa's list. Now, nobody had a stocking. Money remained short, though Pixie was collecting food stamps and Sherri welfare. There was no special Christmas meal or picnic. On Christmas, the Florida sky pelted the Challenger, virtually alone in the campground, with a half inch of rain.

Soon more winter campers and seniors would arrive. Rangers wouldn't be granting extensions so readily. They had already been at Campsite Number 18 six weeks.

Eddie Sexton said, "We've been in one place too long."

They were sitting outside by the Challenger one day, watching new campers roll into the park—Sexton, Willie, and Pixie. An unfamiliar motor home glided by on the camp road. It was a shiny, long Winnebago pulling a Bronco II, a lone man at the wheel.

Willie asked, "Did you see that camper?"

"Yeah," Eddie Lee Sexton said, his eyes following it around the bend.

It was the New Year, 1994.

Soon, they would have new names. *Wise.* Willie Wise. Pixie Wise.

Ed Wise, the Indian author, thought it was time for a new plan, as well.

3

He drove into Little Manatee State Recreation Area on New Year's Eve, but had to wait in the campground's holding area, then a small campsite, until rangers found a better campsite for his 33-foot Winnebago.

Raymond Hesser had the Cadillac of motor homes, a bachelor's degree in natural science, a specially equipped Bronco II, and a post office box in Sarasota where he got his mail. He had a three-wheeled electric scooter to get around on, profits from a motor home parts business, and friends all over the United States.

What he didn't have was a good set of legs or hands.

Hesser suffered from Friedreich's ataxia, a disease that caused loss of balance and coordination. But he had no trouble driving, or handling the big Winnebago. And as long as he could make friends in campgrounds, he was going to see these United States.

He followed the weather, attending camping conventions and staying in parks throughout the north and south, venturing into Mexico as well. It was no easy procedure leveling out the motor home from a scooter, or unhitching the Bronco II, something most campers did in minutes. That could take him a couple of hours, but it hadn't deterred him. Hesser had been on the road for six years, living a fuller life than many of the perfectly fit.

He was sitting on his scooter at the back of Campsite Number 27 when he first saw the bearded man and his wife, walking hand in hand. The man looked like he wanted to say something, but didn't. The next day, the couple passed again, this time a young girl riding along next to them on a bike. The following day, there was a third pass.

"I'm Ed Wise," the man said. "And this is my wife."

The wife didn't say a word, but Ed Wise struck up a pleasant chat, a chat with a few questions.

Hesser answered, no, he didn't have a wife. That's right. He traveled alone.

Ed Wise wanted to know why he was on the scooter.

"It's called Friedreich's ataxia," Hessler said, adding an explanation of the symptoms.

"That's good you can get around that way," Ed Wise said.

Wise told him he had MS. He said he was an Indian, some obscure tribe. He also said he was blind in one eye.

The next day Ed showed up again. The hydraulic pump in his motor home was out, Hesser complained to his morning visitor. The pump helped level the motor home. He was going to fix it himself. He had to crawl underneath the Winnebago to get it out.

How do you do that, Wise asked, with your disease and all.

"It's not that my legs are weak," Hesser explained. "I've just lost balance and coordination in them."

Wise wondered about his arms.

Same, he said.

"That's good for you that you can get around and do that stuff," Wise said. "You travel a lot?"

"Well, my motor home is my home," Hesser said.

"You on disability?"

Hesser nodded.

"Me, too," Wise said. "But I'm having a problem getting my checks."

Hesser told him that his were wired directly to his account.

The next day, Hesser was underneath the Winnebago

when Wise stopped by again, wondering if the repair was going okay.

"Everything's fine," Hesser said.

Hesser had just taken apart the motor and cleaned it when the young man who introduced himself as Willie Wise showed up at his campsite.

"You know my father," he said. "He told me you were working on your motor."

Hesser said he still had to test it.

Willie had an idea. They had a battery charger down at their campsite. They could test it with that. That would save a lot of time and energy, Hesser thought. They went to Campsite Number 18. It was just around the bend, on the opposite side of the camp road.

As they tested the motor, Hesser met the boy named Skip and chattered more with the old man. They talked about towing vehicles behind motor homes. Wise said he put some 48,000 miles on his car. He was an author, and he had to drive back frequently to see his publisher in Ohio.

Ed Wise asked him about his motor home registration, saying he'd been having trouble registering his Challenger in Florida. The state wanted several hundred dollars. As far as Hesser knew, it was about $50.

"That doesn't seem right," Hesser said.

Willie followed him back to the campsite, offering to put the motor back in his motor home. It took him only a couple of minutes, the young man very handy with tools. But the motor also had a broken solenoid. Hesser had broken the part taking it out.

"Well, let's go get it," Willie said.

It's Sunday, Hesser reminded him. Auto parts stores were closed. Willie said he and his father were going to Ohio, but would be back on Wednesday.

"I'll go with you when I get back," he said.

Willie left, but returned later that day. His father wanted

him to take a look at his motor home title, he said. He was still curious about the registration fee.

Hesser showed him his registration.

"I need to see the title," Willie said.

Hesser told him the title was in a safety deposit box in Sarasota. He lied. Ed Wise seemed to be awfully curious about the 1988 Winnebago. How much he paid for it, its estimated value now. His better judgement told him to keep the title to himself.

On Wednesday, Willie was back, and the boy named Skip. They drove toward Ruskin, but found the solenoid at a K-Mart along the way. Willie saw a repaired heater core on the floor of the Bronco. When they returned to the campsite, he designed a new mount for the part. He put in the heater core in the Bronco, too.

It saved Hesser days of work.

The kid was a whiz with tools, Hesser thought. He spoke with a slight speech impediment. Willie told him it came from a head injury he got as a kid. They talked about camping, the states Hesser visited. During one conversation he mentioned to Willie that he was sick of traveling alone. He was looking for a female companion to join him on the road.

That week, Hesser was getting ready to drive into town to buy a new bolt for one of his crutches. He also planned to stop at a couple of nearby banks.

Willie showed up at his campsite, wanting to go. At first, Hesser tried to dissuade him. He didn't want a relative stranger to see him doing his banking.

"I thought I was your friend," Willie said.

Hesser felt sorry for him. He not only took Willie, but brother Skip. When it began pouring rain outside the hardware store, he was glad they came along. He would have been soaked trying to get the scooter out of the car.

On the road, Skip made a couple of comments about the can of pepper spray he kept in his console. But in all his years on the road, Hesser had never had any trouble. People were helpful everywhere he went.

He made the deposits at drive-in windows. Cash sealed in envelopes with deposit slips.

That evening, Willie showed up at his motor home again. He said he had somebody outside he wanted Raymond Hesser to meet.

"Now don't be shy," he told Hesser.

The young woman was wearing pants and a knit top. Willie introduced her as his sister.

"This is Pixie," he said, his eyes twinkling.

There was no doubt about it, Raymond Hesser would later decide. Willie Wise was playing matchmaker, trying to set them up.

4

Steve Ready was losing hope they'd ever find them.

In December, another call had come into FBI agent Randy Howell from May Sexton. She and her husband were surrendering, she said. They'd even set a date, December 21, at 11 p.m. at the FBI office in Canton. Ready waited at the office. He was in another room when Howell walked in at 11:20. May had just called, he said. She claimed they'd run into bad weather.

"She's full of shit," Ready said.

The weather bureau showed it clear up and down I-75.

Steve Ready also took a call from Tuck Carson. The Sextons had stolen his car, he said. They'd promised to make payments, but just found out payments were three months overdue. Yes, they'd been at their home in Indiana in early 1993, he said. By all appearances, the Carsons had stonewalled Clark County cops, he thought. Now they wanted his help.

They spit on you, Ready thought, until they need a cop.

Ready wrote down the details on the Nissan, then told Carson to file a stolen car report, and hung up.

On January 13, Ready was slugging through more reports at his cubicle in the Renkert Building when his beeper went off. He called headquarters. Sheriff Bruce Umpleby had made the page.

"These Sextons called again," the sheriff said. Orville and Sarah Sexton. "Could you please talk to them for me, Steve."

Shit, Ready thought. What now?

The Orville Sexton who answered the phone was as friendly as a long-lost brother.

"Steve, how ya doin'?" he drawled.

"How's Sarah feeling these days, Orville?" Ready asked.

"You know, Steve, I forgot to tell you the day you was here. Eddie did make two phone calls."

"He did?"

"Yeah, they were long distance. I got my phone bill right here."

As he sped over to the house, Ready couldn't remember if he'd even bothered to hang up the phone. The bill soon in his hands, he looked at the two phone numbers. One he recognized as Dave Sexton's. The other, in the same area code, didn't look familiar.

The detective phoned the number in to Randy Howell at the FBI. Howell didn't get back to him until the next afternoon. He said the bureau's Tampa office had traced the number. A state park called Little Manatee, he said.

Howell told Ready agents had already visited the park.

"The motor home is there, Steve," Howell said.

"They doing it?" Ready asked.

"No, they're going to wait until tomorrow."

Ready pulled the phone back, looking at it a moment. "Randy," he said. "If these people leave, it's my ass."

5

Eddie Lee Sexton told the entire family his plan as the sun burned through the treetops early in the morning of January 14. They were all sitting in the cramped Challenger. Today was the day, he said.

Today, they were going to "pull it down."

The patriarch had been discussing Hesser for days with Eddie, Willie, Pixie, and Skipper. "I'm going to become a good friend with Ray," he said at first. Then he dispatched Willie, Skipper, and Pixie to find out everything they could about the handicapped camper, telling Pixie to "be friendly" with the man and learn everything she could about his family and his bank account.

The brothers reported Hesser making the deposits, saying they'd seen $5,000 in cash. There was a safe in the back of the Winnebago, Skipper said.

Eddie Lee Sexton wanted his motor home, his money, and his very identity. He'd take some of Hesser's IDs and apply for a lost driver's license.

Then they would be on their way.

The old man laid it out. Skipper would hide the Challenger while Willie and Pixie would go somewhere with Ray. When Ray returned, Willie would take him down. Skipper would tie him up with tape. They'd drive off with the Winnebago and transfer their belongings from the Challenger. Ray would be ordered at gunpoint to write checks to Willie, Pixie, Skipper, and Sherri. Tap all his money. If he cooperated, they'd keep him alive on the road with them. If he didn't, Willie and Skipper would kill him. Willie would be rewarded for his work, the patriarch said. After it went down, the Bronco II was his.

"What happened when the checks and money ran out," someone would later ask Skipper.

"You know, we never thought of that," he said.

Sexton showed his sons how to tie Hesser up with tape, around the wrists, then a strip across the mouth. They practiced on each other and Christopher, but the father decided the tape didn't hold as well as he liked.

"We need handcuffs," Sexton said.

He sent Willie to buy them. When he returned with a set, he berated his son for the price he'd paid.

"They were the only ones there," Willie said.

Now, on the 14th day of January, they were all gathered together. Sexton told the family to get their clothes and personal effects together. Pack up the campsite. They were going to move the camper. Today, they were going to kidnap Ray Hesser, get his money. But they weren't taking him along.

The patriarch said he was going to shoot him.

"We're going to pull it down," he said. "Today, I'm going to take Ray out."

6

By that morning, park ranger Yale Hubbard couldn't believe the operation the FBI was mounting. They'd moved in a camper and a truck into campsites kitty-cornered from the Sextons', agents seeing the great outdoors undercover. They had an airplane doing periodic flyovers. They'd parked a surveillance van up the road. Two of the Sexton boys approached it, trying the door handles, but it was locked.

The FBI men had sworn Hubbard to secrecy, then asked him to find ways to move campers away from the Challenger. They needed a buffer zone for a SWAT team. They didn't want innocent campers in the line of fire. They were hoping they could arrest the Sextons away from the campground. If only the couple would take a drive and leave the teenagers behind. What the FBI didn't tell Hubbard was they'd interviewed Tuck Carson. He'd told the bureau he'd seen at least five weapons with the Sextons, including two pistols and an "Uzi-like" weapon. The FBI didn't want another Ruby Ridge.

That day, as campers left, the ranger did not assign any new campers to sites near Campsite Number 18. Soon he had a third of the circle vacant around the Sexton motor home.

Hubbard was worried about Raymond Hesser. He knew the handicapped camper from previous stays. For several days, Hubbard and another long-time camper had been teasing him about Pixie, calling her "his girlfriend." They knew she'd been visiting Hesser's trailer.

"Ray, you know she's a married woman," Hubbard joked.

They'd busted his chops, Hesser playing coy. Guy stuff. Hubbard didn't know if he was actually sleeping with the girl, or just wanting them to think he did.

Now the ranger was concerned. He tried to drop subtle hints.

"You know, Ray, all that glitters isn't gold," he told him. "You don't really know these people at all."

Hesser did say they seemed awfully nosey. He told the ranger that Pixie and Willie followed him to the camp pay phone when he transferred electronic funds. He felt like they were trying to learn his PIN.

"Ray, just be careful," Hubbard said.

7

Raymond Hesser hadn't even washed up yet when Willie showed up at 9 a.m. Soon, they were shooting the breeze at the dinette. Then Ed Wise was at the door.

Inside, Ed Wise did all the talking. He began talking about the Winnebago again. How many people did it sleep? Where would they sleep? His eyes kept going toward the back of the motor home, then at the ceiling.

He stood up and said, "Well, Willie, you ready to be my eyes?"

The two of them left. At 11 a.m., Pixie was at his door with her two children.

"I wanted you to meet the two girls I was telling you about," she said.

She'd been over the night before. She'd already told Hesser she was divorced, had the two kids, and that her ex-husband was in Arizona. She was a very pleasant girl, Hesser later said. Seemed normal. She liked to joke and laugh.

Hesser gave the kids a couple of Pepsi's. Dawn, her 5-year-old, asked Hesser to come with them to see the ducks. They walked down to the canoe launch on Little Manatee, but there weren't any ducks that day.

On the way back, he saw Ed Wise, his wife, and Willie drive by, Ed driving. He thought it strange, considering Ed Wise's comments about his eyes. Pixie walked over to the car. They seemed to be having some kind of discussion among themselves.

The car turned around and drove back the other way.

Pixie continued walking next to Hesser's scooter, but left when they reached his campsite. She said something about having to take her parents up to a local store.

When Raymond Hesser got back to his camper, Willie was waiting.

"Are you and my sister going to be friends now?" he asked.

8

Eddie Lee and Estella May Sexton were arguing in the Nissan as they drove to Sun City. Christopher, Kim, and Pixie were in the back. Sexton had been looking into Seminole Indians and local reservations, still clinging to the idea there might be sanctuary for them with an Indian tribe. That had brought up the subject of Mel Fletcher, back in Canton. May later said her husband was accusing her of sleeping with Mel Fletcher again.

Sexton parked the car in the large Winn Dixie parking lot, a supermarket. They'd driven to Sun City for milk and juice.

"Pixie's going in," Sexton told May. "Your ass is staying in the car."

"Fine," she said.

It was 1:36 p.m., January 14, 1994. They had been on the run for 13 and a half months.

Both doors flew open the moment Eddie Lee Sexton turned off the ignition.

Doors pulled open.

Eddie Lee snatched out one side, May the other. Then the kids.

Men in camouflage clothing, shouting "FBI!"

They were both facedown on the pavement, guns pointed at their heads.

The children, too.

"Go ahead and move and you're dead," somebody said.

9

As the news broke in Canton newspapers of the couple's arrest, Steve Ready's name and the leads he'd developed that resulted in the capture were never mentioned in the newspapers.

It didn't bother Ready a bit. They got 'em, that was the important thing. He had work to do.

He worked the phones all week with the Hillsborough County Sheriff's Department, the FBI, Florida social services, riding herd on the children's whereabouts as Eddie and May Sexton were held in the Hillsborough County Jail on the fugitive warrants, an extradition hearing set.

Christopher, Matthew, and Kimberly were taken into

custody by Florida child protection workers and were flown back to Ohio into the custody of the DHS. Rangers ordered Willie, Pixie, and Skipper to leave the campground hours after the arrest. There would be no more extensions. They left in the Challenger and the Pontiac, leaving the Nissan behind. Ready tipped the Hillsborough County sheriff's office that it was a stolen car. As he talked with officers and agents, the only people he hadn't accounted for were the boy named Joel Good and the Goods' son, Skipper Lee.

Ready was anxious to pursue a full-blown sexual assault case against the parents, and anxious to glean more information from the rest of the Sexton kids. That week, Eddie Jr. drove to Florida and picked up Skipper, Sherri, and her son. But Willie and Pixie, with her two children, wanted to stay at their Uncle Dave's.

On Thursday, nearly a week after the arrest, Ready sat down with Sherri Sexton at the Renkert Building. Her appearance moved him more than any Sexton to date.

Her vacant eyes. She seemed only a shell of a human being.

He went slowly. She denied she'd been sexually abused by her father at first, but in time she began disclosing. He'd started when she was 13.

"It hurt," she said. "He told me he was going to make a woman out of me."

They'd had intercourse five times from 1985 until 1991. Her father, and her father only. Christopher was born during that period. She'd also had a miscarriage while living in the house on Caroline Street.

"How would you feel about taking a blood test with Christopher?" Ready asked. "That would prove it."

She agreed.

Ready talked with Charles "Skipper" Sexton. He bore little resemblance to the teenage wrestler Ready had seen in family photos. The road had hardened him. His face was long and gaunt, his hair disheveled, a cigarette hanging from his lip.

They talked about his sexual abuse of his siblings. He was adamant. No way. Ready kept working him, slowly, reading from the DHS reports from Lana and James.

"Skipper, look," he said. "I can understand you not knowing any better. From what I gather, this kind of thing was going on in your family all the time."

He said Lana once asked him to "do what our mom and dad do."

He started to sodomize her, he said, but "chickened out."

He was beaten severely for it.

Then he said, no, he made it all up.

He's all over the place, Ready thought. He could have worked him hard, like Orville Sexton. But he decided to go easy. The kid already has been through a meat grinder, the detective decided.

Plus, he might need Skipper Sexton later on.

Ready switched subjects.

"Where's Joel Good and the baby?" he asked.

"Haven't seen them," Skipper said.

He said they'd left a couple weeks before Christmas, heading back to Ohio.

"Him and Pixie weren't getting along," Skipper said.

"You saw them leave?"

Skipper shook his head.

The detective wondered what car they left in.

"A grey Buick," Skipper said.

Otis Sexton told Ready he was told by family members Joel Good left the Sextons sometime between Thanksgiving and Christmas. A woman picked him up in a red Nissan, they were saying.

Grey Buick. Red Nissan.

Ready picked up the phone and called Lewis Barrick, Joel Good's grandfather.

No, they hadn't seen Joel at all, he said.

10

On January 19, Willie, Pixie, and their aunt Jean Sexton sat in the visiting room at the Hillsborough County Jail in downtown Tampa, the patriarch talking to them one at a time. It was one of three visits the two siblings would make to the jail to see their father in the 10 days between January 17 and 27. Pixie visited her mother only once, Willie not at all.

The plan was still a good one, he told them individually. They could still get the Winnebago and the money. They could post bail for him when bond was set back in Ohio.

Eddie Lee Sexton leaned forward, whispering to Willie.

"Do you think you can pull the job off?" he asked.

11

When Raymond Hesser drove up to his Winnebago the next day in his Bronco, he saw them at his campsite, sitting on the hood of their car.

He was surprised, considering everything. Hesser not only knew about the arrest, but the stolen Nissan and their phony names. On the day of the arrest, they'd visited his campground, wanting to borrow $20 for gas. That same day, Skip had also shown up, wondering if he could "buy a piece."

"I don't carry a gun," Hesser told him. He wondered why he needed it.

"My father told me to uphold the family name," he said.

Now, on January 20, he got busy.

"I'm getting ready to leave," Hesser said, as he went about the time-consuming process of getting himself out of the Bronco. "I don't have much time."

"Where you going?" one of them asked.

He said he was going to a place called Camping World to stay overnight while some repairs were done on his motor home.

"Did you drive the motor home back to Ohio?" he asked.

"No," Pixie said.

"Yes," Willie said.

At the same time.

They said they wanted to tell him the whole story, about their parents' arrests, about the FBI.

"We want to tell you inside," Willie said.

As they moved toward the motor home, Willie told him, "Pixie is ready to get close to you."

Moments later, they were at his table, telling him about false charges against their father. Willie seemed to be trying to control the conversation. He seemed like he wanted to control everything. He was pushing Pixie on him.

Hesser asked Willie to go outside. He wanted to talk to Pixie alone. He complied, but soon came back inside the motor home.

Hesser saw a ranger drive by. He pointed. "He doesn't drive through here very often," Hesser said. "He must be keeping an eye on you guys."

Get going, he told himself.

They helped him pack up, but were trying to convince him to come over to their uncle's house near New Port Richey.

"What is it you guys want?" he finally asked them.

"Well, I want to go traveling with you," Pixie said.

He told her he was looking for a woman, but not one with two kids who smoked. Smokers bothered him.

"What do *you* want?" she asked him.

"I just got to get going," he said.

They helped him hook up the Bronco, Pixie driving it up the hitch. They said they would follow him to the park dump station and help him unload waste. Willie drove their Pontiac, Pixie rode along with him in the motor home.

They worked on him more at the dump station. Come to Uncle Dave's. But already, Hesser had caught Pixie in a half dozen lies. Now, Willie was talking about wanting to ride with him to Camping World, then he could show him where his uncle lived.

They had something planned. Hesser was convinced now. They were after his motor home, his car, and his money. That's how they were going to leave Florida.

Hesser came up with his own story. He proposed that Willie could meet him at Camping World. He couldn't come along because he had personal, private meetings in Sarasota to attend to first.

"If you don't let me go now, I'll never make it back to Camping World tonight," he said.

The place was just north of Little Manatee.

The Pontiac was parked in front of the Winnebago, off to the side.

"You leave first," Willie said.

"I can't get around your car," Hesser said.

He waited two minutes after they drove off, then he drove south, in the opposite direction.

Later, he'd count himself lucky to get away with his life.

12

Teresa Boron and sister-in-law Sue Barrick called the campground, the FBI, Florida police departments, welfare officials. Then they dialed Tampa area shelters and YMCAs.

There was no sign of Joey. He'd gone back to Ohio with his son, an FBI agent said he'd been told by the family. Picked up in a red Nissan.

"But there is no car," Teresa told him.

They considered driving to Florida themselves, asking Pixie face to face, where was Joey? But where was she? How would they find her?

Teresa talked on the phone with Steve Ready when he called her father. A few days later, she went to the Renkert Building. She talked to the detective, telling him the whole story about the strange family.

He gave her the number of the Hillsborough County Sheriff's Department, suggesting she call them and file a missing persons report.

No, not again, she told him. She'd been through that.

"Drop my name," Ready said.

He added, "They're saying he left in a red Nissan."

"It's not a Nissan, it's a Mazda," she said. "They think it's a Nissan. That was *my* car. But he couldn't have left Florida in it. With me, or anybody else."

"Why are you so sure?" Ready asked.

"Because it was totaled in March of 1993."

xi

The Devil Made Me Do It

1

Skipper Sexton remembered hearing the truth about the baby, his namesake. He was sitting at the picnic table with Pixie before the arrest.

"I'm thinking, what are we going to do when all this was over. And thinking, I wonder where Skipper went? And Pixie was like, 'I don't know.'

"I said, 'Well, it was a kid. It probably went to heaven.' I said, 'You think you'll ever tell authorities where that kid is?'

"She's like, no.

"And I go, 'Why's that?'

"She said, because she'll be put away for life. For murder.

"I was like, 'Murder? I thought you overdosed it.'

"And that's when she slipped up. She said, 'No, I suffocated it.' But they covered it up as an overdose."

Skipper later recalled, "That's when it all was over."

Sitting at Eddie Jr.'s house in Canton now, a Sunday

night, back from Florida only a couple of days. Skipper hadn't breathed a word.

Burning some herb, and thinking about it again.

Skipper told Eddie Jr., "I need to tell you something, man."

2

The same Sunday night. Another phone call from Otis Sexton. Steve Ready hadn't had an uninterrupted evening in front of the television in weeks. Eddie Jr. and Skipper were at his house, Otis said. They were talking about murder.

"Steve, I think you better get over here," Otis said.

When Ready arrived at the two-story on 15th Street, Sherri Sexton also was in the living room with her two brothers. Ready took Skipper into the dining room and turned his tape recorder on.

"I understand, Skipper, you want to tell me something about what happened to Skipper Lee Good," Ready said.

Skipper took a hard drag on a Marlboro.

Little Skipper Lee was dead, he said. Pixie had slapped him up and fed him Nyquil in Hillsborough River State Park. The baby was dead in the morning. It lay in the camper for a couple of days, then Willie and Joel had buried it in a grey gym bag.

"Willie showed me," he said.

"Nearby?" Ready asked.

Near Campsite Number 89.

There was more from the 19-year-old. Joel Good also had been killed, about a month later, at a different campground. Coming home from a picnic, he saw his father, Pixie, and Willie go into the woods together. When they came back, he sent Skipper and Pixie to buy a shovel. Alone in the car, Pixie told him Joel was dead, that Willie had stabbed him in the chest. When they returned, his father and Willie went into the woods for two hours. When his father returned, he threatened to kill them if they revealed what happened to Joel.

"Did Willie tell you what happened?" Ready asked.

Yeah, later, Skipper said. Willie told him that before they buried Joel, they'd cut off his head, hands, and feet and buried the torso in a separate spot.

"Willie bragged Joel's head was purple and his eyes were bugged out," Skipper said. Willie later showed him that grave.

"Could you locate both these graves?" Ready asked.

Skipper nodded. "On the baby's, I made a mark on a tree."

Ready asked, "Why didn't you come forward earlier with this information, Skipper?"

He said he was worried his father would kill him. Now his father was in jail.

Moments later, Ready talked to Sherri Sexton.

She told Ready she was at the campsite when Joel Good was killed. While the parents were at the picnic, Pixie had asked her to watch Dawn and Shasta while Pixie, Joel, and Willie went for a walk in the woods. Fifteen minutes later, she heard Joel yelling, "Eddie!" from the woods behind the motor home. She started back into the forest, but then saw Willie.

She said he told her, "If you go in the woods, I'll fucking kill you."

She confirmed the rest of Skipper's story.

"Did your mother know about this?" Ready asked.

Sherri shook her head. Some of the younger siblings didn't know either. And everyone was to say Joel left in a red Nissan, she said.

It was past midnight when Ready left.

Driving back to North Canton, past darkened homes and unlit stores on Market Avenue, Ready thought, no way. Chopping a guy up. It's too diabolical. Two people are killed and the rest of the family doesn't know shit.

Maybe Skipper Sexton was trying to take some heat off himself. He knew Lana had accused him of rape.

Ready knew he was only guessing. He'd been a detective nearly two years now, but he wasn't a homicide cop.

The next morning the detective did the only thing he knew how to do. Believe it or not, you check it out. He drove to the Stark County Detention Center cottages the next morning, where Matt and Christopher were staying, waiting for DHS placement.

He approached Matt as if it were fact.

"I know all about Skipper Lee," Ready said.

Matt hesitated, then told the Nyquil story.

Christopher gave a nearly identical account.

He also asked them both about Joel Good.

Independently, they both said: "He left with a woman in a red Nissan."

When he returned to his Renkert Building cubicle, Ready picked up the phone and called the Hillsborough County Sheriff's Department. He talked to a corporal named Lee "Pops" Baker, then played phone tag with a homicide detective named Mike Willette. By Tuesday, Ready was telling Willette about the interviews.

"Let me get back to you," Willette said.

On Wednesday, he called back.

"How'd you and this boy Skippy like to come to Florida tomorrow?" Willette asked.

3

Steve Ready and another deputy, Shirley Rebillot, already were scheduled to fly to Tampa to transport Eddie Lee and Estella May Sexton back to Ohio that Sunday on the sex charges. A round-trip ticket for Skipper Sexton was waiting at Cleveland-Hopkins, paid for by Hillsborough police.

It was the first time Skipper Sexton had set foot in an

airplane. He sat quietly next to Ready, hardly saying a word.

When the jet landed at Tampa International, Ready's stomach was in knots. Maybe it was the $700 ticket on another department's tab. Or maybe it was the way Ready's witness looked, Skipper sitting there in a black motorcycle jacket, his pineapple top hair. Or maybe it was what had happened to Glenn Goe, the way Machelle Sexton had bailed. Ready felt like he'd put something into motion he now had no power to stop.

A homicide detective named John King and Pops Baker met them at the gate. As they wove through the crowd at Tampa Airport, Baker said they'd gotten Skipper Sexton a room at the Sheraton. Skipper could charge meals and essentials to his room.

"But first, we got a contingent waiting at Hillsborough Park," Baker said.

Contingent. In money-strapped Stark County, Ready thought, that meant five cops having a cigarette. Minutes later, as they sped in an unmarked car north on Highway 301, Ready realized he was sweating. He hoped they weren't throwing too much manpower at this thing.

He looked over at Skipper, sitting with him in the backseat.

"Skipper, look at me," he said. "I never lied to you, and I never will."

Skipper nodded.

"But I want to tell you something," Ready continued. "And I'm not threatening you. But I've got a lot of work in this. And if you're making this up, I'm going to *kick your ass.*"

When the car rolled up to Campsite Number 89, Ready's hands were shaking. *Contingent?* Waiting were a lieutenant, a sergeant, five detectives, a pack of deputies from two counties, two park rangers, a half dozen evidence techs with a video crew, an assistant prosecutor, and two K-9 units of cadaver-sniffing German shepherds, borrowed from Sarasota, an hour south.

Ready watched John King, a dog, and its handler disappear into the brush behind the campsite with Skipper. Just the three of them. They didn't want to contaminate the area with scent.

Ready lit a cigarette and began pacing.

After 15 minutes, he sat down on a picnic table. Shirley Rebillot rubbed his shoulders, saying, "Steve, it's going to be fine." No, he thought, he was about to find out what Geraldo Rivera felt like when he opened Al Capone's empty vault.

Twenty minutes later, the evidence crew disappeared into the brush. The dog had hit a scent.

A Hillsborough deputy gave Ready a thumbs-up sign.

One hundred-and-fifty feet into the woods, a tech was pulling black peat away from a clear plastic tube.

Inside was a perfectly-preserved red silk rose.

4

Thirty minutes later, in his Tampa office of the Criminal Investigation Division near historical Ybor City, the old cigar-rolling district, Hillsborough homicide detective Mike Willette finished pounding out arrest warrants for William L. and sister Estella M. Sexton. He'd been on the phone and radio all day. He'd received photos of the family, fugitive reports from the FBI, and from Ready a location in Moon Lake where Willie and Pixie might be staying. Another crew had already staked out the location. After a judge signed the warrant, Willette sped north to join them, weaving through traffic as he perused reports.

After nearly 13 years in police work, Mike Willette considered himself to have one of the best jobs in local law enforcement. He'd seen the sheriff's department grow from 20 deputies on the midnight shift in 1981 to well

over 100. The department was a full-blown metropolitan
police agency, covering everything but Tampa city, ever
expanding with the Sun Belt population explosion. The
detective worked one homicide at a time, a rare luxury in
police work. About a dozen a year, usually. If he needed
help, he got it. Already, Pops Baker had three squads of
a half dozen men and women working or on standby.

Not only homicide cops. As he parked his Crown Vic
up the dirt road from Dave Sexton's compound, Willette
knew a child sexual assault detective named Linda Burton
was waiting in another car nearby.

By late afternoon, word came that Ready, Skipper Sexton, and another evidence crew were at Little Manatee
state park. Dogs had hit on four locations behind Campsite
Number 18, but a body had not been found.

Almost three hours into the stakeout, Willette got tired
of waiting. It was 6:30 p.m., well past dinnertime. In four
years of investigating killings, the detective had learned
there was more than one way to do surveillance, and they
had nothing to do with coffee and doughnuts.

Willette took off his badge, removed his Ruger 9mm,
then strapped a Walther .380 on his ankle. They might be
expecting cops, he thought. But a social worker from the
Florida Department of Health and Rehabilitation Services,
the HRS, that wouldn't set off any alarms.

Willette parked the Crown Vic in front of Dave Sexton's
mobile home. He saw the Challenger motor home parked
out front, but still no sign of the Grand Prix Ready had
told him the Sextons might be driving.

He walked up to the front door and knocked.

Dave Sexton rolled up to the door in a wheelchair.

"I'm here to check on the welfare of the children,"
Willette said.

"You from HRS?" Sexton asked.

Willette smiled and said he just wanted a little family
background. After a few minutes of visiting, he wondered
where Pixie and Willie Sexton might be.

Willette heard gravel grinding behind him, turned and saw department cars sliding to a stop near a black Pontiac on the road.

"They're visiting their father in jail," Dave Sexton said.

Not anymore, the detective thought.

5

An hour later, Willette and John King were smoking cigarettes in the hallway outside the small interview rooms at the Pasco County sheriff's sub-station in New Port Richey.

"How do you want to do this?" Willette asked.

"I say we just go right at it," King said.

A few minutes later in the room, Willie Sexton signed a consent to interview form. Yes, he could read and write, he said. He'd graduated from 12th grade in Ohio, he added.

They felt like they were talking to an 8-year-old. Ask something, he answered. Single sentences. Yes. No. He seemed to have no grasp of the big picture. Willie Sexton seemed to have no idea of the deep trouble he was in.

By the time they gave him a coffee and cigarette break not an hour and a half later, he'd sketched out his personal history, the family's, the fugitive flight, the way the Sextons supported themselves on the run—and the death of his nephew Skipper Lee. Pixie gave the baby Nyquil, he said. He, Pixie, and their father decided to bury the baby at the camp, he said. He and Joel buried it. He checked the grave for seven days in a row afterwards.

"Why would you do that?" Willette asked.

"To see if there was any smell coming from it," Willie said.

After the break, Willie signed a consent to search the Challenger. The motor home was in his name, he said.

Willette and King turned up the heat a couple of degrees.

"Where's Joel Good?" Willette asked.

A woman, probably his aunt, picked him up about a week before his parents were arrested, he said. In Little Manatee. He was probably in Ohio.

"At his grandmother's," Willie said.

"*His* grandmothers?" Willette asked back.

"Or his brother's."

Willette paused, then said, "Willie, Joel Good never left Little Manatee state park."

Willie Sexton became quiet and still, his eyes locked on to Willette's. They stared at each other, Willie's eyes never going to King's.

It was a bluff. They still hadn't found Good's body.

Willette waited. Through five minutes of complete silence.

Then Willie said, "I buried Joel."

And he said he'd strangled Joel Good. It was Pixie's idea to kill him, he said. And one more thing about Pixie. There was more than Nyquil involved.

"I saw her jap slap the baby," he said.

Then, he said, she covered the child's mouth with her hand.

6

Down the hall, in another interview room, Detective Linda Burton had been asking a lot of questions of Estella "Pixie" Good, also getting a lot of one-word answers.

Burton, 43, had been working child sex crimes for four years, at a grueling rate of a case a day. The job had taken her everywhere from white trash trailers and migrant camps south of Tampa to the million-dollar homes in Avili, an exclusive, guarded suburb in north Tampa.

"Incest," she would say. "It's always occurred, rich or poor. You can read about it in the Bible. Up until the

1980s, you kept it hidden in the family. Why do they do it? It's a form of control. It's not sexual. It's all about power."

Burton had seen only one trend since taking the job four years ago. It had become a division joke. They seemed to get a lot of cases from one particular state. It wasn't West Virginia, or parts of Appalachia. It was the heart of America.

"Are you from Ohio?" she'd ask victims and perpetrators.

"I don't know what it is about that state," Burton later said. "But a lot of them say yes."

But by 10:30 p.m., three hours after the arrest, Linda Burton had never seen anyone like the young mother sitting across the table from her. From any state, or social strata.

Totally flat. No hand movement. No body language. No smile or frown. Not a tear or a tinge of emotion, even when she talked about the death of her own child.

She was unnerving. Pixie Sexton's eyes were dead.

Pixie said her father gave the baby the Nyquil. He wouldn't let her seek medical treatment.

Her father made them bury Skipper Lee.

Her father and Willie killed her husband Joel. He was killed because he wanted to go back to Ohio.

Her father held his hand over her baby's mouth.

The door from the interview room opened. Mike Willette came in, sat down, and told Pixie Sexton that her brother Willie had told them the entire story about the baby.

"Estella," Willette said. "He saw you hold your hand over the baby's mouth."

Willette got up and left, closing the door behind him.

Burton stayed with the death of Joel Good.

Willie wanted Joel to go into the woods, she said. To get a stack of camping gear stolen from another campsite. Her father was at the picnic, but she knew that Willie and her father were planning a murder. They'd never said how it was going to be done. Willie came back to the camper, took something out and returned to the woods. After about 45 minutes, Sherri reached for the TV, turning it down and saying, "Listen."

They heard Joel yelling "Ed!" Like he needed help.

She and Sherri went back in the woods, getting above the high brush by standing on a fallen tree. Willie had a rope around Joel's neck, an arm across his face.

"Get back to the camper," she reported Willie said.

Back at the motor home they found her father.

Her father walked into the woods to help Willie. She knew they were going to bury him.

Burton went back to her baby's death.

Yes, there was Nyquil and aspirin and Tylenol, she said. But the baby wouldn't stop crying. Her father became angry and told her to keep the baby quiet.

That's when she put her hand on its mouth, she said.

Afterwards, the detectives compared notes.

"Zombie-like personalties," Burton said.

Later, as they met more Sexton siblings, they came up with other nicknames.

"Not zombies," somebody said. "Flatliners."

"And they're the Sexton Family Robinson," Mike Willette said.

7

When they lost the sun at nine, evidence techs packed up their gear and suspended the search at Little Manatee. They left behind three small flags in the leafy cover of dead cypress and ferns 50 yards behind Campsite Number 18, places where the dogs reacted. They left behind a deputy in a county cruiser to preserve the suspected crime scene.

Just before midnight, a detective's car returned to the

campground, park ranger Yale Hubbard following behind. Soon flashlights pierced the woodsy darkness as a small contingent of deputies and detectives gathered at the campsite's edge. It was a cold night, the temperature heading toward the 30s. Somebody was trying to find a spare pair of gloves for the young man who had agreed to go to the crime scene with police.

Moments later, they all walked into the woods. The young man stopped at a 30-foot-long tree not 100 feet from the camp picnic table. He turned and bummed a cigarette from Yale Hubbard.

"This is where I did it," Willie Sexton said.

"Did what?" Hubbard asked.

"This is where I strangled him," Willie said.

They continued into the lowlands behind the camp, stopping at the bank of a flood plain. Willie pointed. It took two deputies to remove a pile of rotting cypress stumps from the spot.

"How the hell did you ever get those big logs on there by yourself?" Hubbard asked Willie.

"My dad helped me," he said.

The deputies stopped digging only three inches into the peat. The bottom sole of a white and blue running shoe faced upwards, as if someone had taken a shallow dive into the black earth.

The rest could wait until morning.

8

At 8:30 a.m. the next day, Friday, an evidence crew slowly unearthed the body as a crowd gathered not far from the police tape strung around Campsite Number 18. The Hillsborough County Sheriff's Department had dispatched Jack Espinosa, its affable media spokesman to handle reporters, photographers, and TV crews arriving at the scene. The Sexton story was breaking in Tampa and

St. Petersburg with the arrest of Pixie and Willie Sexton the night before.

Joel M. Good's head was three feet into the dirt, his face in the water table. The day he died, he'd layered himself in blue plaid flannel, a sweatshirt, and a pair of white denim pants. A crudely made garrotte of two tree branches and hardly pencil-thick twine remained twisted tightly around his neck. There was a chop wound just above his right wrist. Lesions dotted his body, likely caused by decay. Short vertical puncture wounds were on the back of his left hand.

Joel M. Good was only a few weeks shy of his 24th birthday when he died. Now he looked 1,000, his skin like a mummy's embalmed with black, wet Florida peat.

That afternoon, Good's body would join his son's remains at the Hillsborough County Medical Examiner's autopsy room. Little Skipper Lee Good had been found inside the duffle bag just as he was buried, the pacifier still in his mouth, the rattle clutched in his hand. The medical examiner noted no bruises on the face or "acute traumatic injuries." Oddly, while Pixie and Willie said the baby was given Nyquil just before it died, a toxicology report showed no alcohol in the baby's system, its stomach empty. Joel Good, however, had traces of alcohol.

The medical examiner would rule that the infant's death had been by suffocation. Joel Good had been strangled to death.

Not 15 minutes after the excavation of Good's body began, Mike Willette and Willie Sexton were sitting in a sky-blue room at the Criminal Investigation Bureau in Tampa. Willie sat alone at a table with a cup of coffee, but his arms hung at his side. Tape was running in a video camera as the two went over the details of the homicides again.

Willie's version of Skipper Lee's death contradicted his sister Pixie's. He'd seen her give the baby Nyquil and "jap slap" the baby from his bunk across the aisle. Then smother it. He kept using the term, "jap slap," like an adolescent who'd discovered a new, hip word.

Finally Willette asked, "What do you mean by jap slap?"

Back and forth with the hand, 10 times, Willie said.

Willette moved on to Joel. Joel wasn't happy about his son's death, Willie said.

Really, Willette thought.

"At some point, it's decided that Joel doesn't want to cooperate anymore . . . is that correct?" Willette asked.

"Yeah," Willie said.

"Something comes up to do something to Joel?"

"Yeah."

Willette asked, what was that?

"What my dad had planned at first, he had it planned at Hillsborough, before we moved."

"Had planned what at Hillsborough?"

"To take Joel out."

"When you say take Joel out you mean . . ."

"Murder him."

"Who was going to murder him?"

"He just wanted me to."

He, his father, and Pixie talked about it, he said. The father walked him and Pixie around the campground, and talked about murdering Joel. One idea was to take Joel back to Ohio and shoot him, bury him up there. The threesome talked about the murder during several trips back to Ohio, he said.

Willette wondered about the trips, why Pixie always went along. She had old state ID with the name Estella May Good, the same as her mother's, he said. She'd cash the checks made out to her mother for Willie's Social Security.

"What else happened on those trips?" Willette asked.

Willie froze.

"You can talk about it," Willette said. "It's all right."

He mumbled something.

"What happened?" Willette asked again.

"They had a relationship in the back of the car."

"What kind of relationship."

He froze again.

"They have sexual intercourse?" Willette asked.

"Yeah."

Willie said he was driving. It was on the interstate, during a trip from Indiana. They had a blanket with them in the backseat.

Willette asked, "Did your sister agree to this?"

"Yeah, she agreed to it."

"Did your dad have sex with anybody else in the family?"

"That's the only one I know of. I heard a lot more things."

"From who?"

"My uncle Dave. My dad told my uncle Dave."

"And your uncle Dave told you?"

"Yeah."

"What kind of stories were those?"

"When this first started, he sent my sister Sherri to Uncle Dave's because he didn't want no blood tests taken. Because Sherri's baby happens to belong to my dad."

Willette moved back to Joel Good's murder. "Let's go back to Hillsborough State Park. What was Joel bitching about?"

"My dad was afraid of him getting loose and calling somebody and telling somebody about his son."

Willette wanted to know what Willie thought about the prospect of murdering his brother-in-law.

"I didn't think it was right," he said.

Willette moved to Manatee.

"Were there more conversations about Joel?"

"Yeah."

More with Pixie and their father, he said, adding, "They decide to take him out up there."

"Who decides this?"

"My sister and him."

"And they tell you how to do this?"

"Yeah. My dad tried to teach me how to use my arm, to choke him."

His father had learned it in Vietnam, he said.

"What was the final decision on how to kill Joel?" Willette asked.

"With a knife or rope."

The detective moved to the day of the murder.

Willie said he was watching TV with Joel, his sister Sherri and Pixie, while the rest of the family was on the picnic.

"My sister Estella came out, took me around the corner of the motor home so Joel Good wasn't there, and she told me, 'Willie, this is the day to take Joel out.'"

"Was this pre-planned?"

"That's what she told me."

"Who planned that?"

"Probably my dad."

"And your dad was going to take other people off for a picnic?"

Willie nodded.

"Did your dad tell you this?"

"Naw."

"Estella told you that?"

"Yeah."

"What did you do then?"

"I said, "Can't you?' Like, 'Do I have to? Joel didn't tell anybody.'"

"And?"

"She said, no."

"What happened next?"

"She says take him back there and do away with him."

"Where?"

"In the woods."

Willie said he had rope in his side pocket.

"How did you get Joel to go in the woods with you?"

"She told me to tell him there was a lot of stolen stuff in the woods that they needed to get rid of."

Willette asked, "How did Joel die?"

They were walking, balancing on a fallen tree, horsing around like young boys.

He took the rope out.

"I was thinking of everything my dad and my sister told me to do, you know. Then I wrapped it around his neck."

"You were behind Joel?"

"I think I had the rope in a knot. With a stick in it."

"But you don't remember?"

"I think I did have a stick in that rope."

"Does Joel know this is coming?"

"No."

He wrapped the garrotte around Joel's neck and crossed it, pulling. They both fell off the tree, Willie landing on top of Good.

Willette wanted to know what Joel did.

He yelled "ahh" real loud, Willie said, adding, "My sister thought he yelled 'Eddie'."

"Were your sisters out there?"

"That's when they heard." They came out in the woods, he said.

"How long did he struggle for?"

"Like a minute. Then I went all paranoid."

"You went all paranoid?"

"Yeah."

"What did you do?"

"Tried to blow my breath back in his mouth. Make him come back alive."

"But he was already dead."

Willie moaned, his only emotion during the interview.

His sisters went back to the campsite and got his dad, he said. "My dad got there awful fast after that."

"What happened then?"

"He says, 'Oh my God.' "

"Then what happened?"

Pixie went to Walgreen's in Sun City to buy a spade after nobody could locate the army shovel used to bury Skipper Lee.

"Who carried Joel back there [to the grave]?"

"Me and my dad."

"Did he get stabbed or cut or anything else?"

On the wrist, Willie said.

"Why?"

"Because my dad told me to chop his hands off so there was no identification."

"Did you cut his hands off?"

"Just a little cut. I couldn't do it, because I was getting sick."

He'd tried with a machete, Willie said. The machete was still under the seat of the motor home.

The night before, Skipper Sexton had told Willette about the plan to abduct Ray Hesser. Willette also committed Willie's version to tape. Pixie was involved in that plot, too, he said.

"My dad was talking about switching his ID, his whole lifestyle," Willie said.

He added, "Estella got fresh with him."

"Did she have sex with him?"

"No. She was going to. They was close." She'd only kissed him, he said.

Willette wondered if there were any other homicides or assaults Willie knew about. "Has anybody else been hurt in this thing?"

"No."

He wondered if his father had ever sexually assaulted him.

"Ever put anything on you, William?" Willette asked.

"No," he mumbled.

"You can tell, William."

"Naw."

Willette paused.

"Anything else you want to say, William?"

Willie paused for a couple seconds, then said, "Yeah, I wish I could take Joel's place."

It was too easy.

In a way, even the seasoned homicide detective felt sorry for the kid.

9

Minutes after he finished with Willie, Willette met with Eddie Lee Sexton in another interview room. Face to face, he seemed hardly the bigger-than-life figure portrayed by his children. He'd been booked into the jail measuring only 5-foot-9, weighing only 140 pounds. Age 51. Hair, brown. Eyes, hazel. Not black and piercing as others would describe him in many interviews to come.

Sexton signed a consent to interview form, and soon was explaining a litany of physical ailments: multiple sclerosis, back surgeries, cancer between his shoulder blades.

The baby died in its sleep, possibly SIDS-related, he said. Willie, Pixie, and Joel left with the baby, later telling him they'd buried it in Hillsborough State Park.

Sexton said he'd discovered Joel's murder when he'd returned from a family picnic. Sherri and Pixie had told him. He went in the woods and saw Willie with the body.

Sexton told him Willie said: "He was going to tell on me."

"About what?" Willette asked.

"Sir, I have no idea," Sexton said.

Willie done it. Willie buried him. He didn't want any involvement in the whole matter, he said.

The whole sad situation was the fault of the FBI and the criminal justice system, he added. They were the ones who had them on the run.

Even before Willette studied Sexton's prison record, he had the impression. He'd seen it hundreds of times with hundreds of subjects in interview rooms.

"Ex-con trying to paint the best picture of himself," he later said.

But as interviews with children, relatives, and other fire

and police authorities would continue over the next five months in Tampa and during a half dozen trips to Canton, Ohio, Willette would amend his description of the soft-speaking, pity-seeking hypochondriac.

"Eddie Lee Sexton is the devil," Willette said.

10

Later that day, they searched the motor home parked at Dave Sexton's compound and found the machete under the driver's seat.

Willette tried not to breathe through his nose in the Challenger. Odors of smoke and urine wafted up from the carpet and beds. Boxes, pots and pans, shoes, toiletries, and clothes were crammed in every nook and cranny. A cross was draped across the driver's seat. Clothes also were piled a foot deep in the aisle. Detectives weren't sure if it had been rifled, or if the Sextons just traveled that way.

They found no guns or other weapons, though they limited their search to the items involved in the homicide. In fact, the initial FBI raid also had turned up no arsenal of firearms, though some of the teenage boys had loose ammunition in their pants pockets. During the FBI surveillance, agents in the FBI airplane had stopped two teenage boys wandering around in the Little Manatee woods with a shovel. They speculated to Yale Hubbard that perhaps the Sextons had buried their arsenal. But when Hubbard searched the area, the ground appeared undisturbed. Some Sexton siblings would say some guns were hocked at Florida pawnshops as the clan ran out of money. Either way, Eddie Lee Sexton appeared totally unprepared for the firefight he'd been predicting for months.

Other, perhaps ill-advised, amateur searches would only spawn more mysteries.

The report was carried in Sunday's edition of the St. Petersburg *Times,* part of an explosion of stories on the

Sexton family and the developing case. The story began
in Shady Hills, culled from an interview with the Sextons'
former Treaty Road neighbor, Bob Wilson. Wilson's
brother had discovered a plywood box a couple of days
before, buried six inches under the ground in the woods
behind the mobile home the Sextons had rented. But the
brother had covered it back up. After reading a Saturday
paper about the death of a 9-month-old baby, Wilson
picked up a shovel and dug up the box. It was 3 feet long
and painted yellow.

He opened it but found nothing inside.

11

Skipper Sexton plopped down in Steve Ready's room at
the Sheraton a couple of days into their Tampa stay.

Saying, "See my ring?"

Ready eyed the large gold nugget on his finger. "That's
pretty nice, Skipper," he said. "Where did you get it?"

"Bought it down in the gift shop."

"How much?"

"Four hundred," Skipper said.

"Where the hell did you get that kind of money?"

"I charged it to my room."

Ready's mouth dropped open. "Skipper, you're going
right back downstairs to that gift shop and take it back,"
he said. He could just see the reaction of the Hillsborough
County Sheriff's Department when that showed up on the
bill.

Earlier, on Friday, Ready had sat down with May Sexton
at the Hillsborough County Jail, sexual assault detective
Linda Burton joining the interview. He asked her to
respond to the charges being made by some of her children
regarding sexual abuse. She denied she'd been involved
in any assaults. Then she denied any of her children had
ever come to her regarding incest with their father.

The whole matter was Otis Sexton's doing, she said.

May maintained Skipper Lee Good was taken to the hospital by Joel and Pixie, but she couldn't name the hospital. No, her husband never got mad about the baby crying, she said. Joel had gone back to Ohio, as far as she knew.

Midway into the interview, she changed her story. Yes, she knew Skipper Lee was dead, but hadn't heard the baby crying that night. The baby was not breathing when Pixie woke everyone up the next morning. Family members tried to resuscitate it in the motor home, then Joel and Pixie took it to the hospital, she said.

May remembered coming back from the picnic and seeing Willie covered with dirt, needing to take a shower. Willie had beaten up Joel once, she said. Willie had a bad temper, she said.

"So do I," she added.

See no evil, hear no evil, Ready thought.

"She's a great con artist," Burton said. "I got the feeling she was happy we weren't getting anything that we wanted out of her."

Maybe in time, they agreed, one of her kids would give her up.

On Sunday, January 30, three days after the baby's body was found, Steve Ready and deputy Shirley Rebillot hooked up with May Sexton again, this time to take her on a flight back to Ohio to face grand jury charges.

Eddie Lee Sexton remained in Florida. He'd been charged with first degree murder in the death of Joel Good. Pixie now faced murder charges for both her son and her husband. Willie also was looking at two counts, one for Good's homicide, the other for being an accessory in the baby's death because he'd helped bury the child.

In a matter of days, Florida social service workers would remove Dawn and Shasta Good from Dave Sexton's house, where they'd been left by their mother upon her arrest. They would be examined for possible sexual assault. And blood would be taken from not only Dawn and Shasta, but

Sherri's child Christopher. Samples also would be taken from Pixie and Sherri. With a search warrant, a nurse would take a vial from Eddie Lee Sexton. It would take several weeks of genetic testing, but soon all the investigators in the case would know once and for all if Eddie Lee Sexton was both the father and grandfather of the children.

Ready and other detectives also would discuss drawing blood from the corpse of little Skipper Lee. But Pixie was saying the baby was Joel's child.

"Leave it be," Ready said. "Why add any more pain to his people back in Ohio. It's already bad enough."

Ready and Skipper had just buckled themselves into their seats when Ready noticed the young Sexton, his leather jacket off, was wearing a new silk shirt and a black leather tie. His hair was combed back.

"Nice tie, Skipper," he said. "Where'd you get it?"

"The gift shop," Skipper said, smirking.

Steve Ready had no idea what his room bill totaled.

This time, he didn't even want to ask.

xii

Best Memories

1

It was a double funeral with a single, closed casket. On February 10, they carried the lone coffin across the snow to the chapel at Forrest Hill Cemetery in Canton, the wind whipping, biting nearly 100 people's cheeks. The family had asked the funeral director to bury the baby cradled in Joel Good's arms. They were laid to rest in the same plot as his mother and father.

He'd always wanted a family, Teresa Boron thought.

Now they were all together. Still, she couldn't shake the memory of her promise to her dying sister. *I'll always be there . . .*

Lewis Barrick had already found Pixie Sexton's letter and given it to homicide detective Mike Willette, the threatening letter Joel had clutched in his hand that rainy night. Teresa told detectives about the beating he'd received a year ago in Canton.

Teresa was buying newspapers now, only to learn new cruelties. Sherri and Skipper and Eddie Jr. were giving interviews, revealing abuse in the home, details about the fugitive flight. Sherri claimed in one story that the infant they'd just put in the grave was her father's.

"The important thing is that Joey considered Skipper his son," Teresa said. "He loved that child, no matter whose it was."

One paper carried a picture of Eddie Jr., Skipper, and Sherri sitting on a couch together. They stared off the page with dead eyes. Everyone in Canton was talking about the Sextons.

Everyone was talking about that Sexton stare.

Five days after the funeral, word came that Eddie Lee and Willie Sexton had been indicted by a Florida grand jury on first degree murder charges for Joel's death.

But another development shocked the entire family.

Pixie Sexton hadn't gone before the grand jury.

Teresa thought, what are they doing? Joey followed that girl everywhere. She had to be involved.

2

A colleague pulled Jay Pruner into the fourth-floor hallway of the Hillsborough County Courthouse Annex. "Hey," he said. "There's a major league meeting on these bodies in the parks."

Soon the 36-year-old prosecutor was sitting among fellow division chiefs in a meeting chaired by Harry Coe III, a former judge and the State Attorney for Hillsborough County. A dozen lawyers attended the two-hour strategy session.

Most agreed: The state's case had a couple of big problems.

As Pruner recalled the session, "It's apparent from initial interviews that Eddie Sr. is the domineering, Machiavellian—no, that's too euphemistic for him—the Rasputin of the group. But for him, it all wouldn't have happened.

We know we've got Pixie involved in the baby's death. We know we've got Willie confessing to the death of Joel. And we know Eddie's involved with him. But at that point in time, the only thing we have linking Eddie Sr. to the murder is Willie's statement."

But it was also likely Willie's statement could not be used in the murder prosecution of Eddie Lee Sexton. A statement by a co-defendant would not be admissible if Willie chose not to testify in his own defense. It was a longstanding rule in American criminal law. Willie Sexton had the constitutional right not to incriminate himself on the stand. Therefore, Eddie Lee Sexton's lawyer would have no way to cross-examine him about the confession, which would negate the patriarch's constitutional right to mount a defense.

In Florida, the law required the state to bring a murder defendant to trial in 175 days, unless waived by the defense. If the defendant demanded a speedy trial, that dropped to 60 days. Under court guidelines, prosecutors also knew Willie and Eddie Lee Sexton would be assigned a top-flight attorney skilled in capital cases. But even a greenhorn would see the problem with Willie's statement. Sexton's lawyer would likely demand a speedy trial before the state had time to shore up its case with other family members who might have heard of the plan to kill Good. Detectives believed the Flatliners needed time away from Dad before they'd be forthcoming.

Eddie Lee Sexton was the bad actor, everyone in the meeting agreed. They needed to prosecute the patriarch like Charles Manson.

They needed to make a deal.

They could offer Willie Sexton a plea, guaranteeing he'd testify. But Willie Sexton had strangled Joel Good with his own hands.

That left Estella "Pixie" Sexton.

The meeting became heated. It was Hobson's choice.

"Judge Coe was not really thrilled about making a deal

with someone perceived to be a baby killer," said Jay
Pruner, an eight-year trial veteran. "But if we didn't get
Sexton, he'd walk away forever."

That soon became Pruner's problem. Days later, he was
assigned the Sexton case.

3

On February 15, they all talked with her. Mike Willette, Linda
Burton, two assistant state attorneys, and later Steve Ready,
who'd escorted Skipper Sexton back to Tampa for more
interviews. They brought Pixie Good to the state attorney's
office. Pixie's court-appointed attorney Manuel Lopez, a public defender, had made her available for the interview.

The deal had been struck. She'd be charged with manslaughter only, for her baby's death, then throw herself
before the mercy of the court.

There were more one-word and one-sentence answers.
Some admissions, too.

Pixie said she'd given the baby Nyquil, as ordered by
her father, and held her hand over Skipper Lee's mouth.
She reported her father saying of the crying baby:

"Quiet that baby, or I will."

She said she was afraid her father would harm the child.
She maintained she had no idea she'd killed him.

Pixie said she'd heard Joel's murder being discussed on
a trip to Ohio with her father, Skipper, and Willie, but
offered few details about the conversation.

The day of the murder, she said she'd seen Willie strangling Joel. When her father returned from the picnic, she'd
followed him back into the woods. She said her father
kicked Joel's body with his foot and told Willie:

"Now, finish him off."

She confirmed the plot against disabled camper Ray
Hesser.

She said Willie told her he'd been sodomized by his father at Bear Creek, the campground in Ohio.

Everybody feared Dad, she said. Everybody had been punished. Sometimes her father beat her mother. Their mother never protected them.

"He controls everything," she said.

Burton and Ready covered her sexual history.

Her father picked her up from work one night when she was 17, she said. She was sitting on the couch when he came out of the bedroom in only his underwear. The rest of the family was asleep.

"Do you know how babies are made?" he asked.

"Yes," she said.

"I want to have some," he reportedly said.

That was the first assault, she said. She struggled, but he held his hand over her mouth. She'd also been raped by her father behind Wales Square. He came to her regularly for sex. He'd hold his hand over her mouth, take her while the rest of the family was sleeping. He took her once while her mother was away at a teachers' conference. She protested, but also feared him. She told her mother once, but May told her, "You're crazy."

Dawn and Shasta were her father's, she said. She told Joel this, she said. Joel confronted her father, saying he wasn't going to be raising his children. Her father beat Joel, she said. She said this was back when they were living on Caroline Street. In other interviews, she'd say the beating took place in Florida, just after Skipper Lee's death.

Linda Burton asked Pixie why her father would want to have sex with her.

"To have more children," she said.

"Why not use birth control?" Burton asked.

"My father didn't believe in birth control," she said.

4

Eddie Jr. and Otis Sexton drove to Florida to retrieve the Dodge Challenger. When they returned to Canton in early February, Steve Ready hit a jackpot of evidence.

The detective was running back and forth daily from the DHS to interviews with Sexton siblings, to assisting Hillsborough homicide detectives to visits with Otis Sexton, who was coming up with one lead after another from conversations he was having with his displaced nieces and nephews.

In the Challenger, Ready found credit and phone cards in the name of "Everett Sexton" and names he didn't recognize. There were pawnshop receipts from Florida. There were videotapes of the Sexton family, the Reno-Clinton tape, and one of the Sexton children gyrating in a house dance on Caroline Street.

Ready found a mauve silk robe and a nightgown and a blue silk bra. He asked Sherri and Skipper about the lingerie. The siblings said Kimberly wore them. Ready took them into evidence. They were inappropriate for a child of 9.

Otis Sexton handed him some photographs he said he'd found in the Challenger. There were three of Eddie Lee Sexton and his daughter Kimberly, one with Lana. The girls were wearing wedding veils and sheer lace skirts. A Christmas tree was in the background. The patriarch stood with the girls as if he were taking their hands in marriage. It seemed to confirm a story Ready had been hearing from Sherri, Skipper, and Shelly Croto. Eddie Sexton married Sherri, Shelly, Lana, and Kimberly. In one account, he took daughters into the bedroom, saying, "This is where we're going to have the honeymoon."

What at first seemed to be a sexual abuse case against

Eddie and May began spinning off in several directions, metastasizing like some kind of family cancer.

Pixie Good told Ready in Tampa that her father had told her he'd buried an infant before for one of her aunts in Ohio. The baby had died after birth, she said. Ready noted it as another lead to chase down.

On February 21 in Florida, Ready got a call from social services in Pasco County, in connection with the blood being drawn from the children. Doctors' examinations had revealed that Dawn and Shasta had both been penetrated anally, Dawn vaginally as well. The children had little control over their bowels, indicating chronic sodomy. Dawn had disclosed that Skipper, Willie, and "Grandpa Eddie" were the perpetrators.

Ready and Willette interviewed Skipper. He adamantly denied abusing the children. But he and Skipper had beat up Joel after Pixie accused her husband, he said. Then Willie told his own story. His father had been sodomizing him since he was 9, he said. He'd sodomized him three times in three different states while they were on the run, he said.

Ready confronted Charles Sexton in an interview after social workers told him Kimberly was disclosing that Skipper had fondled her. He denied assaulting Dawn and Shasta. But he admitted touching Kimberly's vagina when the family was staying at a motel in Indiana.

The last day in February, Ready reached May Sexton's sister in Ohio to talk about Pixie's story. She denied ever having a baby die, let alone ever having her brother-in-law dispose of it. Ready asked her about Eddie Sexton's general background. She seemed terrified of reprisals.

Then she told him another sister had been raped by Eddie Lee Sexton and another Sexton relative. The sister bore Eddie's child, who was now 14. After the Sextons' arrest, the sister had fled Ohio and was in hiding, fearful police would question her and bring Sexton's wrath. The story matched the charges discussed by Sexton personal attorney James Gregg.

By March, Ready was hunting for "Uncle Toehead," trying to confirm Shelly Croto's story that he'd been killed and put in the trunk. He found him in Toledo. His name was Eddie Cline, and he was very much alive. Cline said he was coming to Canton anyway. Sure, they could talk about Eddie Sexton. Two days later, Ready got a call from Cline's attorney. He wouldn't be making any statements, he said.

There were more stories of fraud and fires and Eddie Lee Sexton soliciting the services of the "Ice Man." Otis was claiming Dave Sexton had hired the con to kill his wife years ago, but backed out of the plan. So the Ice Man's crew robbed the brother, leaving him tied up in his living room. Ready got a name, and later a three-page sheet of convictions—burglary, bad paper, and assault with a deadly weapon among them. His name was Paul Shortridge. He was in a West Virginia penitentiary doing time for counterfeiting.

During one interview, Sherri Sexton disclosed one alleged rape after another, not only by her father, but relatives. She'd been fondled at 9, then later raped by her late uncle Joe Sexton and a cousin, she said. She told her parents, she said.

"But they just yelled at me," she said.

Sherri said she'd been raped in Florida. One night, after her aunt Jean Sexton left for the evening, her uncle Dave asked her to clean his trailer. She had her son Christopher with her. She said her father's older brother asked for sex. She refused. He pushed her on the floor, pulled off her shorts and panties and raped her, she charged.

Sherri began shaking and crying, showing the first emotion Steve Ready had seen from the young woman with the vacant eyes.

She continued, saying a week later, she was raped by a cousin. She moved out of the compound, she said, first staying with another couple, then moving into a battered woman's shelter until her father came to Florida.

In March, another tip came Ready's way. Dave Sexton allegedly had fathered an incestuous child with a daughter when the family was living in Ohio years ago. The daughter now was married and lived in Canton.

Ready interviewed her at her home, going slowly, using his best hands-on approach.

Yes, she said, her father had raped her when she was a teenager. She'd lived with the secret for 13 years. She'd not been sexually active before that. She had a boy. That boy was Tommy, the teenager living with Dave and Jean Sexton in Moon Lake. They'd adopted him after birth. She'd always told her mother the boy had been fathered by a neighborhood teenager. But she said she'd revealed the true story to her mother after her uncle Eddie Lee Sexton was arrested.

Ready asked her what she'd like to see done.

"I'd like him punished for what he did," she said.

Ready filed a detailed police report. Later, he talked to her again. She had talked to her mother, she said.

"I've decided I don't want nothing done," she said.

Back at the Renkert Building, Ready was swimming in paperwork. There were more sex charges to be written up on Eddie Lee Sexton, as well as letters to jurisdictions in other states where assaults had allegedly occurred. The leads were coming faster than he could keep up with them. Plus, May Sexton had been scheduled for trial on Lana's sexual abuse charge. Her trial was set for April. Ready was helping local prosecutors reach witnesses for that trial.

Ready thought, where did this case end? Or, more curiously, where did it all begin? Where in the Sexton family tree was permission first given to violate one's own flesh and blood?

One day, Ready was talking to Anne Greene.

"Sexton," Anne Greene said. "Think about it. *Sex. Ton.* Ton of sex."

A *sexton* also was someone who maintained a church and its religious articles.

"A sexton also maintains the church graveyard," Otis said.

As more stories of rituals emerged from siblings, Eddie Lee Sexton certainly maintained his own place of worship. But nobody could figure out what gospel he was preaching. A little general occult. A little fundamentalism. A little Satanism. A little sci-fi hustle called the Futuretrons.

The children still were paying for his little church.

Ready made the 30-mile round trip to Shelly Croto's trailer in Bolivar dozens of times. He'd make appointments, but when he arrived no one would answer the door even when her car was there. He suspected she was hiding inside. Sherri Sexton succumbed to past traumas. She was hospitalized in a psychiatric ward, suffering from depression and PTSD. Social workers were reporting more Satanic manifestations with Lana.

Pixie Good, meanwhile, appeared to have suffered a complete mental breakdown at the Hillsborough County Jail. Psychiatrists put her on anti-depressants and anti-anxiety drugs. She suffered from ulcers. By April, she was on an IV because she was not eating or drinking. In May, she tried to cut herself and was put in restraints. She was having auditory hallucinations, hearing her father's voice. She was sleeping only four hours a night, experiencing nightmares and flashbacks. There would be another suicide attempt as her father's trial approached.

Ready began typing reports at home. A lot of leads never were committed to paper. There just wasn't time. His family life was suffering, not to mention the rest of his caseload.

Ready, Judee Genetin, and other DHS officials met with the Stark County prosecutor's office to consider filing sex assault charges against Skipper Sexton. The office wanted to wait and see how Lana Sexton held up on the stand at her mother's trial. Luckily for Ready, much of the mother's case was being coordinated by county attorneys.

A DHS supervisor called over to one of Ready's superiors at the sheriff's department, telling him Ready was bogged down with the Sextons. DHS needed more manpower, not only for Sexton, but the other cases Ready was supposed to be working.

"If Deputy Ready can't do it," the command officer said. "We'll find somebody else who can."

"Do what you got to do on the Sextons," she told Ready. "And forget everything else."

5

After weeks of motions and an unsuccessful attempt to move the trial out of Canton, a jury was impaneled on April 12 to weigh sex charges against May Sexton. Her court-appointed attorney Jean Madden wanted May's husband and two children in Florida to testify on her behalf. The state wouldn't fly them up for the trial, and a plan to have them testify live by satellite TV was scrapped because of costs.

The trial would last only two days.

Social workers Bonita Hilson and Tracy Harlin set the stage with the family's DHS battle. Psychologist Robin Tener's evaluation of Lana was introduced. Tabatha Fisher told the jury of the disclosures and seizures in her foster home. Psychological reports from her hospitalization at Akron Children's were introduced.

James Sexton, now 18, testified. James was working as a cashier now at a gas station and living in a foster home. He'd been the most vocal of the Sextons all along. He appeared to relish the chance to strike back with words.

He told the jury about the Futuretrons, the mark on Lana's hand, and an expected "$2.5 million" advertising campaign. He testified he saw Lana whipped for failing to smile at the dinner table. He detailed various Sexton household punishments and the occult atmosphere.

Jean Madden cross-examined him. She introduced to the jury that he'd been under a psychologist's care.

"Do you feel you were picked on?" she asked.

"Picked on?" James asked back.

"Yes."

James shot back, "Sexually molested. Abused. Beaten."

She tried to discredit the occult stories.

"Now, you saw devils floating around the house?" she asked.

"Yes . . . I actually seen them."

"Um-hmm," the attorney said.

"And my dad was the leader of it."

"Your father threatened you if you told anybody about that?"

"Yes. One time he had a baby sitting in the middle of the table, all cut up and baked."

"Where did he get the baby?"

"My mom had her."

"When?"

"I'll say in '87."

It was one of several "babies" his mother had given birth to in the house, he claimed, babies who later disappeared.

After a 10-minute mid-afternoon break, Lana Sexton took the stand. Assistant prosecutor Kristine Rohrer spent a half hour on the basics, warming her up with the size of her family, siblings' names and ages and nicknames, descriptions of the house on Caroline Street.

They covered the Futuretrons and the whippings.

Dressed in blue, May Sexton cried at the defense table, dabbing her eyes with Kleenex. Lana would say later in the trial she didn't want to see her mother punished. She wanted her to get counseling.

Then Rohrer headed for the heart of the felony charge, an incident when Lana was 8.

The attorney asked, "Did anything besides being whipped with a belt happen that made you uncomfortable with your mom?"

"Yes," Lana said. In her parents' bedroom.

Lana continued, "Sometimes us kids would take a shower in the bathroom by her bedroom. And I was drying off from my shower and she called me in there."

"What did she say?"

"She told me to sit on the bed."

"And then what happened?"

"She would feel me in the wrong parts."

Rohrer wanted a more specific area.

"Private parts," Lana said.

"Which private parts are you talking about?"

"Your front private parts."

"Front private parts on the top, front private parts on the bottom?"

"On the bottom . . . she started to rub me."

Lana said she went to bed afterwards, crying. The fondling lasted only a couple of seconds, she said.

But it was long enough for the jury. May Sexton called no witnesses. Her attorney argued the prosecution failed to prove its case. The panel came back with a guilty verdict in two hours. May dropped her head onto her arms, then cradled her face in her hands.

As deputies put the mother in irons, Skipper Sexton, sitting in the courtroom audience, said, "This is bullshit. I know she's innocent." They were after the wrong parent, he said.

Judee Genetin told reporters May's case might not be a "one-shot deal," hinting further charges could arise.

The following week, May Sexton appeared in court for sentencing. Jean Madden argued she had no criminal record. She asked the judge not to be influenced by the stream of stories about the Sexton family still appearing in local newspapers.

Common Pleas Judge John W. Wise looked at Estella May Sexton and asked her if she had anything to say.

"Yes, Your Honor," she said. "I would like to maintain

my innocence and I'd just like to get it straightened out, and then I'll accept anything the court wants to give me."

Judge Wise told her she'd violated a parent's prime responsibility. "You have to protect them, take care of them," he said. He sentenced her to two years in prison, the maximum under the law.

Authorities had two good weeks.

In Florida, Pixie Good pled guilty to manslaughter charges, agreeing to testify against her father and brother. The day May's trial started, a fax hummed off a machine in the Renkert Building for Judee Genetin and Steve Ready.

The documents were from Gene Screen, a Dallas genetic testing lab. The blood testing was completed. According to genetic markers, Eddie Lee Sexton was the probable father of Dawn and Shasta Sexton. The lab fixed the percentage of paternal probability at 99.99 percent.

6

"We want to get Momma," detective Mike Willette said.

Willette and Linda Burton wanted to connect May to the homicide. Through the spring and summer, they talked to all the Sexton offspring.

"Nobody would give her up," he later said.

Willette, Burton, and John King did find plenty of support for Jay Pruner's theory of Manson-like control. Sexton siblings disclosed their home life, the assault drills, the robberies on the road, the burning of the trailer on Treaty Road.

Detectives talked to Herb Shreiner, Jackson Township's fire investigator. He detailed the two suspicious fires on Caroline Street. They also saw the FBI report on Clyde Scott, May's father, about Sexton's fire schemes.

Later, Steve Ready showed up with a file from the Canton Fire Department. There were eight fires in the city of Canton among the extended Sexton family, two undetermined, six arson. Three of them were in homes owned by Eddie Lee Sexton on Third Street and Fifth Street. One file reported that someone in the family had earned the name "The Mechanic," for his ability to rig a blaze.

A retired Canton fire investigator named Dave Demeo later recalled his dealings with the clan. He said Eddie Lee Sexton appeared to have burned his way up the real estate market, eventually making enough profit to buy his Jackson Township home.

"They made a living out of the profits from insurance companies," Demeo later recalled. He believed Sexton was working a particularly crafty scam. Sexton would sell slum properties he owned on land contract at inflated prices to relatives, then burn the homes and get a pay-off well over the home's value.

But Demeo could never directly link Eddie Lee Sexton to the fires. He was always out of town when they occurred. In the rubble of two homes, Demeo found rigged heat-producing wires and a fish aquarium heater, ways to delay ignition so the arsonist could distance himself from the scene.

A 1977 fire on Fifth Street, three years before they bought the house on Caroline, paid off $16,000. Another Fifth Street landlord later recalled Sexton chatting with him after the fire. Sexton told him if he ever wanted to start a fire, he knew how to do it. You put a candle on a paper plate, he said, placing it in the basement.

"He said that he would pile a bunch of clothes under the stairwell and the candle would burn down, light the plate and then the clothes," the landlord recalled. "Then it would go right up the stairwell."

It wasn't long before Jack Espinosa, Hillsborough's police spokesman and a former stand-up comic in Cuba, was proposing a new test question for the local academy: "What is the one crime that Eddie Lee Sexton did not commit? Answer: petty theft."

In Tampa, Willie Sexton kept requesting interviews with

Willette, despite the advice not to do so from his attorney, Nick Sinardi. He changed his story, saying his father had held a 9 mm to his head and ordered him to kill Joel. Then he threw the gun away in the woods behind Campsite Number 18. Willette, Willie, and a crew with metal detectors combed the site for a day, but found nothing. Then Willie admitted he'd lied.

In Canton, the bizarre stories from siblings within the house on Caroline increased in intensity. Patrick Sexton, the oldest half-brother, said, "I'm embarrassed to have the name Sexton." He said he kept his distance from the family after he moved out of the house. He told Willette his father used morphine and syringes for his back pain. His father had predicted the problems with social services would one day have a deadly result. "Somebody is going to get killed before this is over," his father said.

Skipper told Willette about his father instructing them in seances and animal sacrifices, but denied he'd ever seen an actual sacrifice. He revealed another punishment. One time his father made a couple of boys rub Ben Gay on their penises after accusing them of putting the ointment on a sister's jacket.

May Sexton, in a jail interview, said her husband was tougher on the boys than the girls, though he did whip the girls. She denied any cult activity. She read the Bible to her children, she said.

Christopher Sexton said he'd heard a conversation between his father, Willie, and Pixie about getting rid of Joel, apparently on the road to Ohio. Willie said, "We'll have to get rid of Joel." His father asked Pixie what she thought of that. Pixie said, "I don't care."

Christopher was uncomfortable talking about life in the house on Caroline, particularly about sex. He said his father hadn't "messed with me since I was a teenager."

Willette asked, "What does *mess with you* mean?"

Christopher touched his pubic area and said, "Up the backside."

Shelly Croto told her entire story, laying out the punishments and abuse now being confirmed by siblings. Shelly remembered seances and her father "calling a spirit" out of Sherri's dead cat on the table.

But more than dead animals were involved in the rituals, she said. Her mother had three or four miscarriages that she could remember. After one, she said a fetus "as big as a notebook" was boiled by her mother and eaten by the family. A hand-holding seance preceded the dinner. Her father said he'd call the spirit out of the fetus and it would speak out of one of the kids.

"I became sick," she said.

Then, she didn't want to talk about the incident anymore.

On May 3, Willette had a long interview with James Sexton in the DHS offices in Canton. He said his father allowed them to have only one friend, but no visitors. He prohibited them from using deodorant. They could bathe only once every two weeks.

James said his father cast Satanic spells on them, using a Satanic bible and praying in "weird" foreign words. He had an occult library, a crystal ball, and a Ouija board. He had a "romance" shelf of pornography. He showed them hard-core porn films.

James's interview also centered around dead fetuses. He claimed his father took his mother's miscarriages and chopped them up, cooked them, and served them on the dinner table. He served one's bones to a dog. He said his father had killed a baby in the 1970s and buried it under the basement at the family's former home on Oxford Street. He'd seen him kill a cat, chop its head off, and hang it on a cross.

James said, "If I didn't do what Dad wanted me to do, he would tell the kids that he would kill us and make us sleep with the dead baby."

Willette said, "James, you understand here that I need

you to tell the truth." His siblings had told him nothing about this, Willette told him.

James said that was because the rest of the siblings liked his mom and dad. James told of his father putting a rifle to Willie's head and demanding secrecy about the family. His mother even told him she'd had miscarriages, he added.

"What did the baby taste like?" Willette asked.

"Chicken," James said, adding he couldn't eat poultry to this day.

James recited a litany of sexual acts. He said he'd been ordered to perform fellatio on his father at age 6. His father drew a face on his stomach and made him suck his belly. He, Matthew, and Skipper had to perform fellatio on each other. He said Skipper told him they could do anything as long as they didn't get semen on the floor. He'd been sodomized repeatedly by Skipper. His father would give the boys a dollar if they'd suck on their mother's breasts. His father made James "shake" his penis until "stuff came out." He saw Skipper make Lana suck on his penis while he looked like "the Statue of Liberty."

He quoted his father as saying: "It's all within the law. It's natural."

His father was also a thief, James said. He said the patriarch didn't mind the children stealing from convenience stores. He's seen his father take a tent from a campground. His father stole brass eagles out of a house. (Later listed as a stolen property on Sexton's own insurance claim.) His father ripped off a boat motor, then ditched it in the family pond.

Before the session ended, Willette probed for a positive experience. He asked James what his best memory was.

James said, "Any day we didn't get beat."

7

The day before, attorney Jay Pruner visited the house on Caroline Street. It was unlocked. He and Steve Ready searched for a Satanic bible, but found none.

Pruner, too, heard all the stories about dead babies and miscarriages from James, and later Shelly. The prosecutor was going through a familiar syndrome common to everyone who investigated the Sexton case. First disbelief, then entertaining the possibility, then discovery of facts that tended to support the children's claims. For several nights he hashed out the details with Steve Ready, Mike Willette, and Linda Burton over drinks in Canton bars.

Ready began analyzing the ages of the Sexton children. Between Eddie Jr. and Machelle, May Sexton had five births, one child every year. She missed a year, then had Skipper, James, and Matthew in one-year successions. Christopher, Lana, and Kimberly's births were spread out over five years. Then she stopped having babies in 1984 when she was 37, still at child-bearing age.

Pixie Good later said, "She was always having babies. And she was always saying she was pregnant." As she had on the fugitive flight.

"We know she has a baby every year," Ready said. "But what happened in those years she missed? Why did she just stop? Did she stop, or were there miscarriages?"

By the evening of May 5, the date of James's interview, Pruner was spent. He'd met with Judee Genetin and prosecutors for Stark County. There had been interviews with two other Sexton siblings and with Augusta Townsend, the woman who'd housed the Sextons after the standoff.

Pruner, Willette, and Burton had one more stop. The family of Joel Good was waiting at Sam Barrick's house in Bolivar. The prosecutor had talked to them on the phone several times, but he wasn't leaving Canton without explaining to them face-to-face why Pixie Good had been allowed to plead guilty to manslaughter.

Half a mile from Sam Barrick's hilltop ranch house in the rolling hills outside Bolivar, Willette pulled out in front of a semi he claimed he didn't see.

The big rig narrowly missed them.

Jay Pruner should have seen it as an omen of what was waiting for him inside.

8

They all crowded around the dining room table. Sam and Sue Barrick, Teresa and Chuck Boron, Lewis and Gladys Barrick, Aunt Velva. Joel's brother Danny was there, and nieces and nephews. There were at least a dozen people.

Pruner had expected four or five.

For an hour and a half they all shot questions at the attorney. They were all upset, and they hadn't even heard yet about the stories of their loved one being abused with hot sauce, being beaten with a sweeper cord, being burned with cigarettes.

"Why did you make a deal with Pixie?"

"You saw her threatening letter to Joey, didn't you?"

"Why isn't Pixie charged with Joel's murder?"

He tried to explain the law, the court rules. They couldn't put Eddie Lee and Pixie away with Willie's testimony.

Pruner said, "We don't like using Pixie. We know what she is."

"What would it take to charge Pixie?" Teresa Boron asked.

"Look," Pruner said. "We've cut our deal."

They had Eddie Lee Sexton on the defensive now, he said. Attorneys for Eddie and Willie had not sought a speedy trial because they needed time to build a defense. The case was expected to go before a jury by fall.

A flurry of questions came from all directions.

Teresa Boron waited for a moment of silence, then said it. "You don't understand. Pixie was the one who brought him into the family. But for Pixie, Joey would still be alive."

Pruner said they'd be seeking the death penalty for Eddie Lee Sexton. But there was no way to convince them they would get justice.

In fact, that was not a guarantee he could make. Under another set of court rules, there was a very real possibility that many of the revelations by the Sexton kids would never be heard by a jury.

Without the stories, they'd have difficulty proving Sexton's control and premeditation. From day one, the strategy had been a calculated gamble. As the family shot more questions, Jay Pruner did not tell anyone that.

xiii

The Big One

1

Tampa attorney Rick Terrana said of his new client, "I can tell you this. I have dealt with all types. Some I've liked a lot. Some I've disliked a great deal. From an attorney-client perspective, he was one of the most cooperative, pleasurable clients I've ever had. And he's very intelligent. Eddie Lee Sexton is no dummy."

Terrana, a 33-year-old former public defender, was homegrown Tampa, a product of the city's Italian community, growing up on the bay. Tall, dark, and shrewd, Terrana dressed meticulously and savored hand-rolled double coronas. He tried about 20 major felony cases a year. Eight had been capital cases, but the attorney had yet to have a jury send one of his clients to death row. On weekends, he made Cabernet wine he dubbed "Italian moonshine" and donned camo to pursue Florida's wily deer herd as a skilled bow hunter.

Terrana and Willie Sexton's Tampa attorney Nick Sinardi also were making trips to Canton, Ohio. Florida has one of the most liberal discovery laws in the country. Defense attorneys not only receive copies of all the evidence gathered by the state, they can put potential witnesses under oath and build their own record in sworn depositions. In late summer, the attorneys deposed the Sexton family, park rangers, homicide detectives, and the state's chief accuser, Estella "Pixie" Good.

A plausible second theory of the murder developed. Joel Good's death was not ordered by Eddie Lee Sexton, Terrana believed the evidence showed. It was planned by Pixie and Willie, who were incestuous lovers. Willie had told police in his video interview that Pixie had set her husband up. Christopher had said she "didn't care" when the murder plot was discussed during an Ohio trip. There appeared to be no independent corroboration from other siblings that Sexton had ordered Good's murder. That was Pixie's version. There were the puncture marks on Good's hand and talk from Willie at the campsite that Pixie had "stabbed" Joel. By many accounts, Sexton showed surprise and concern when he was told of the murder. Pixie had driven to buy the shovel, and participated in the cover-up well after her parents' arrest.

The depositions only fortified the theory. Siblings told of the alleged plot to kill Joel for insurance, the couple's frequent arguments, and the outright torture of Good in Moon Lake and Shady Hills. Terrana later recalled, "We also had endless testimony on how well Joel and Eddie got along. It was never controverted by anyone—except Pixie."

Terrana took Pixie's testimony in three lengthy depositions. She distanced herself from every bad act or premeditation. She denied accusing Joel of sodomy, or torturing him. She denied any complicity in the plot of kidnap camper Ray Hesser, also the subject of depositions. She admitted Joel had yelled "Ed" as Willie attacked. In her last deposition she sounded as if she might be covering for Willie when his attorney Nick Sinardi took over the questioning.

"Did you ever warn Joel that your father may have been considering taking him out?"

"No."

"Why not?"

"Because I didn't think he was going to actually do it."

In that August deposition and a previous one in July, Pixie said when she took her dad into the woods Joel still was alive. Her father kicked his leg, she said. Joel moved.

"Now finish him off," she quoted her father as saying.

Standing near the body, Willie was saying he didn't intend to hurt Joel, she said.

Willie apologized a short time later, she recalled.

"He just told me he was sorry for it," Pixie said.

"What did you tell him?"

"I told him I accept his apology, but it ain't going to bring nothing back."

There was no objective, outside observer of this family, Terrana discovered. Park rangers and others described the family as placid and well-behaved. Terrana would argue that the new stories about dead infants and rituals in Canton should not be heard by the jury. At the same time, he believed they were symptomatic of their credibility. The state was about to base a death penalty case on accounts from what Terrana called "the most dysfunctional family in America."

Sherri Sexton was under psychiatric care when Terrana took her deposition in August. A psychiatrist had prescribed her Depakote and Xanax. She said she and Pixie were not close. She maintained Joel and her father got along well. He was always trying to counsel Joel and Pixie, help their marriage.

She remembered her father's reaction when he arrived from the picnic, Pixie reporting that Willie had killed Joel.

"He said, '*Shit,*'" she recalled.

Willie and Pixie blamed each other in an argument just

after the murder. In the following days, Sherri heard her father tell Willie, "You shouldn't have done it," and "I can't believe you did it."

"Do you remember Willie's response?" Terrana asked.

"He never said nothing," Sherri said.

"Why do you think Willie killed Joel?"

"He was afraid that he'd tell about the baby's death . . . I feel Willie and Pixie got together."

Pixie was no helpless victim, Sherri also said.

"I feel she was in love with my dad," Sherri said. "Because I read a note once."

"And what did that note say?" Terrana asked.

"There's nobody like him. She really loves him, wants to have kids by him, and she would like to marry him."

Sherri said she'd found the note after her parents were arrested, in the motor home's safe. Then she burned it.

Charles "Skipper" Sexton's deposition in August also produced for the defense. Skipper painted a damning portrait of Pixie, saying she was Willie's sexual partner. He'd seen them having sex in Florida by peeking through a window with Matt, and another time in the motor home. In a deposition hours earlier, Matt had denied this, saying he only saw Pixie having sex with one of Dave Sexton's sons.

Pixie spawned the atmosphere for the beatings of Joel by accusing him of sodomy, Skipper said. Willie pushed the plan to kill Joel, Skipper said. His father told Willie he was "crazy." He recalled an Ohio trip after the baby's death and more discussion. Willie was saying Joel was going to get "the heat" on them; "We should take him out."

"Was there any response by either Pixie or your dad or you at that point?" Terrana asked.

"You know, Pixie had a smile on her face because she was wanting it done."

Skipper continued feeding Terrana what he needed. Pixie called Joel an "asshole," wishing he was dead. Pixie tried to solicit him to do the killing the day of the murder, Skipper swore.

"She said, 'I'll give you a million dollars if you kill Joel.' I was like, 'You're stupid.'"

Skipper said when they drove to get the shovel, Pixie told him, "I'm glad it's finally done."

"And what did you say?" Terrana asked.

"I called her a sick bitch . . . [Joel] was like a brother to me, you know."

But Skipper's story also shifted during the deposition. He said Willie had told him that "Dad thinks I should do it," when Willie brought up the plan a couple of days before the killing. His father told Pixie she would be "erased" if she didn't stop "running her mouth" about the murder.

Terrana had compared Skipper's statements to Steve Ready with a previous conversation he and the attorney had.

"Charles, you've given me a statement about the death of Joel Good today that's now different . . . Now, in my head, you've told me four stories. Why should I believe what you told me today?"

"Because that's for me," Skipper said. "The other stories wasn't for me."

"What do you mean?"

"The story I gave you today, that's a true story."

"The stories you gave Ready weren't true?"

"Half and half."

A jury would appreciate that kind of honesty, Terrana thought. He had scores of inconsistences to shoot at in cross-examinations with many of the state's witnesses.

Rick Terrana couldn't wait.

2

She was back, this time with her 3-month-old daughter, Courtney, needing a place to stay again.

Anne Greene looked at Shelly Croto. She'd gained at least 40 pounds. She bore little resemblance to the frail girl with the pleading blue eyes. Anne had attended her baby shower, showed her how to nurse in the hospital, and counseled her on marital problems. Now, on a warm day in July, Shelly Croto was telling Anne that her husband had smacked her. She was leaving him. She also thought she might be pregnant again.

The Sextons had turned Anne's life upside down. Over the past two years, they'd endured one Shelly crisis after another. Anne thought, and what was Shelly doing? Was she getting therapy, or joining an incest survivors group? No, she was living in what appeared to be an abusive situation and having babies. Just like her mother.

One more time, Anne decided.

Anne made arrangements to find the young mother housing. She lined up other support services.

Then, after two days, Shelly left, calling Anne from a pay phone, telling her she was at the bank, telling her she was doing errands.

Then nothing.

Anne called Steve Ready and they went looking for her. They stopped at her trailer and looked around Bolivar. By the time the night was over, they learned she was back with her husband. Anne called local social services.

Machelle had told social workers a different story. No, she hadn't been abused.

David Croto, meanwhile, was saying he'd never touched her, and never would. Shelly had told him she'd gone to visit an aunt. Shelly seemed to be playing Anne and Dave against each other, the allegiances always shifting, just like in the house on Caroline Street.

Dave Croto later said sometimes he felt like he was living with three or four different people. "She exaggerates, sometimes makes up stories," he said. "Sometimes for no reason. Simply to get attention."

Maybe, Anne figured, it was because the trial was approaching. Maybe that's all she knew how to do. Maybe she needed more emotional support to face her father in court.

Shelly Sexton Croto, Anne decided, would have to find it somewhere else.

Anne Greene had nothing left to give.

3

He reached out with letters and phone calls, writing almost daily—to May or Pixie, Eddie Jr. or Skipper or Sherri. He told his correspondents to pass his words along to those he could not reach directly. Eddie Lee Sexton had plenty of money for stationery. He was still getting compensation checks. He paid Dave and Jean Sexton $500 to retrieve his backlog of checks from his Massilon post office box and deposit them into his inmate account.

The letters were a study in manipulation, half truths and changing alliances.

In his early letters, he called Pixie his "Little One." He sent her money, gave gentle fatherly advice, and promised exoneration.

"Don't worry, honey, they are not going to convict you on the baby or Joel, cause I will go all the way with you," he wrote.

He exhorted her to tell only "the truth." But in all the letters, he reviewed "the truth."

Writing: "I told them that Joel and Willie was suppose

to take the baby to the hospital to get a certificate of death and make sure it wasn't in a coma, and they left in the car and came back in about two hours . . . it was about three or four days later that they told us that they buried it."

Or, on Willie killing Joel, claiming it was Willie's plan: "[Willie] said I told him to hurt Joel, but you know that I didn't, and I know you that you didn't know either . . . Little one, you are not to blame for Joel. Willie made that decision on his own."

He wrote that Willie was in Otis's camp, that Otis had secured power of attorney and was receiving Willie's Social Security checks. Willie was telling "lies."

He told her to "keep her chin up" during her psychological collapse. He advised her to take a plea deal for manslaughter on the baby, writing that a prison term of "two to five years won't be bad."

The tone was always serene, except one letter sent on Valentine's Day. Investigators had just taken Sexton's blood. The search warrant had tipped him that she'd accused him of rape and incest. Sherri and Machelle had accused him as well.

"Honey, I don't know what the hell is going on," he wrote. "Let me know if it's any truth or not."

When it became clear she'd turned on him, he went to work on Willie, through letters to Eddie Jr. Tell Willie, he wrote, that Pixie had "turned state's evidence."

Tell Willie: "Why don't you involve Pixie? Are you going to let Pixie lie on you and get out of it, or are you going to tell?"

Then he came right out with it. "Willie, if you want a good defense, use the fact that Joel molested the kids Roach and Tigger and you and Pixie wanted to stop it . . ."

He pushed different buttons with each child. He called Skipper "Running Bear," writing from "Big Running Bear." He promised him money, saying he was being offered "from $50,000 to $75,000" from Maury Povich,

Montel Williams, and Geraldo Rivera, but "I have to put it in your name."

He made it sound like the rest of the siblings were supporting him. "I guess the only one against me is Sherri," he wrote Skipper in an August letter. "Remember son, I love you and trust you."

In another, he made Skipper feel like the chosen, writing, "I guess I can only depend on you."

Eddie Lee Sexton had a name for his pending murder trial.

He wrote Skipper: "I'm sure that I'll beat The Big One ... Soon we'll be on that highway, heading for parts unknown."

4

Dave Sexton rolled into his Tampa deposition in a wheelchair, black sunglasses on. He told attorneys he was "legally blind."

It was an odd inconsistency, considering that in a later interview he'd say he "saw" the burn and whip marks on Joel Good's back. His interviewer also noticed in their session that he appeared to be watching an Elvis concert on his living room TV. But Dave Sexton told the attorneys he "knew" all about Joel's beating and Pixie's involvement. He also said he didn't know Eddie had any "legal problems" when he showed up in Florida.

Dave Sexton also would maintain Sherri had never been raped when she was staying with the family. Pixie had not had sex with anyone in his immediate family.

"My sons wouldn't do nothing like that," he said.

He implied the family's problems were all his brother Otis's doing, saying "I wouldn't turn my back on him." He had a running feud with Otis Sexton as well, he said, claiming Otis once called his wife "a whore."

Pruner found "The Ice Man," Paul Shortridge. From a

prison phone, he denied any involvement with any of the Sextons. He told Pruner: "I wouldn't believe a damn thing Eddie Lee Sexton said."

But as the heavy heat hit Tampa Bay, it was not Dave Sexton who had Pruner concerned. His best witnesses to the immediate aftermath of the murder were in trouble. Pixie suffered from continuing psychiatric problems. And Charles "Skipper" Sexton's impeachability was growing by leaps and bounds. In the spring, after a police foot chase, he'd been arrested and confessed to a home burglary in Massilon. He faced certain conviction. His address now was the Stark County Jail.

The state had only one outside observer of bizarre behavior by the Sexton Family Robinson, Augusta Townsend and her story of the Sexton's stay at her Canton home after the standoff. But she was emotional, flamboyant, and furious at Eddie Lee Sexton for scamming her out of money. "She was a walking mistrial," Pruner later said.

Pruner feared the siblings wouldn't hold up on the stand, their father only feet away. Pixie and Skipper had handed over some of the letters they were receiving from the patriarch. It didn't surprise the prosecutor that Skipper seemed adrift.

Pruner began to focus on the disabled camper named Ray Hesser. As the accounts of the planned kidnapping unfolded, it occurred to the assistant state attorney that all the elements were in place for another case. On June 22, the state filed a conspiracy to murder charge against Eddie Lee and Willie Sexton. If Pruner could try the conspiracy before the capital case, it would be a telling dry run, and more.

It was another calculated gamble.

"This a nineties' word, but we had the potential to 'empower' those kids," he'd later recall. "They see that they can testify and convict Daddy, Daddy's hold over them is, maybe not cut, but less. The flip side is that if they testify and Daddy walks, I'm shit out of luck in the murder trial."

5

On Tuesday, June 28, Hillsborough Circuit Judge Bob Mitcham brought all parties together in another of several hearings on the growing Sexton case.

Judge Mitcham, known as "Brother Bob" among his admirers and adversaries, was one of Tampa's most formidable defense attorneys before joining the judicial ranks. As a jurist, he sometimes quoted scripture and posted passages on his office wall. The white-haired judge also was known for his folksy humor as he sent scores of defendants off to prison or freedom in one of the county's busiest courts.

There was nothing funny about Willie Sexton as he sat rigidly in the jury box next to a uniformed deputy, shackled and wearing jail blues. His left arm was bandaged at the wrist. In jail, he'd tried to slash his veins with the broken parts of a radio headset. His attorney Nick Sinardi was asking for additional funds for more psychiatric exams.

Mitcham granted the request, and also granted a request by Sinardi and Terrana that Willie and Eddie Lee be tried separately. Sinardi had argued his client was terrified of his co-defendant in the case.

There were a couple more matters. Mitcham set the first murder trial for September 26, then the conspiracy trials for August 29, saying the conspiracy should be tried first because the state could use the outcome as an aggravating factor in seeking the death penalty.

Judge Mitcham also was prepared to rule on a request made five days earlier by Eddie Lee Sexton. The patriarch wanted his guilt or innocence to be decided by the tribal council of the Eastern Allegheny Indian Nation. He claimed to be a member of the tribe. He'd presented Judge Mitcham a membership card with his Indian name on it: "Running Bear."

Mitcham ruled Indian status didn't apply to a murder case. Eddie Lee Sexton was not entitled to immunity for events that happened "off the reservation," he said.

As Sexton watched from the defense table, Mitcham reached from the bench, giving Sexton's membership card to a court clerk.

"Hand this back to Running Bear," the judge said.

Pruner would soon hear about other Indian matters.

Not 10 days later, the prosecutor took a phone call from homicide detective Mike Willette. A witness had come forward after seeing the Sexton coverage in the newspaper. Willette was calling from Sarasota.

"Jay, I've got a librarian down here who seems to know something about these people," the detective said.

6

He didn't play organized sports. He didn't lift weights, he told a jailmate. He'd pumped those bulging biceps by throwing yards of dirt in his little landscaping business back in Ohio, sometimes with his helper, the boy he also called his "best friend," also his victim—Joel M. Good.

He'd never had a date, except his sister Sherri, whom his father allowed him to take to the senior prom. He liked to fish on the family pond for bass, and when it froze, he skated. He liked music, country-western mostly. His favorite song was "Pin A Note On My Pillow" by Patsy Cline.

Once, when he threatened to leave the house on Caroline, he'd been tied to a tree, his father pressing the tip of a rifle to his head. Another time he'd been carted back by the police as a runaway. He'd received $446 a month from Social Security, but hardly saw a dime. He'd been whipped, pummeled, and sodomized by a father. He was big enough to beat his father until he couldn't walk.

But by all accounts, he'd never raised a hand.

By September 21, Judge Bob Mitcham had received

three psychological evaluations of William Sexton from the defense and prosecution.

He was virtually illiterate. He'd been in special ed classes all his life. He had an IQ of 80. He couldn't count backwards from 20. On the Vineland Social Maturity Scale, he registered the age of an 11-year-old.

One official diagnosis: Major depression, congruent with severe psychotic features. And Post Traumatic Stress Disorder. He claimed to be hearing voices about Joel. He had flashbacks. He hid under beds and in cell corners. He was on two medications for depression, anxiety, and seizures.

He was not necessarily insane, everyone concluded, but was "incompetent" to stand trial under the law. He was competent at the time of the murder, one psychiatrist wrote.

But he wasn't now.

"Mr. Sexton does not have the sufficient present ability to consult with his lawyers with a reasonable degree of rational understanding," reported psychiatrist Bala K. Rao, M.D. "He does not have a rational or factual understanding of the proceedings against him . . . He can't provide a reasonable description of the roles of the judge, the prosecutor, or defense attorney." He couldn't understand "the concept of plea bargaining."

Two psychologists believe he might be competent at a future date following extended therapy in a state mental health facility.

Judge Mitcham ruled Willie Sexton incompetent to stand trial. Less than a month later, he would commit him to the Mentally Retarded Defendant's Program at the Florida State Mental Hospital at Chattahoochee. He'd be evaluated every six months for competency, and brought back for trial if his condition improved.

Later reports would surface of Willie being raped by inmates at the Hillsborough County Jail. Before the judge's ruling, Otis Sexton spoke to Willie on the telephone. His uncle told him he'd see him during the trial. He seemed

oblivious to the potential consequences of strangling Joel
Good.

Willie asked, "Uncle Otie, will you be able to take me
home?"

7

The jury was seated, the opening arguments held that
morning on the last day of August.

Eddie Lee Sexton, 53, sat at the defense table, wearing
a brown suit and red power tie, his hair combed back.
During voir dire the day before, he'd worn a pair of Rick
Terrana's shoes, three sizes too big. Now he had a pair of
Bass Weejuns. The clothes came from the county public
defender's office, which kept a wardrobe of suits for indi-
gent clients.

Without his beard, his weight up from jail food, Eddie
Lee Sexton looked as harmless as Art Linkletter. His eyes
followed Jay Pruner's first witness to the stand.

Charles "Skipper" Sexton was dressed in jail blues. His
temporary Florida residence was the Hillsborough County
Jail. He easily answered the prosecutor's first 46 questions.
He told the jury he'd pled guilty to burglary in Ohio. He
told the jury of camping at Little Manatee and seeing
the large "mint" Winnebago with Raymond Hesser. He
recalled a discussion between his father, Pixie, Willie, and
himself.

"And what did your dad say about Mr. Hesser, this disabled camper?" Jay Pruner asked.

Skipper answered quietly, "You know, we're just having
a discussion about how good the motor home—you know,
the condition the motor home was in and everything."

"Okay. Was there any plan to do anything with Mr.
Hesser?"

"Yes, there was."

Pruner asked, "What was that and who said it?"

"Well—"

Skipper paused. Frozen. Then he began to cry.

Jay Pruner could feel his own pulse thumping. It would be the attorney's most vivid memory of the entire Sexton case. He posed the question again, number 50. From the back row, spectators could see Pruner's neck turning bright red.

"Mr. Sexton, what did you father say he wanted to do with Mr. Hesser?"

Rick Terrana objected. "That's a mischaracterization of the evidence."

But there was no evidence, not yet.

Mitcham overruled.

Skipper finally answered, "He wanted to get his identity."

Pruner pushed him now. "What did his plan involve as how to get his identity?"

Terrana objected again.

"Sir?" Pruner demanded.

"Kidnap him."

"And to do what with him in addition to kidnapping him, if anything?"

"Take him out."

"Take him out, meaning what, sir?"

"Kill him," Skipper Sexton said.

For the next hour, he detailed the entire plot.

There were a half dozen more witnesses waiting. But after Rick Terrana couldn't shake Skipper Sexton on cross-examination, the attorney conferred with his client. Then the attorney had an announcement for the court.

Eddie Lee Sexton was prepared to plead guilty to conspiracy to murder, a potential 30-year felony.

The conspiracy trial was over by the Tampa rush hour.

Said Terrana later, "We determined that it would be in our best interests, and Eddie's best interest, from a strategic standpoint and for other reasons, to discontinue the trial at that point. And Eddie, for some reason I don't know to this day, he wanted to get that trial out of the way.''

8

''The Big One'' had some of the trappings Americans have come to expect from high-profile trials.

Judge Bob Mitcham's large courtroom just off a busy hallway on the first floor of the Hillsborough County Courthouse Annex was at capacity. Photographs and video cameras were allowed in the courtroom. But Mitcham also would allow witnesses to avoid being shown on camera if they so requested. Considering the subject matter, several witnesses took advantage of the option. TV stations secured copies of Sexton's Clinton-Reno videotape for viewers. Newspapers and TV news weighed in daily with coverage.

Joel Good's aunts, uncles, and grandparents strolled the hall, wearing pins made from Good's bright-eyed high school portrait. The Sexton Family Robinson had been put up in a nearby Holiday Inn, along with witnesses Steve Ready and Judee Genetin. The Stark County DHS also sent a social worker to look after the minor Sexton kids. They planned a trip to Busch Gardens for the siblings, but it rained through most of their stay. They amused themselves by feeding pigeons from the balconies overlooking a nearby canal. At night, they talked deep into the early morning hours, making more disclosures about family life.

Eddie Lee Sexton also had his supporters. His older sister Nellie Hanf had arrived from Canton and was expected to be a witness in the penalty phase of the trial, if the jury convicted her baby brother. Dave and Jean Sexton arrived, Jean a witness. On breaks, Dave Sexton sat in the hall in his wheelchair, sunglasses on. During one, Steve Ready stood down the hall and flipped him obscene gestures every time Sexton looked his way. If he couldn't see him, Ready figured, no harm. If he could, he deserved it. Ready remained frustrated that Sexton's daughter had chosen not to pursue a rape and incest charge.

Otis Sexton wandered the halls, talking to reporters, commiserating with Good's family. Eddie Jr., not a witness, also showed up at the Holiday Inn. The state picked up the tab until Jay Pruner learned he was siding with his father, asking his siblings, "Are you for us, or against us?" The patriarch's letters had him all twisted around. Pruner checked him out on the county's hotel tab. Eddie Jr. went to Rick Terrana for help.

Before everyone gathered, there'd been weeks of motions, including an attempt by Terrana to move the trial to another county, but it had been denied. More crucial to the defense were hearings to limit the evidence to the facts surrounding the murder itself. Terrana had made a preemptive strike at the prosecution's theory of dominance and control by Eddie Lee Sexton. He wanted Mitcham to prohibit testimony of rape, incest, and brutality by Eddie Lee Sexton. It was basic criminal law. Previous bad acts by a defendant could not be introduced to prove a crime, lest they prejudice a jury. They were only relevant if they had probative value related to the crime. Jay Pruner had argued exactly that in an evidentiary hearing. He wanted it all. The abuse, the Satanism, the dynamics in the house on Caroline Street. They were part of the "iron-fisted" control that allowed Sexton to order the murder of his son-in-law.

"The State must be able to accurately depict the true nature of Sexton's relationships with family members," the state argued in a brief. "Absent such evidence, a jury shall be left wondering why William would kill for his father, why other adult offspring would acquiesce in their father's plan and why they shared in their father's desire to avoid arrest and the dissolution of the family."

After hearing arguments, Judge Mitcham put both sides in a state of legal suspended animation. Rather than limit the evidence up front, he told attorneys he'd rule witness

by witness during the trial. For Terrana, that meant a flurry
of objections in front of the jury. For Pruner, that meant
he faced the very real possibility of watching his entire
theory crumble before the gathered crowd.

In the first trial phase, the prosecution would present
17 witnesses and 23 exhibits. Crime scene photos. Pictures
of Joel Good, one from high school, the others after he
was unearthed. The crude garrotte. Polaroids of the Dodge
Challenger. Pixie's plea agreement. She would not be sentenced until after the murder trial.

There was a noticeable absence of one prop: a time-line
card common in a trials of such complexity. Jay Pruner
planned to steer clear of dates and times, putting Good's
death at somewhere between Thanksgiving and Christmas
of 1993. A few of the Sexton children had been able to
name a day of the week for particular events, but that was
it. Their depositions about the length of stays at the state
parks didn't even match camping receipts. Through thousands of pages of reports and depositions, the Sexton Family Robinson seemed to have been living in a time warp.

A jury of eight men and two women would hear poten-
tially two phases, the first to determine guilt or innocence.
Under Florida law, if the jury determined Sexton had
planned the killing, he could be convicted of first-degree
murder, even though he himself had not strangled Joel
Good. During the second, they'd determine if the death
penalty was warranted.

In his opening, Jay Pruner said good morning to the
jury, then went right at Eddie Lee Sexton.

"For all of his adult life, it is apparent that Eddie Lee
Sexton had a secret," he began.

9

She was the state's second witness, the first Flatliner, walking slowly to the stand. Pixie Good wore a padded-shoulder

blazer with a hounds'-tooth-like pattern and a black shirt that seemed to accent the dark circles under her eyes. Her first words were nearly inaudible, even to the court reporter five feet away. Mitcham exhorted her to speak up. Finally, the court adjourned early for lunch so a microphone and speaker system could be installed. Even then, the microphone had to be continually readjusted. Someone finally propped it on top of a phone book, the microphone almost touching her lips.

Still, the jury strained to hear.

She told the story she'd been telling in depositions. She'd heard Joel yell "Ed" and rushed into the brush to find Willie strangling Joel. Her father returned from the picnic. She took him to Willie and the body. He lowered his ear to Joel's mouth to see if he was breathing, then kicked his leg and ordered Willie: "Finish him off." He ordered her and Skipper to drive and buy a shovel. Her father ordered the cover story about the woman in the red Nissan.

Then she surprised attorneys on both sides of the courtroom. She said she heard more conversation the night of the murder in the motor home, between her father and mother as they lay in bed in the Challenger, only "six steps" from her bed.

"What did your father say?" Pruner asked.

"He was telling my mom what actually happened."

"What did you hear him say?"

"That he had Willie kill Joel."

It was the first time any Sexton sibling had said May Sexton had been told about the murder plan. Terrana wanted a bench conference, complaining he'd been blindsided. He'd received no police statements concerning this testimony, he complained.

Terrana told Judge Mitcham, "That's the first time I've heard that statement."

"That's the first time I've heard it, too," Pruner said.

When they resumed, Pixie told of two conversations in

which her father told of planning to kill Joel. One was during a trip to Ohio two weeks before the killing. The other was at the camp picnic table a week later.

"He said that he wants to get rid of Joel because he knows too much," she said.

They moved into life in the house on Caroline Street, her father's discipline, Pixie saying, "Until you're 18, you get it with the belt. After you're 18 you get his fist."

Terrana objected, telling the judge at a bench conference, "Judge, now begins the trip into the land of collateral matters. This is where I would suggest the inflammatory nature outweighs any probative value it may have."

The jury was removed. Both attorneys argued for 10 minutes, citing case law.

Then Mitcham ruled.

"It's the theory of the state that the deceased, Joel Good, was killed by Willie Sexton at the direction of the defendant. If I understand it correctly, the state is going to further try to show this jury that had it not been for the will and the exercise of the defendant's will over Willie Sexton and the others, that Joel Good would not have been killed. The court, therefore, will overrule your objection."

Judge Mitcham let it all in, not only the physical beatings, but the sexual abuse, the robed rituals, the Jackson Township standoff, the flight from authorities, the military drills, the videotape, the video rehearsals, the order for Pixie to silence her crying baby, the makeshift burial.

Then the incest, over Terrana's objections.

Pixie said she told her husband that Dawn and Shasta were her father's after Skipper Lee's death.

"Were you present in any conversation between Joel Good and your father where this subject came up?" Pruner asked.

"When Joel asked my father about it."

"What did your father tell Joel?"

"He told Joel he [Joel] is still going to raise them even though they're his."

Pixie talked about the trip to a library. She said she was curious whether her son had really died of crib death, as her father maintained.

"At the library did your father lay hands on you in any fashion?"

"He grabbed me by the shoulders."

"What were you doing at the time?"

"Trying to talk to the lady."

Then Pruner introduced the Clinton-Reno video. The jury watched an edited version, showing only Eddie Lee Sexton's opening soliloquy and his closing remarks.

Rick Terrana questioned Pixie relentlessly, not only pointing out her plea deal, but covering inconsistencies in her depositions. He introduced her threatening letter to Joel before Christmas of 1992. In her deposition she'd claimed it was written before they were married. Now she was saying it was after they were married.

"That's because I didn't read the letter [in the deposition] to see what was said," she explained.

The PA was turned up so loud to catch her voice, the system squealed after some answers. Judge Mitcham likened the feedback to a temperamental, screaming child. He ordered the bailiff to turn it down.

Terrana set Pixie up for later testimony about the torture of her husband.

"You've never physically abused Joel, have you?" he asked.

"No."

"Never even raised a hand to him?"

"No."

"Didn't accuse Joel of sexually molesting your daughter Shasta?"

"No."

And later, "You ever beat Joel with a vacuum cleaner cord?"

"No."

". . . ever burn Joel with cigarettes?"

"No."

"Did you ever direct Willie and Skipper to hold Joel down on the ground while you inserted a funnel into his rectum and poured hot sauces and salt into his anus?"

"No."

"Isn't it a fact that while that was going on you were laughing?"

"No.

"You loved Joel, didn't you?" Terrana said sarcastically.

"Yes, I did."

She seemed incapable of taking the bait, showing no emotion, save her brooding raccoon eyes.

She denied her father ever tried to mitigate marital problems. She denied she gave her baby the Nyquil. She denied she ever slapped little Skipper Lee. She denied she smothered it.

"When you found out the baby had stopped breathing, isn't it true that your dad tried to administer CPR to the baby?"

"No, my brother Skipper did."

She denied the insurance plots and arguments and offering Skipper a million dollars to kill Joel. She denied her own testimony, saying there were no physical altercations in the Sarasota library. She denied ever talking to the librarian about the death of the baby. She denied ever having sex with Willie. Her only admission: Yes, she carried her husband's ID.

Terrana moved to the murder.

"Isn't it a fact . . . that you coaxed your husband into the woods?"

"No."

"And when you went into the woods you got his attention while your brother Willie strangled him?"

"No. That's not true."

"Well, let me ask you when you were watching your husband strangled . . . the husband that you loved so much, that you cared for, that you never had problems with, while he was being strangled by your brother with a rope around his neck, did you ever help?"

"No."

She said she ran back to the camper to get help.

Terrana demanded, from who? The little kids?

The attorney wanted to know who she heard Joel yell for when he was being attacked.

"Ed," she said.

Closing, Terrana asked, "Pixie, you hate your father, don't you?"

"For what he did to me, yeah."

"And that is abusing you way back, right?"

"For abusing me and taking my family away," she said.

10

After he'd interviewed her in a deposition, Jay Pruner described librarian Gail Novak as a "quivering bowl of jelly." She looked as if she were about to pass out from fear at times. Rick Terrana tried to get her to admit in her deposition that she was under psychiatric care, but she said she'd only had some counseling for everyday problems.

More dangerously for the state, elements of her story about the Sextons in the University of South Florida library simply did not add up. What were they doing with a baby at the library? It was nearly six weeks after Skipper Lee's death. There was no evidence Joel had money to fly back to Ohio. Eddie Lee Sexton burying something in the vacant field on campus didn't match the facts. Skipper Lee was unearthed in Hillsborough State Park, on the other end of the county, not nearby Manatee. The librarian sometimes sounded outright paranoid in the dep. She claimed strangers visited her at work after the Sextons arrest, including Sherri Sexton, who said, "What have you got on Pixie?"

The flip side was that the family's behavior in the library matched, particularly Eddie Lee Sexton's control. Gail

Novak was his only independent witness, with no apparent stake in the trial's outcome. He scheduled her near the end of the trial, but before a couple more witnesses. Pruner hoped that if she did fall apart, the jury would diminish her testimony as the trial went on.

Gail Novak took the stand in a beige suit, her glasses secured high on her nose.

Pruner introduced photographs of the library. He kept her story simple—the visit, the Sexton's appearance, their names, the apparently drugged Joel Good, their requests for information on crib death, Sexton's subtle hand grips on Willie and Joel.

"At any point in time in the library did you observe . . . Pixie or Willie tell Mr. Sexton that Joel wanted to go back to Ohio?"

"Yes."

"And who was that?"

"Willie."

"And what did the defendant say?"

Terrana objected. He knew what was coming. The jury was taken out while the attorneys argued the objection before the judge. He was overruled.

When the jury came back, Pruner resumed. "Could you tell us, please . . . what Willie told the defendant."

"That Joel wanted to go back to Ohio."

"And what was the defendant's response?"

"There's no way that boy is going back to Ohio. The only way that boy's going back to Ohio is in a body locker."

Through much of her testimony, the librarian appeared terrified. She was out of breath. Her eyes darted to Sexton. She needed water.

Pruner took her through the library photographs, showing her proximity to the family's actions and statements. Pruner wondered about Sexton's behavior with Pixie. She told the jury how he'd pushed her into the computer table.

Gail Novak began to break down. She was blurting out

the story now, getting ahead of the questions as she'd done frequently in the deposition.

"You better get your story straight," she sobbed. "That's what he was saying to her."

"Okay," Pruner said, trying to regain control.

"I'm sorry," she whimpered.

Judge Mitcham stepped in, saying, "That's all right, ma'am. You just relax. All right?"

The judge decided she needed a rest. He broke early for lunch. When they returned, Mitcham said, "Now, I want you just to relax. All right?"

"Yes," Novak said timidly.

"And if you need a break, you let me know and we'll give you whatever time you need to compose yourself."

As Terrana began to cross-examine, he was in somewhat of a no-win situation. If he went after the librarian too hard and she cracked up, the jury might hold it against his client.

Terrana solicited material Pruner had avoided. The migrant clinic. The search for a funeral home. The pleas to see the dead baby in the car. He wondered why if this family was so bad, she hadn't gotten campus police involved. She tried to explain that her emergency calls weren't being taken seriously. He got her to describe the digging in the vacant lot. The Indian ritual.

She gave the date of the visit, November 30. But Terrana failed to point out the time span between then and the baby's death. Still, the testimony sounded disjointed, almost fantastic. What was Eddie Lee Sexton doing revealing so many secrets in the presence of a stranger?

Terrana tried to suggest she'd pulled her story from newspaper clippings. She admitted she'd saved three stories on the murder after seeing Sexton on TV, which prompted her to contact police.

Terrana walked back to the defense table. He whispered to his co-counsel Robert Fraser that he had a few more points he could cover. What did he think?

"God, no," Fraser said. "You've destroyed her already. Quit while you're ahead."

Later he said, "If I had to pick the most non-credible witness of all, it would have been the librarian."

Later, Terrana didn't even bother to address her testimony in his closing argument. Neither did Jay Pruner in his.

Gail Novak, they both thought, was a wash.

11

Over five days of testimony, they came to court in clean dresses, sport shirts, and slacks. They looked like all-American kids, until they took the stand.

Flatliners in hardly audible voices. Christopher, Matt, Shelly, and Sherri. None of them looking at their dad.

The testimony was hit-and-miss. Christopher told how his father called Joel a "snitch" the night of his death. Matt put Pixie right in the middle of the gasoline parties and the abuse of Joel. Then Pruner culled some important testimony from the boy who'd shared little during the investigation. Matthew said his father didn't want Joel beaten because it would draw attention to the family, he said.

"Whose physical well-being was your father looking out for when he told you not to beat Joel, Joel's or his?" Pruner asked.

"Himself," Matt said.

An objection was sustained, but the point was already made.

Shelly, the daughter who began it all, locked her eyes on Ohio DHS social worker Joanne Shankel in the audience. She fought terror through her entire testimony. Shelly detailed the horrors in the house on Caroline.

"I thought maybe my father would be in chains," she later recalled. "But he wasn't. I thought, he has nothing to lose. I thought he was going to jump from that table and kill me right there."

Local news organizations couldn't report some of Shelly's disclosures simply because there was no way to address them in a family format. When she revealed that her father had measured her brother's penises with a ruler, Terrana's co-counsel Robert Fraser moved for a mistrial.

"All this stuff about measuring penises and all the rest of this evidence, all it's doing is throwing mud on our client," he boomed.

Pruner responded, "Judge, it's part of the pattern of this defendant to use every means possible, social, sexual, emotional, and physical to exercise dominion and control. And one way to do that was to keep the kids under his feet by belittling them to keep him elevated."

The trial went on.

Skipper Sexton was not the same reliable witness of the conspiracy trial. He tried to invoke the fifth. Mitcham appointed him an attorney who tried to explain to Skipper that because the state had granted him immunity, the right not to incriminate himself didn't apply. When he took the stand the next day, he was little help to Pixie's credibility.

"Mr. Sexton, whose idea was it to kill Joel Good?" Pruner asked.

"Estella and my dad's."

Later, "Have you ever told anybody that your dad was involved in the plan?"

"Yeah, a couple of times."

"Was that the truth?"

"It wasn't."

He was a package of contradictions. Sometimes he implicated Pixie, exonerating his father. Then he'd turn around, say the opposite. He distanced himself, and sometimes Pixie, from the abuse of Joel.

Terrana had a field day, wondering about all the stories in his depositions.

"Well, are you telling me today everything you told in the deposition is not true?" Terrana asked.

"I told you some of the truth."

He went to the August deposition, where Skipper had also changed his story.

"And I said you've told me so many stories, what makes this the true story and you said because now 'this is for me.' ".

"Yeah."

"And I asked you what do you mean, *this is for me* . . . And you said, well, the other stories weren't for me and this one I'm telling you today is for me. *This is the truth.* Do you remember that?"

"Yeah."

And later, "So your deposition was another half-and-half, is that right?"

"Yeah."

"Well, today are you testifying for you, Mr. Sexton?"

"I'm testifying for the family."

"So today is the truth?"

"Yeah."

"Nothing else you said before is the truth?"

"You know, just whatever," Skipper Sexton said.

Pruner tried to put his vacillations in context, getting Skipper to admit his father had offered him money from talk shows, offers that never would materialize.

Later, several jurors would say they found all the siblings lacked credibility.

After Skipper, the state rested and Terrana launched his defense. It would consist of only two witnesses. He'd already been building his theory in cross-examination, that Willie and Pixie had killed Good to hide their involvement in the death and burial of baby Skipper Lee. Pixie not only set up Joel's ambush, she'd probably stabbed her husband as well.

Earlier, a medical examiner acknowledged some of the holes in Joel Good's skin might have been superficial stabs, but most likely, she insisted, they were part of natural decay. He also had the puncture marks on his left hand. No one, however, testified to seeing any blood on Pixie Good.

The stabbing dispute drove home the gruesome nature of the crime. Pruner brought in Mike Willette to introduce a box of Good's clothes, the detective insisting he'd seen no knife holes in the material. The box remained closed as Judge Mitcham told the jury they could examine the clothes later. But he had a warning. He complained he could detect a "very strong stench and odor" from the box. He warned the jury to use rubber gloves if they chose to examine the clothing during deliberation.

Sherri Sexton took the stand on behalf of her father, detailing Pixie's arguments with Joel, the gasoline parties, Pixie beating her baby, and events the day of the death. She said she'd seen Willie and Pixie have sex "a lot."

"Describe the events leading up to [Pixie, Willie and Joel] going into the woods, if you know," Terrana said.

"They asked Joel if he wanted to go get some wood with them."

"Who asked Joel that?"

"Pixie and Willie. And Joel said no and then Pixie forced him to go . . . She grabbed his arm and made him go."

Later, she heard Joel yelling, "Ed!"

She told her father that her brother and sister were "hurting Joel" when he returned from the picnic.

The patriarch saying, "Oh, shit!"

That night, Pixie told her she sliced Joel's wrist, Sherri swore.

"She was happy," Sherri said. "She said that she was glad that he was dead."

"What was your dad's attitude toward Willie Sexton?" Terrana asked.

"He was mad and upset."

"Did your father ever talk to Willie or say anything to Willie to express this feeling he had?"

Sherri said, "He said if anybody else gets killed he's going to call the cops."

During cross, Pruner asked, "As a matter of fact, you hated Pixie growing up and even while you're down here, right?"

"Yes," Sherri said.

Pruner had her tell the jury about her flight to Florida with her son to avoid a blood test. The incest.

"On at least one occasion [your father] made you have sex with an uncle, correct?"

"No."

"Uncle Dave? No?"

"My Uncle Dave raped me and I told my father about it."

Pruner made several more points. She admitted she'd only seen Willie with a machete. She didn't see Pixie with a knife. She admitted her father was worried about Joel going back to Ohio.

"Your father often said a good snitch is a dead snitch, right?"

"Yes."

"And after Joel's death, your father referred to Joel as either a rat or a snitch, didn't he?"

"Yes."

Terrana finished with one more witness, Jean Sexton, who confirmed the beating of Joel Good.

Eddie Lee Sexton did not take the stand. In some ways, Terrana figured, the jury got a good look at his witness in the video, without a cross-examination. Several jurors later said they thought he sounded believable on the videotape.

After lunch, the attorneys gave their closing arguments.

Jay Pruner began with the video.

" 'I would gladly die for my country because my family is my country.' Those are the words of Eddie Sexton captured on the videotape that he created for President Clinton. And no truer words were ever spoken by Eddie Lee

Sexton, because he ran his family as a dictator would a country. He wasn't a benevolent dictator either . . .

"Much as the forefathers of our country blew holes into the mountains for transportation for the train system, Eddie Lee Sexton dynamited the bedrock of the personality and the will of his children through the incessant bombardment of abuse . . . Why? To preserve the national security, the security of the family, to preserve the national secrets, the family secrets, the secrets that he spoke to his children, his daughters who then became his wives."

But there was a traitor in their midst, Pruner argued. Joel M. Good. And for that, he faced the penalty of death.

Terrana's argument didn't skirt the family history.

"I suppose if he were on trial for all the other things we've heard about, being a dictator, sexual abuse and on and on and on, and being the worst father of the century, I would tell each of you, yeah, the state's proven its case. But Mr. Sexton stands trial for his life for a crime he did not commit. He stands trial for first degree murder."

Simply, he argued, motive didn't support the state's theory. What did Eddie Lee Sexton have to fear from Good disclosing his son's death? There'd been no testimony that he'd ordered the baby killed. He wouldn't have been charged.

But, "Pixie Good had her husband tortured. *She* tortured him. And when he was speaking his last words because she loved him so much, he didn't call for her. He didn't call for Willie. He didn't call for Skipper. He called for the man sitting at the table right there, Eddie. He called for *Eddie,* the man who hated him, if you believe Pixie Good. That's who he called for in his last-ditch attempt to stay alive."

Pruner answered in his rebuttal.

"Joel Good yelled for Ed. Does that surprise you? Who ran things? Who was the arbiter? Who was the one who had physical domination and control?"

12

The reality of their father on trial for his life, seemed to open a new gate back at the Holiday Inn. The siblings, including the oldest half-brother Patrick, talked deep into the night with authorities staying in nearby rooms.

The house on Caroline Street was a temple dedicated to meeting their parents' insatiable carnal needs. Shelly and Matt told of taking a candy bar out of the master bedroom and being punished by being locked up in their rooms without food for three days. Food from the locked refrigerator was used to show favoritism. Once, when boys brought back regular Kentucky Fried Chicken instead of "extra crispy," they were forced to eat nothing but chicken for days.

Their parents locked them in closets for wetting themselves as young children, then beat them when they were let out the next day. The Christmas tree was taken up and down during the holidays, the holiday canceled. Once, their father threw it across the room.

The patriarch ran around the house naked, draped in an American flag. He claimed to have an 11-inch penis, calling himself "Super Dick." He flashed them every day. The father sent Patrick out to buy condoms and "hard-on" cream, a numbing lotion to deter male orgasm. Eddie Lee had a blow-up sex doll. Girls went to the master bedroom for "private talks." He raped some of them with the hard-on cream. He used a hand-held dildo and a strap-on. Both parents shaved the girls' pubic hair. They instructed the children on how to have sex with one another.

When Pixie testified her mother knew about the murder, the children became agitated. They said their mother knew "everything" going on in the house and on the road. Their mother sometimes restrained them during their father's sexual assaults. Sherri said her mother was present during her rapes, three or four times a year in the master bedroom. She'd ask for her mother's help, but the matriarch would only laugh. She was lured to the bedroom after being accused of telling family secrets at school.

Sherri described the marriage ritual. She was 17 at the time, she said. Her father read vows from the black book with a "star" on it. Her mother took photographs. Lana and Kim were married, too.

Shelly became very emotional. She said she was made fun of by her parents because she was not as sexually developed as her sisters. She began crying, saying every time she looked in the mirror she saw a "monster" because of the trauma she'd been through.

She felt the whole world could see it, too.

Judee Genetin later would decline to discuss the details of the hotel room sessions, but talked about the impact after the bodies were discovered and her Florida trip. In the two years she'd spent on the case, she'd had doubts about some of the most outrageous stories, believing some disclosures were "one step beyond reality."

But no more. The true evil was not in the rituals. It was much more basic.

"For the most part, I think my children have the nicer things," Genetin would say. "For the Sextons, it was all under lock and key. It was all backwards. Everything, and every child, was kept to benefit *them.*"

Genetin, and others, had also discerned structured roles within the family madness. Eddie was the patriarch. Pixie was his lieutenant, his watchful eyes. Skipper was his sergeant, a wily enforcer. Willie was his muscle. Lana was his mystical figure. Christopher, the loved one. James, the runt. Shelly, the outcast. Kimberly, the innocent mascot. Matt, the quiet one.

"Sherri," Genetin would say, "was pure victim."

That left the matriarch. As the trial wound down, Genetin was thinking about May Sexton. Back in Ohio, there appeared to be no solid plans by the Stark County authorities to pursue more charges.

"She's worse than him," Genetin later said. "She's such a liar. She knew all this was going on. She participated in it. She was part of it. She tried to latch on to this battered woman thing, and that's just crap. She was no battered woman. She was part of the plan."

13

The jury began deliberations the next morning. They lasted only 2 hours and 35 minutes. Jay Pruner and others thought the fast deliberation meant they'd rejected the state's entire case.

As the verdict was read, Eddie Sexton sat impassively, his head slightly bowed. Sherri Sexton broke into sobs in the audience. Otis Sexton hugged Sherri and his sister Nellie, then crossed the aisle and whispered to Teresa Boron, "Congratulations. We got him."

Later, one after another, the jurors told Rick Terrana and reporters why they'd convicted Eddie Lee Sexton. It wasn't Pixie or her siblings or the stories of graphic abuse that tipped the scale of justice. "It was the greatest single lesson I've ever learned in the practice of law," Terrana later said.

The reason was the only emotional witness sandwiched between all the Flatliners.

It was Gail Novak, the librarian.

"She had no reason not to tell the truth," one said.

The next day, on October 7, after three witnesses testified to Eddie Lee Sexton's character, the jury met for another 2 hours for the trial's second phase. Their vote was 7–5. One less, and the law would have required Sexton be given mandatory life imprisonment. The patriarch stood calmly, chained, wearing prison overalls, as the punishment was read.

When he left the courtroom, he was taking his first steps toward Old Sparky, Florida's electric chair.

Afterwards, Sexton's sister Nellie, who'd testified on her brother's behalf in the penalty phase, said if all the stories she'd heard were indeed true, there was a place for his wife Estella May Sexton.

Nellie said, "She ought to be sitting on his lap."

xiv

Preservation of the Seed

1

Eddie Lee Sexton squatted on the concrete floor like a catcher in the triangular holding cell at the Hillsborough County Jail, fielding questions from St. Petersburg *Times* reporter Bill Duryea in the patriarch's only interview in the days after the trial.

Sexton had been sentenced not only to death on October 6, but given 15 years on the conspiracy to murder charge. Later, Estella Sexton Good would be sentenced to six years in prison. She broke down sobbing, the first public emotion she'd shown through the entire Sexton ordeal.

Duryea, who'd covered the trial, was struck by Eddie Lee Sexton's hands. They were as smooth as a surgeon's, and his long fingers made the kind of graceful movements people expect from an artist.

Eddie Lee Sexton likened himself to the Savior.

"I know what Christ felt on the cross," he said. "He was condemned to death for something he never done."

An analytical savior.

Sexton said he believed he knew what had happened. The jury had convicted him for outrageous stories—the "lies" his children had told. He claimed to have an IQ of 160, saying "I'll match my IQ with anybody."

He said, "I'm innocent of anything and everything."

He denied rituals involving dead babies.

"My God, no," he said. "That's ungodly."

Pixie and Willie had planned the murder, he claimed. She was not the girl he raised.

"She was always a good child," he said. "It started after she married Joel."

Duryea asked him about the drills, the instructions on how to make a garrotte.

"I was teaching my one young son how to protect himself from sex offenders," Sexton said.

They were discussing why the jury had convicted him when Sexton said something rather odd, or perhaps telling.

"Let's take the Menendez brothers," Sexton said. "They killed their mother and father. It was a vicious act. Their defense was sex abuse. But society accepted it."

Eddie Lee Sexton had never claimed to be a victim of sex abuse in his criminal defense or during the penalty phase of the trial. He didn't claim it with Duryea, either.

He'd only admit he'd erred in his fatherly role.

"I don't know where I went wrong," he said. "But evidently I went wrong somewhere. Maybe I was just too good to them."

He added, "I'm guilty of one thing. And that is trying to preserve and protect my family."

2

For months, the conviction split the extended Sexton family into two camps—everybody versus Otis. The whole affair just didn't square with the Eddie Lee they knew, some of his own siblings said.

Sexton's 65-year-old sister Nellie Hanft had taken the stand in the penalty phase. She told of comfortably taking her granddaughter over to visit the house on Caroline. She'd seen one child spanked, Patrick with a belt, for stealing a walkie-talkie. Eddie was a "jolly" man, she said. He cut the hair of her husband, a stroke victim. He and his boys fixed things around her house. He played Santa Claus, bringing gifts to her daughter's children.

Eight months after the trial, Nellie Hanft sat near a framed, vintage portrait of her parents in her neatly kept Canton home and explained to a visitor the childhood she remembered. She was 13 when Eddie was born. Her mother Lana was 42. All her mother's children were born at home, not unusual in the remote hollows of southern West Virginia. A doctor for the Island Creek Coal Company signed his birth certificate five days after his birth. Eddie Lee was born in a small house just up the hill in a little group of homes called Baisden Bottom, a half mile from the Verdonsville, West Virginia, post office. Most of their lives, the large family made do in three-bedroom homes.

"I suppose we were poor," Nellie said. "But we didn't know we were poor, because everybody around was poor, too."

The family was frequently on the move, William Dewey Sexton taking new jobs. They stayed in the counties that hugged the rivers, the Big Sandy and the Ohio, America's Bible Belt. They left one house in Logan County after a house fire. Their father served a stint as the sheriff of Pike County, Kentucky. When Eddie was seven, the family moved to Ironton, Ohio, just across the Ohio River from Ashland, Kentucky, where he preached in a mission. After William Dewey's death, family members began migrating to Canton for better work and pay.

William Dewey was a sick man by his late 40s, Nellie said. He suffered from black lung, a heart condition, "and a lot of ailments."

"My dad was stern, but he was fair," she said. "He listened. I never got a lickin' in my life I didn't deserve. And never in front of other family members. He disciplined the boys, my mother the girls. He believed a man could hurt a girl, so he left us girls to my mom."

However, according to their silver-haired younger sister, Maggie Sexton, the rule didn't always apply. Her father was a controlling patriarch, she recalled. He didn't allow the girls to date. When they did go out, he sent a chaperone. Maggie remembered her late sister Stella running away at age 15.

"Daddy whipped her," she said, "for disobeying his wishes."

Maggie also lives in Canton, in a small, modern apartment. She collects Social Security for epilepsy. Her siblings describe her as "slow," but she had no trouble recalling youthful memories. She is five years older than Sexton. She remembered a brother who was frequently ill with colds and other ailments.

"When Eddie was a child he was ill," she said. "He was a change of life baby. Momma was putting all her attention to Eddie. And Otis, the second youngest, got jealous. Otis was always jealous of Eddie."

She said Otis frequently tried to get Eddie in trouble, snitching on him, setting him up to fight neighborhood kids. Understandably, both sisters believed their youngest brother's troubles were only a continuation of the rivalry, with Otis working behind the scenes in his criminal case.

Orville Sexton, the oldest living brother everybody called "Big Chew" for his love of Red Man, remembered a father not as righteous as many around him assumed. Orville had just come back from World War II when he first learned of his father's indiscretions. William Dewey worked as a minister for the Salvation Army in Logan for three years. But he was defrocked, Orville recalled, for his involvement with a woman whose husband was in the service. Orville remembered at least four extramarital affairs. In Ironton,

William Dewey took up with a woman who lived across the river in Ashland, and fathered a child with her.

"He'd live with Mom one night, then stay with that woman the next night," he recalled. "The night he died, he just happen to come home. He told Mother he was going to quit. About two in the morning he had a heart attack and died."

Orville said his father suffered from intense guilt, a condition he poured into preaching a gospel that promised deliverance from sin. "He was a strict man. And strict with the kids. He wanted to live religious. He'd see a picture of Jesus in a window on the street and he'd sit there and cry like a baby. He wanted to live right. But he had a weakness for women."

After his death, the long-suffering matriarch made some small investments in rental properties. She married another man, who eventually died an alcoholic, family members said. The matriarch joined her children in Canton in the early 1960s, living for a short time with her Eddie Lee's family.

"She was an invalid and while she was there we got into a couple of fights," May would recall. "Eddie started calling the children names and that in front of her. And she said if they're 'little bastards' [as he was calling his kids] you're a little bastard also, and he got upset with her."

The mother died close to Thanksgiving in 1976. Oddly, considering their relationship, the most affected offspring was not Eddie Lee, but Dave Sexton, who nearly knocked over his mother's casket, collapsing on it in grief. Eddie Lee's short stint as a minister followed.

There was also some mystery surrounding both Eddie Lee's and Otis's birth certificates. Both their county birth records report nine children were in the family at the time of their births two years apart, with no dead or stillborn children listed. Both list their father as age 42. Eddie Lee's

mother is listed as "Lana Toler," Otis's as "Leona Toler,"
the name, Otis believes, of an aunt.

The documents certainly were no proof Eddie or Otis
were products of incest. Perhaps they were only clerical
errors. Eddie's sister Nellie was 13, Stella, 11, and Maggie,
5, when Eddie, the last child, was born.

Shelly Croto reported her father once told her that his
father had sex with some of his sisters. But Nellie Hanft
was adamant, as was Maggie.

There had been no incest in her family, both said.

3

It took nearly a year for the news of Eddie Lee Sexton's
dubious fame to reach the hollows and bottoms of his
Logan County birthplace. Today, the green treetops on
mountains around Verdonsville hide dozens of closed
mine shafts. They're the remnants of war-time coal booms,
a time when it took 100 men, many of them transients and
immigrants, to do the same work that three men and a
mining machine can do today.

Still, it was coal country, "Home of the Billion Dollar
Coal Field," one sign near Williamson proclaimed. Here
and there, the brown iron sculpture of mine processing
stations just out of the lowland, looking like smokeless oil
refineries.

Unlike the mountain men of *Deliverance,* people in these
parts are gracious and helpful, seemingly endowed with
the luxury of time. A dozen vehicles stack up behind a car
parked in the street. Someone runs inside to fetch milk
from a grocery. Not a horn will sound, unless a rare big-
city visitor happens to be in the line.

On a muggy August day, Florence Baisden worked the
phones to relatives for two hours for a visitor, trying to
locate someone who remembered William Dewey Sexton,
his wife Lana, and the boy born halfway up the nearby

hill. "Sextons" were all over the county. But "that was a different string of Sextons," 76-year-old Henderson Baisden finally reported from his hospital bed.

Coal miners were always moving in and out, he said.

Florence Baisden converted her local filling station to a recycling center and bow hunting shop after her husband died. The bottom—the mountain's bottom land—was named after her husband's great-grandfather, Julius Baisden. Several generations were born, lived, and died in the same group of houses up Mud Fork Road where Eddie Lee Sexton's mother gave birth. Before the four-lane came through, a 30-mile trip to the tiny city of Williamson could take a couple of hours on twisting mountain roads. In the 1800s, it took a couple of days. Isolation and limited population almost dictated marriage among cousins.

But Baisden Bottom and Little Italy Bottom and Black Bottom and countless others had their rules. Pentecostals and Baptist churches abound. The revival meeting remains one of the most popular venues for local enlightenment and entertainment. The blind see. The crippled walk. The afflicted are delivered.

The cures, however, may be more moral than physical.

In these parts, there's no shortage of funds for the disabled. Simply by being a late miner's wife, Florence Baisden said she could receive Social Security, free medical care, and payments from black lung and miner's welfare funds. Her two sons were eligible for black lung payments because they'd driven coal trucks. They declined.

Many others take advantage, she said. "There's people on it that never worked a day in their life. The black lung. Your daddy drew black lung, and his name was Paul Jr. and you're named Paul Jr. Your daddy dies. You cash his checks well after he's gone."

In Logan, a police sergeant named Glen Ables also noticed distinct cultural differences from his home near the Virginia border when he transferred to the Logan detachment of the West Virginia State Police 20 years ago.

Most local violence is over male dominance and territory, he said. Fights with friends and neighbors over women and property. Wife beatings. Child abuse.

Said Ables: "In one way, even the bad people here aren't fundamentally bad. A local criminal may steal everything you have—your gas, your TV, your car—but if they pass you on the road and you're down and out, broken down, they'll stop, pick you up, and take care of you, or fill your car with the gas they stole. They'll take care of you.

"But there are some fundamental rules of life that people here live by," he added. "Some of those rules are not what we accept. But they're solid and consistent with these people. We don't have street crime as most people know it. But they'll kill you and shoot you over the fundamentals of life. Property is mine. Possessions are mine. Family is mine."

Incest, he said, has only recently emerged from the closet. "It's taken people a long time to realize there's some scientific problems with it," he said.

There have been no studies examining the stereotype, the old West Virginia slam: "My parents met at a family reunion."

Up a few miles Mud Fork from Baisden Bottom, a librarian at the new Southern West Virginia Community and Technical College said her most frequent research requests from local students are for materials on child abuse and incest. She asked that her name not be used in fear of ostracization.

"It's a taboo subject," she said. "But growing up here, I would say if people would be truthful with you, it's seven out of ten families. It's still going on."

A culture, perhaps, where Eddie Lee Sexton learned many of his moves.

4

Thirty miles away, near Delbarton, a 52-year-old disabled West Virginian named John Runyon was putting a new engine in a Chevy when a daughter ran out of their mobile home, yelling, "Eddie's on TV!"

Runyon had seen Eddie Sexton only three times in the last 25 years, most recently in Canton in 1988. In 1963, when a Mingo County court sent Eddie Lee Sexton to prison, John Runyon was at his side.

He'd been Sexton's best friend for almost five years. They met at 16 in West Virginia. Runyon's sister had married Eddie's older brother Joe. Sarah, Orville's wife, was also kin. Eddie always said he was a year older than Runyon. He was shocked to find out later they were born the same year.

As teenagers, they worked odd jobs together, scrapping cars and selling produce in Ironton. They followed relatives to Canton, working for a Manpower office there. On weekends, they cruised towns back in their home state, picking up women. Drag racing with Eddie's 4-year-old Buick. Sowing wild oats.

They never hurt for money or a place to stay, Runyon recalled. Eddie's mother and sisters gave them money when they needed it. They crashed in their bedrooms, never putting down stakes. "Eddie was the type of feller, his whole family went out of the way to help him," he recalled.

They hooked up with a married woman in Canton, Runyon recalled, carrying on an affair with her while her husband was at work. It ended when Otis told the woman's husband, he said.

"There'd always been bad blood between those two brothers," he recalled.

"We'd work all week, take the money, and run around

all weekend. Typical teenage stuff. We never got in trouble with the law, though. We didn't even get a traffic ticket during that whole time."

That all changed the last weekend of May 1963. They'd cruised into Delbarton on a joy ride, stopping to visit brother Orville, ending up at a place called Betty's Beer Joint. "It was the first serious drinking we'd ever done," Runyon said.

That night they bought a case of beer and went home with a local. When the man passed out, Eddie made a move on his 15-year-old daughter Sarah.

"She was a brown-haired girl, five-five, about 110 pounds," Runyon recalled. "We'd had dozens like her. But Eddie fell head over heels in love. Next thing I know, he says he's gonna marry her."

They drank all weekend, Runyon finally talking Eddie into going back to Canton with the last few dollars they had. It was around midnight when they finished their last beer in the car. They were driving through Naugatuck, maybe 20 miles down the road, when they passed an all-night gas station.

Then, "Eddie brought it up," Runyon said.

He wanted to turn around and marry the girl.

"We hardly have money to get home," Runyon said. "How you going to get married? I just couldn't figure it, either. I don't know what set him off so much about this girl."

A few minutes later, they pulled into the gas station with a tire they'd purposely flattened. A 20-year-old man was working in the station alone. As he fixed the tire they jumped him, knocking his head into the tire machine.

They took the entire cash register, $309 inside. That night they slept at Orville Sexton's. The next day, Eddie was married to Sarah by a local preacher.

"The girl's family thought the Sextons had money," Runyon recalled. "They were the kind of family that did a lot of bumming, so they didn't mind."

They wanted the money close by. When Eddie decided to take the girl back to Canton, her parents called the law. State police showed up the next morning at Orville's. Runyon and Sexton had dumped the cash register and its contents. But the police produced a gas station receipt from the Buick and jailed them both.

Eddie Lee had been married only one day.

A few weeks later, they pled guilty to armed robbery, both of them sentenced to Moundsville Penitentiary, serving five years of 5-to-18-year terms.

In the pen, Eddie dropped him, Runyon recalled, picking up with his cellmate, Paul Shortridge, the man later known as the "Ice Man." Sexton and Shortridge ran a poker and dominos games and made book on sporting events, Runyon said.

"As far as I know, him and Eddie never was in a fight in prison," he said. "Eddie was Eddie, no matter how you sliced him. His attitude never changed. He was not the type of person who had a lot of friends. He'd pick one person, and stay with him.

"I can't understand how Eddie turned out this way, if it's all true. From the time we met to the time we got out of prison, he wasn't criminal-like. He didn't have a con mind. If he got that, he got it from Shortridge."

There was one more revelation from that period. Eddie Lee Sexton had never even been in the armed services, Runyon said. It was a cover story to account for his years in prison, he said.

Runyon now belonged to the Church of God in Hatfield Bottom. Otis Sexton, he said, helped him get his life back together after he got out of prison. Otis helped him get a job in Canton, but he later moved back to his home state after he hurt his back in a battery salvage job.

As far as Runyon could tell, Eddie was totally reformed when he and his wife stayed with the family one night in Canton in 1988. His children were perfectly behaved. They served house guests coffee and made their beds. Eddie

talked about the Bible and preaching. But he also showed
Runyon and his wife a collection of videotapes. Three trays,
kept near the family pictures. They were labeled "Family
Movies," "Children's Movies," and "X-rated Movies."

Still, he couldn't shake the feeling that Eddie Lee Sexton's problems were Otis's doing. "He's getting his
revenge," Runyon said. "For all those hard feelings he
had against Eddie years back."

5

Sixty miles up the Big Sandy River, in Ironton, some folks
remembered quite a different Sexton family, and a different Eddie Lee Sexton in the years before he and John
Runyon hit the road.

Eighth Street was one of the town's black blocks. Across
the alley, Seventh Street was white. When the Sextons
moved into the shotgun next door at 914 South Eighth, a
black woman named Gwen Collins said the entire neighborhood "went to pot."

Now a retired social worker, Collins was 13 at the time.
She still has vivid memories of the Sextons, particularly
Eddie Lee.

"All the time they were fighting and running out of
the doors, and just acting crazy," Collins recalled. "The
mother would run out of the door and fuss at them. Then
they'd curse her out."

There were frequent visits by police cars. The Sextons
had old cars and a chicken coop behind the house. The
homestead bothered Collins's mother, who was a cook,
and her father, a shoe repairman. "Mother was very clean
and neat," she said.

Maggie Sexton, just a young teen, often sat on the back
porch alone, Collins recalled. "She acted like she was
scared of things, or just stared into space."

Eddie, not even 10, sat on the porch, too. He played

with kitchen matches incessantly. He'd sit there for hours, sticking one after another into the porch, gazing at each match as it burnt down to the floorboards.

Eddie tormented animals and picked on vulnerable neighbors, Collins recalled. He threw things at fenced dogs. He'd lure small, harmless neighborhood mutts to his hand with a treat, then kick them viciously. He pinched the bottoms of young girls. When one of Collins's sister married and became pregnant, he teased Gwen.

"Ha, ha, your sister's gonna have a baby," he'd say, as if being pregnant was some kind of serious mistake.

Across the alley, Phillip Martin, now a food broker in his 50s, watched Eddie hang chickens on the clothesline and lop their heads off with a knife. It wasn't necessarily farm chores, Gwen Collins recalled.

"One day, Eddie came storming out of the house, *mad,* and went to the chicken coop," she recalled. "He came out with a chicken by the head. Then he fetched a hammer and just beat that chicken to death in a rage. It sent chills down my spine."

Both Collins and Martin remembered an act of animal cruelty that alarmed the entire neighborhood. A widow on the corner kept a half dozen cats. They disappeared. Then all six showed up in the Sextons' backyard, dead, strung up by their necks on the clothesline by Eddie Lee, 13 or 14 at the time.

"It was very traumatic," recalled Martin. "I was six years older than he was at the time and it was traumatic for me. But he thought it was the greatest thing in the world."

"It darn near killed that old woman," Collins recalled. "She loved those cats. They were her family."

Eddie appeared to face few consequences. Collins remembered the father often gone, or sick. "The mother always treated Eddie a little different than the rest of the kids. You often saw her with her arm around the boy, but not the other boys or girls."

When William Dewey Sexton died, the Sextons held

visitation in their small house. Collins remembered peeking through the window, seeing them all sitting around his coffin. "It was so strange," she said.

When she learned of Sexton's murder conviction, Collins thought of a connection. Eddie often hung around with Collins's youngest sister, several years Eddie's junior. The sister grew up with a host of emotional problems and psychopathic tendencies. She sent their father to an early grave, running him $50,000 in debt in forged credit cards in his name, then died of cancer at 42.

It was as if they were some kind of soul mates, she said.

Collins remembered the words of her mother as she watched Eddie and his mischief from her kitchen window one day.

"That boy is going to amount to nothin'," she said. "Just look how devilish he is."

6

Three days after Sexton's death sentence was finalized by Judge Bob Mitcham in Tampa, Otis Sexton was picketing outside the courthouse in downtown Canton again. He'd have a T-shirt made up. It read:

STOP INCEST. BELIEVE THE CHILDREN.

The day before, Stark County Prosecutor Robert D. Horowitz had announced he was not going to bring Eddie Lee Sexton back to Ohio to try him on sex abuse charges. He said it was a "security" issue. And a trial wouldn't be worth the cost to the county. His critics cited cannibal Jeffery Dahmer, who had been brought back to nearby Summit County for trial, even after he'd been sentenced to 15 life terms in Milwaukee.

Otis was fuming, as were Steve Ready and many social workers at the DHS. Stark County needed to make a statement against abuse and incest, they argued. But there were other concerns as well.

In Tampa, prosecutor Jay Pruner was saying it was only "50-50" that Sexton's conviction would hold up in appeals. Judge Mitcham had pushed the envelope by allowing Sexton's bad acts into his murder trial. There was a real possibility Sexton could serve five or 10 years on the conspiracy charge, win his murder appeal, and be released just about the time the sex charges expired.

Sheriff Bruce Umpleby went to bat for his detective, saying his department would be the one absorbing much of the costs. He wrote Horowitz a detailed memo.

Still, the prosecutor didn't budge.

For Steve Ready, it was more than legalities. It was personal. His solo, year-long investigation had produced more than a 100 counts of rape and sexual battery against the patriarch. Now he'd been denied the closure, the satisfaction, every cop savored when a criminal was convicted in court.

"The cost to the taxpayers? What? A plane ticket?," Ready later said. "Those kids had stood up finally and said, yeah, I was sexually abused by my father—and nothing has happened. And nothing is going to happen. It just isn't right."

For Otis Sexton the new scenario was entirely too reminiscent of what had happened in Jackson Township and Massilon. Now he'd heard from his many sources that May Sexton, who would be released from prison in a year, also might not be pursued on more sex-abuse charges.

Otis's advocacy bordered on obsession. He wrote compelling letters to local newspapers urging the passage of a new crime tax. He lobbied Ohio legislators. The state's specific statute against incest had been repealed in 1974. Like many other states, incest fell under general sexual battery laws. He wrote Bill Clinton, and hung the president's response proudly on his wall. He called reporters, stoking the Sexton story, tipping them off to new developments. He continued calling Steve Ready, offering new sibling revelations. He appeared on Geraldo Rivera's daytime show and confronted his younger brother on a satellite feed from his Tampa jail, causing Eddie Lee to walk out. Local *Stark Magazine* would name him one of the county's "20 most interesting people" before the year was done.

His brother's children kept him hopping. Sherri married a man she'd met in a psychiatric ward. She told him one day she couldn't care for her incestuous child Christopher. "Every time I look at my son, I see my father," she said. Otis started the process to adopt the child. He talked to Willie Sexton by phone from Chattahootchee. He claimed in interviews that the DHS had ignored his pleas for action against the Sexton family in the 1980s, though records didn't appear to support that. Relatives accused him of wanting to skim the siblings' government support payments. He tried to sell the Sexton story for a book, saying he only wanted the money to set up a fund for therapy for the children.

Some, including Ready, Shelly Croto, and Judge Genetin, began to question his motives. At times he seemed like a benevolent version of his brother. Finally, he relented on the demands for the book money, when the writer, after nearly two years, prevailed with his argument that payment would only discredit the credibility of the work.

"I've never profited off these kids and never would," Otis Sexton later said. He estimated he'd lost $25,000 dealing with his brother's legacy.

Steve Ready said, "And what does it really matter why Otis Sexton did it? Without Otis Sexton, we would have never put an end to all of this."

On November 4, as he picketed with his wife Jackie, Eddie Jr., and Sherri, money *was* the issue. The taxpayer's money. His leaflets were no longer handwritten or crude, but professionally typeset and biting with sarcasm.

The protestors were demanding May Sexton be brought

to trial on the sex charges Otis was hearing from his displaced nieces and nephews. Prosecutor Horowitz was complaining about lack of money. So Otis Sexton—under the leaflet's title "Stark County Prosecutor's Office Dragging Feet?"—concluded:

"If the lack of money is all that's keeping her from being prosecuted, will you as a concerned citizen please drop off a dollar to the prosecutor's office and join me in raising money to prosecute Estella May Sexton?"

The office never reported whether it received any money. But that wasn't the point.

Said Otis Sexton later, "I was out to embarrass Bob Horowitz. Plain and simple. And I believe I did."

7

After nearly two years of grand jury subpoenas, months of spade work by assistant prosecutors, and various legal delays, a jury was finally impaneled on August 7, 1996.

May Sexton was standing trial again. She'd face the same assistant prosecutors and have the same public defender, plus a co-counsel. But there were quite a few more charges this time, a herculean effort by attorneys Jonathan Baumoel and Kristine Rohrer Beard.

In 1995, the matriarch had been talking about reuniting with her children upon her release from the Ohio Reformatory for Women at Marysville. She never drew a free breath. A grand jury had charged her with 31 counts, among them rape, complicity to rape, child endangering, and gross sexual imposition. She waited trial for nearly a year in the Stark County Jail. By August, the charges were split into two scheduled trials.

As the first unfolded, the entire story might have seemed familiar, had it not been for the many disclosures of May's direct involvement in her husband's brutality and sexual obsessions.

Kimberly, now 12, told the jury both parents "rubbed her private parts" as she slept with them in the master bedroom. She told of playing the Hershey Kisses game with her mother, being french-kissed during her wedding ceremony, and being forced to model for her dad the bra and nightgown Steady Ready had retrieved from the Challenger motor home.

She saw her mother fondle Christopher in the motor home in Florida, she told the jury. Then her mother gave her Nyquil and ordered her siblings out of the camper. Her mother and father then shaved her legs with a razor they kept in the Challenger's safe. They both fondled her, then put the razor away, "until next time," she said.

The shaving episode appeared to be another family ritual, to which both Lana, now nearly 16, and Shelly Croto, 23, testified. Their mother helped their father shave their pubic areas. The patriarch cut both the girls.

"He put blood on my finger and made me sign a piece of paper and he said I was selling my soul to the devil," Lana told the jury.

Shelly testified she had a scar on her private parts she had no way of explaining to her husband. "They didn't want us to grow up," she told the jury. "They wanted us to be kids, stay babies."

Using diagrams of the house on Caroline, prosecutors portrayed the master bedroom as a virtual sexual torture chamber run by both parents.

Shelly testified her mother rubbed her breasts in fake breast exams and sodomized her with her fingers under the guise of "looking for worms." She'd also undergone a marriage ceremony with her father when she was 13, she said.

Kimberly, Lana, and Christopher, all of them now in stable homes, held up well on the stand. Shelly, six months pregnant with twins, had thrown up in the bathroom before she took the stand, and also during a break.

But it wasn't morning sickness. "Seeing her," she later said. "I just couldn't handle it."

There were more revelations about play and punishment. Kids were forced to stand, holding pennies against walls with their noses for five hours at a time. The family dances were held every weekend in the summer, once a month during school. The children were allowed to drink beer during the parties, Christopher testified.

No account was more brutal than Lana's revelation of being raped at age "8 or 9," her mother a willing accomplice. Her parents took her into the master bedroom one night.

"What's the first thing that happened after they closed the doors?" prosecutor John Baumoel asked.

"I asked them what they were going to do, and they said they were going to punish me," Lana said. She couldn't even remember for what.

Her mom took off her shirt, her father her pants and panties. Her mother got on the bed, holding her arms down, Lana's ankles propped over her own shoulders.

Her father then raped her. "It hurt," she said.

Lana said, "I kept screaming but they wouldn't listen to me."

Baumoel asked her what her mother said.

"She just said this was for punishment," Lana said.

Medical reports, school absentee records, and psychological reports supported many of the accounts. There also were far more subtle looks at the tattered fabric of America's most dysfunctional family.

Shelly identified herself to the jury as "Shelly Sexton," not Shelly Croto, as she remained tied forever to the Sexton name.

The prosecution introduced a letter May wrote to her husband, calling him "sweetheart." Apparently it concerned Kimberly.

It read: "Our little one is doing pretty good so far. I'm sure it will stay that way for its daddy. Our little girl has really straightened up a lot. She's being a lot more grown up too since the secret was told to her."

It will stay that way.

Lana was asked what she remembered good about her mom.

"We always went camping together, swimming together, and it's like when my dad is not there, my mom's really nice, but when he's there, she gets real mean."

"Lana, how do you feel about your mom today?" Baumoel asked.

"I just want to tell her I still loved her," she said, using the past tense. Then she added, "I am upset at what she done and let my dad do to us."

Christopher, when asked why he never reported anything, said, "I thought it was a normal family."

Estella May Sexton's defense consisted of telling a long story of abuse, unsuccessful escapes, and fist fights with her husband. She denied every bad act. She said her husband handcuffed her to the bed and sexually assaulted her. She'd never escaped because she was worried her husband would kill one of her kids, she said.

Baumoel mocked what he called her "duo defense" in his closing argument. "First off, none of this happened . . . They all lied. They all made these things up. It's all part of their imagination, but in the alternative, if this did happen, forgive this lady. This lady was justified because of domestic violence. There's only one victim in this trial and that's her, according to her."

After three days of testimony, it took a jury of six men and six women only 120 minutes to convict her on eight counts. Stark County Common Pleas Judge Harry Clide immediately sentenced her to life in prison for helping her husband rape Lana. Later, she would plead guilty to 13 more counts and avoid a second trial.

At sentencing, May maintained her innocence and said,

"All I can say is God is the only one who can help me now."

She will be eligible for parole in 2011, when she's 64.

8

May Sexton finished her coffee, glanced around the interview room at the Ohio Reformatory for Women in Marysville, then recalled her involvement with the Futuretron project.

"He had me call different chains of restaurants, Burger King, McDonald's and Wendy's. Burger King said send them some drawings and information and stuff and we did. The lady on the phone said they'd send it to their office in Chicago, maybe, and keep it for down the road. And that's what got him all excited.

"Eddie just kept pushing and pushing and pushing, and traveling back and forth to Florida, wasting all kinds of money. I told him, you can't just walk in there. I tried to set up appointments, a Chris somebody, and he said he had a lot of things to do. He wouldn't be able to see him right away. But he'd go on a whim. Eddie thought, if I get down there and I get my foot in the office, I'll be able to talk to him."

May was asked, what were the Futuretrons, what was their selling point?

"They're just, you know, the way they were dressing. If anyone asked what a Futuretron is, well, maybe future generations would all look the same.

"That's what Eddie said."

9

The tendency among some chroniclers of the Sexton case was to look for the easy explanations. But they were as elusive as the patriarch had been during all his months on the run.

On the surface, Sexton appeared to fit the profile of what author and former cult member Linda Blood calls the "new satanists," in her 1994 book of the same name. Literature on ritual abuse abounds with stories of baby sacrifices and dead fetuses. Skeptics doubt their credibility. But that's exactly the point, ritual survivors argue. The key element of ritual abuse is to make the reality of the victim's experience so outrageous, no one will believe the child.

Blood also makes observations about contemporary Satanism astoundingly similar to Eddie Lee Sexton's claim that he was "both God and the Devil."

She writes:

Contemporary satanism, however, is based not so much on the explicit worship of evil but on the contention that "good" and "evil" do not exist in any objective sense. Modern satanists proclaim that their goal is to rise above these mundane human designations into a godlike position of total, unrestricted freedom and power that places them beyond "good and evil."

Blood also provides a chillingly familiar description of the activities in organized satanic cults:

They engage in the sale of narcotics, weapons, kidnapped children, and child pornography, as well as burglary, insurance and computer fraud, and arson for hire.

However, no evidence has yet to link Sexton to any kind of organized Satanic group. More likely, Satanism was just one more tool of control. In fact, Eddie Lee Sexton was a loner. He interacted *only* with family. Other than John

Runyon in his teens, he appeared not to have a single close friend.

On the other end of the morality scale, Sexton also seemed to embrace scripture. Pixie Good would tell a story about the time she'd returned from church and confronted her father with a sermon she'd heard with Joel Good. Incest was a sin, the pastor said. Her father countered with scripture, but she couldn't recall which passages.

Incest is dealt with in the Bible in the story of Lot in Genesis, and also in sexual guidelines in the book of Leviticus.

After failing to marry, Lot's two daughters have sex with him: "Come let us make our father drink wine, and we will lie with him, that we may preserve the seed of our father." The storyteller appears to absolve Lot of guilt by having the patriarch in a drunken blackout during the act.

Likewise, Leviticus lays out a dozen prohibitions by God against a man having sex with relatives, including in-laws. Curiously, one is never mentioned—a man having sex with his daughter.

Some incest survivors also believe the gospel's essential message of forgiveness serves as an easy balm for perpetrators and victims alike. Anne Marie Eriksson, a former Manhattan probation officer, founded one of the first incest-prevention organizations in the country in 1983, called Incest Survivors Resource Network International, now based in New Mexico. A survivor herself, she said perpetrators are often former victims.

"When they've had that trauma, they busy themselves in that black and white religion, seeking relief," she said. "If only they follow this, their life will be peaceful and okay. Of course, it doesn't work. When I was in probation work and I saw a Bible come into court in somebody's hand, I used to joke, 'Okay, here comes a sex abuse case.'"

But at the same time, the good and evil in Eddie Lee Sexton's world appear only as components in a greater pathology. Anthropologists and sociologists report that incest remains a taboo in every known culture on earth. Yet, it has continued for centuries. One study based on the Kinsey sex surveys among middle-class households reports at least 1 in 100 women have had sex with their fathers. Experts suspected the practice to be more rampant in impoverished homes. Other, less scientific estimates, claim incest occurs in as many as 1 in 7 American homes.

One nationally respected researcher and thinker in the field makes a convincing case for the reasons, and draws conclusions hauntingly revealing when applied to the Sexton case.

In her thoroughly researched work, *Father-Daughter Incest,* Harvard psychiatrist Judith Lewis Herman delved into previous sex and incest studies and conducted her own detailed look at 40 women survivors. The women were all white, educated, and middle-class, many of them church-going Catholics and Protestants. They may have not been of the same social strata as the Sextons. But in almost every way, the study's results could have been mirrors in the halls of the house on Caroline Street.

Dr. Herman writes the taboo of incest has been explained by three different schools of thought. It is biologically unsound, with data showing a higher incidence of stillbirths, early infant deaths, and mental retardation. It is a psychological threat because it disrupts the organization and harmony of the family. And socially, it needs to be deterred among patriarchal societies that view "brides" as "gifts" that are exchanged between fathers and young men of contemporary tribes.

Yet, Dr. Herman argues, tacit permission for incest abounds. She cites articles and images from *Hustler* and *Penthouse,* promoting it as a form of sexual liberation. She cites the Biblical references that seem to absolve males in the act. Girls are portrayed as young seductresses in pop culture and literature like *Lolita.* She blames psychologists for dismissing incest reports, arguing that the father of psychology started the trend. Sigmund Freud stumbled upon incest reports in his landmark work, she writes, but incorporated them into his psychological theory as a form of female fantasy, a clinical notion that prevails today.

Incest families, however, have particular characteristics, accounts from Herman's study group clearly show.

In the study, fathers, without question, were heads of the households, their authority absolute. They ruled with force if necessary. They secluded all the women in their families from the outside world. But they, themselves, were usually viewed as "sympathetic, even admirable" men by outsiders.

Mothers were full-time homemakers, depending entirely on their husbands for income. The fathers considered the mothers inferior, not only in their achievements, "but simply in their status as women." Males in the family were considered superior, granted more freedom and privileges. Daughters were prohibited from establishing outside social lives.

Dr. Herman writes:

> Fathers exercised minute control over the lives of their wives and daughters, often virtually confining them to the house. The boys in the family were sometimes enlisted as deputies in this policing role.

It's a patriarchal structure sanctified by many strident Pentecostals and fundamentalists with scripture, like Eddie Lee and his father before him as well. Half of the study's survivors reported physical abuse to enforce the father's authority.

> Other children in the family were beaten as well. Their fathers were selective in their choice of targets: One child was often singled out as a scapegoat, while a more favored child was spared.

There were also limits.

No family member was injured seriously enough to require hospitalization . . . Although the fathers often appeared to be completely out of control in their own homes, they never made the mistake of attacking outsiders. They were not known as bullies or trouble-makers; in the presence of superior authority, they were generally ingratiating, deferential, even meek.

Herman cites other studies that seem to reinforce Eddie Lee Sexton's profile, a man who relied on inferiors for his dirty work. Incest perpetrators appear to be both tyrants and cowards.

The solution to this apparent contradiction lies in the father's ability to assess their relative power in any situation and to vary their behavior accordingly. In the presence of men much more powerful than themselves, such as police, prosecutors, therapists, and researchers, the fathers knew how to present themselves as pathetic, helpless and confused.

The fact that the Sextons had so many children was consistent with the study. The number of offspring in incest families is well above the national average. Pregnancies are usually imposed on women for a reason, Dr. Herman writes. "Economically dependent, socially isolated, in poor health, and encumbered with the care of many small children, these mothers were in no position to challenge their husband's domination."

The psychiatrist also studied daughters. Sexual contact followed predictable patterns similar to the Sexton case. Fondling and oral contact in early years, moving to inter-course at the average age of 13 in the study. Many daughters held their mothers in contempt for failing to protect them, or to believe them when they disclosed. At the same time, they found attachment in the special treatment they sometimes received from their fathers. It was not unusual for daughters to "fall in love" with their fathers and compete with their mothers. As they got older, they often became more rebellious, and faced physical and social restrictions.

Other researchers have studied the pathology of the incestuous patriarch. Incest allows the father to structure sex exactly as he wants it, without worrying about performance or rejections. Secrecy adds to the pleasure. In some cases, the daughter's unhappiness also contributes to his enjoyment. Like rape, for some perpetrators it's an act of hostility and aggression.

The perpetrator's experience cited by Dr. Herman is eerily familiar to the West Virginian weekend that put Eddie Lee Sexton in prison, and perhaps motivated him after his mother's death.

In the father's fantasy life, the daughter becomes the source of all the father's infantile longings for nurturance and care. He thinks of her first as the idealized childhood bride or sweetheart . . .

Another observation explains Sexton on death row thirty years later. Dr. Herman writes:

Disclosure disrupts whatever fragile equilibrium has been maintained, jeopardizes the functioning of all family members, increases the likelihood of violent and desperate behavior, and places everyone, but particularly the daughter, at risk for retaliation.

However, the Sexton case also seemed to break even the boundaries of studies. Detectives and social workers discerned a predictable MO by both parents. Girls and boys first were fondled by siblings and parents. At 13, Eddie Lee Sexton approached girls seeking full intercourse. When boys reached puberty, Sexton sodomized sons, asserting his dominance and authority. With the mentally helpless, like Willie, the sodomy continued.

With the sodomy and May's sexual involvement, the Sextons ventured into extremely rare statistical territory. Mother-son and father-son incest accounted for less than three percent of incest cases in key studies.

The Sextons were an anomaly within a deviancy, their house of secrets a warlock's brew of good, evil, and fantasy.

Largely, Eddie Lee Sexton's fantasy.

Indeed, they were Futuretrons. Procreating a new generation of children who "would all look the same."

10

The Greyhound rolled to a stop in front of the Canton bus station a half hour before midnight on a frigid night in February, 1997.

The passenger from Tampa stood for a few moments, looking around as the bus pulled away in a blast of diesel smoke. She carried only a small cardboard box and had less than $100. She was wearing a flimsy blue cotton suit and a pair of white tennis shoes with "GOOD" printed in marker across the heel.

Estella "Pixie" Good had been paroled after serving two years and three months of her sentence. She'd wanted to return to be near her siblings in Canton, Ohio. Otis Sexton had informed several siblings of her arrival time, hoping one would pick her up. His own family was in turmoil, some of his daughters urging him to let go. He'd done enough, they urged.

But Otis was waiting a block down the street in an idling car. When no other Sextons arrived, the uncle drove up. Pixie was shaking, hardly able to light a cigarette.

"To leave her standing there, to abandon her, would go against everything I believe in my life," he later said.

A few days later, she came down her uncle's stairs for

her first journalistic interview since the entire saga had begun. She clutched a dozen prison certificates of accomplishment. Titles such as: Basic Personal Skills. Industrial Sewing. Employable Skills. Bible Correspondence Course. Insight and Feelings. She'd started a job search, and expressed interest in working in hospice care.

Pixie Good had gained weight; not obese, but no longer the thinnest daughter dispatched to seduce Ray Hesser. The voice was still quiet, the words few. But she laughed here and there, and when she talked, she held her head up, looking her interviewer in the eyes.

She told largely the same story as she did to police, distancing herself from all abuse. She accused Sherri of being the abusive mother, saying she was "always throwing her baby around."

She also filled in some gaps. She discussed the trip to the college library. She revealed the purpose of the secret attic compartments in the house on Caroline.

"We hid in there," she said. "That was the only safe place in the house."

She appeared to have lost entire blocks of her teenage years. She couldn't even remember her two high school friends, identical twins Terry and Traci Turify.

She also may have lied. She said she never knew the contents of the letter Teresa Boron had sent her husband saying his grandfather was deathly ill. She didn't know that her interviewer had the statement from Eddie Sexton Jr. And Eddie Jr. could not know the contents of the letter, unless she told him.

"Eddie [Sr.] tore the letter up," she also said. "Joel never saw it."

She seemed unmoved by the notion that some people thought she was a murderer, an ally of her father. She had no words for them specifically.

"I don't know what I'd say to them," she said. "Everybody has the right to feel what they want. As long as I know I'm telling the truth, it doesn't matter to me what anybody thinks."

For two hours, she never called Eddie Lee Sexton her "father" or her "dad."

She called him Eddie.

"I call him Eddie because I don't consider him my father," she said. "Because of Eddie, I lost everything I had."

11

More than two years after the murder trial, the courtroom revelations of her nephew's torture and death still hung with Teresa Boron and the rest of the family like an old, chronic injury. It would be a long wait for justice. Appeals made the average stay on Florida's death row 10 years.

Joey's brother Danny sued the Sextons in a multi-million-dollar lawsuit. Joel Good's estate won by default against the penniless defendants. The family felt some gratification. The judgement would allow Good's estate to attach any money Eddie Lee Sexton might receive from tabloids or talk shows. No money ever came.

For remembrance, the family hunted down the name of the hospital in Kentucky where Skipper Lee was born and ordered baby pictures. They put up Joey's groomed high school portrait. The prom pictures with Pixie were kept put away.

When Teresa found out that Pixie had told her brother, Eddie Jr., that she knew of her letter to Joey, Teresa wept.

"At least, then, he knew we loved him," she said. That was some consolation.

Then Pixie claimed her husband never saw it.

Or did he? Why was he so adamant about flying back that day in the library?

"I chose to believe he did," Teresa said.

Many months earlier, across town, an ongoing argument raged between the identical twins, Traci and Terry Turify.

Terry thought Pixie Good was a victim.

Traci recalled, "I thought, Stella, you bitch. I wanted to kill her."

For days after news of the murder broke, Traci didn't make contact with Joel Good's family. She was too embarrassed. She thought, I introduced Joel to Pixie.

Then she heard about the funeral. At the last minute, when she learned the details, she raced to the funeral home, but found no one there. The service was over, the procession gone. She sped to the cemetery. When she arrived, the dirt was still fresh on the grave, the area scattered with flowers and snow.

Traci Turify Dryland stood there in the wind, weeping.

Thinking, what have I done?

"I thought, if I would have just went out with Joel, he probably would have never met her," she later recalled, crying again over the memory. "It was all my fault."

She found Teresa Boron's new address in North Canton and drove over, but spent an hour going up and down her street. She couldn't find the house.

Finally, she knocked on the door to Boron's newly-built Victorian.

Traci told Teresa she wanted to apologize for introducing them.

They hugged and cried a lot.

He was her Forrest Gump. "Joel never had a chance," Traci said.

She felt better, but not serene.

"She's a baby killer," Traci later said. "She's a fucking bitch. Joel's not at rest. It's not complete. The Sextons. All of them. I just feel they all should die."

The ambivalence of the identical twins found its way into dozens of individuals touched by one of the most brutal public cases of family abuse in American history.

Steve Ready, Otis Sexton, and Judee Genetin were among them.

Ambivalence not just toward Pixie, but Willie and Skipper.

For Steve Ready, even May.

"Look at their world," Ready said. "Their existence. What else did they know?"

All the patriarch's creations.

On another cold day in February, when she found out that Pixie Good had returned, Teresa Boron began thinking about making plans. When the time was right, she planned to drive over and knock on the door of Otis Sexton.

Saying, "I'd like to have a talk with Pixie."

Teresa Boron planned to take her pastor. She'd need a minister, and some kind of miracle.

She was looking for some kind of peace.

The Bottomless Pit

When Steve Ready visited the house on Caroline Street with Jay Pruner, the Tampa state attorney immediately saw the handless Jesus—and wanted it.

"God, what a perfect memento," Pruner said. "I want that sitting in my office."

Ready considered returning at night and outright stealing it. He thought, pack it up in a big box and send it off to Tampa. Then better judgement took over, a cop's judgement. He could see the headline: SEXTON DETECTIVE ARRESTED IN SEXTON BURGLARY. Perhaps appropriately, a Dumpster truck carted off the statue with the rest of Eddie Lee Sexton's trash.

The patriarch had left much behind, years after the case. Judee Genetin and social workers put together a Christmas party for the siblings, only to have them argue and start pointing fingers at each other over petty jealousies. They seemed to clamor for each other's company and love, but couldn't form any lasting, healthy relationships.

The Exchange Club named Steve Ready deputy of the year for his work. Before Eddie Lee's trial, he was assigned to a federal fugitive task force. But cops and lawyers and social workers and relatives still called Ready with tips. There was a hazy report from Skipper of an unidentified adult male being killed by Eddie Lee years ago and buried in a park called Ohio Powerland. Ready, working part-time, was never able to develop enough evidence. The unidentified body Machelle Sexton saw in the trunk haunted the detective. One day, Otis Sexton revealed a relative said it was him. He'd apparently been beaten by Eddie Lee and dropped off next to a freeway near Toledo, presumed dead. He woke up in a ditch and needed a month in the hospital to recover. But he wanted nothing to do with the law. He was still terrified of Eddie Lee.

Other agencies started reaping Eddie Lee's harvest. Some siblings needed psychotropic drugs to control depression and hallucinations. Eddie Jr. showed up at the Jackson Township Police Department, wanting to be admitted to a mental hospital. In the summer of 1996 he was arrested for theft from Sears and picked up with a crack pipe. His wife Daniela left him. In 1997, he went into treatment. Sherri had more breakdowns and marital trouble. Skipper seemed incapable of serving out his burglary sentence on good behavior and was placed on extended probation. He was not charged with abusing his siblings. Shelly Croto miscarried her twins after testifying at her mother's trial. Willie was continually ruled incompetent in Florida. Like other siblings, he kept having flashbacks and auditory hallucinations. Sherri's son Christopher, Eddie Lee's son/grandson, remained in foster care. Dawn and Shasta were in custody of Florida social services, their fate confidential. It appeared unlikely their mother would ever get them back.

In early 1997, psychologists evaluated Willie Sexton again and declared him competent to face charges. A murder trial was scheduled later in the year, his fate uncertain.

He wasn't the only sibling with a pending homicide case. In November of 1996, James Sexton, 20, was arrested and charged with murder. He'd allegedly burned his 38-year-old roommate to death in a house fire as the man slept on the couch. The man had sex with him, he said. In one interview, James claimed he'd seen his father sitting on the couch. He was trying to burn the old man, not the roommate.

"Just because I'm a Sexton, that doesn't mean they have to charge me with murder," James said. "Maybe felonious assault, 'cause I burned my dad's arm."

Said Ready, "As we speak, there's some kid somewhere who's going to go into law enforcement or social work who's going to find himself dealing with these kids."

All wasn't lost. Social workers were hopeful for Kimberly, Lana, Christopher, and Matthew. They had been adopted, their names changed. Some were in long-term therapy. But others, such as Shelly and Skipper, lacked either the will or the money.

Those involved in the case paid a price. Frustrated with Sexton's house of mirrors and enraged by the graphic disclosures, Steve Ready found himself trying to understand. "These people changed my whole life," he said. "You find yourself lying in bed at night, unable to sleep, and trying to think like them. And that makes me crazy, doesn't it?"

Then, Ready had a heart attack. "As I lay in the hospital, the first thing I thought was: Did that sonovabitch down on death row put some kind of mojo on me?"

Judee Genetin, after returning from the Florida trial, went into a deep, month-long depression. She'd bought a Rottweiler for protection. Wayne Welsh, who started carrying a gun, had a heart attack. And Anne Greene, after leaving Canton for Florida, largely to get away from the Sextons, developed a rare brain tumor. After surgeons removed it, she was left with speech and motor skill problems and faces extended therapy. It's not even clear if she remembers the Sexton case.

For me, unlike most true-crime accounts, it simply

became clear that the Sexton story was endless. The principal perpetrators had been exposed and imprisoned, but
many secrets remained buried everywhere, still waiting to
be discovered. The case had an obsessive pull. The depth
of Sexton's pure evil both repulsed and fascinated.

Yet, I was not disappointed when he promised an interview, but never delivered. I'd done it with other criminals
many times before, but I wasn't sure I had the patience to
sit very long in a small room with the man.

Incest network founder Ann Marie Eriksson told me, "I
tell professionals, if you're going to get programs for incest,
you need to make them suitable for your local banker and
senator. It cuts across all groups, all religions, all incomes."

But for me, the Sextons broke the true-crime book mold
of the perfect family concealing unthinkable crimes. The
fact that the Sextons were so dysfunctional, and Sexton
himself an ex-con, made it even more astounding that he'd
pulled off what he did for years.

I tried to understand May Sexton. She was courteous
and helpful in interviews, but remained a Flatliner herself.
She took a Millon personality test for me. It showed her
to be obsessive-compulsive, self-destructive, and a patholog-
ically dependent personality who clamored for social
approval.

My obsession concerned the babies. The fact that no
alcohol was found in Skipper Lee was troubling. Was the
Nyquil story just a cover for his suffocation, or was something far darker going on?

The biggest riddle began at the J.B. Cook Library in
Sarasota. When I first interviewed librarian Gail Novak
there, she broke down, as she had with authorities. She
complained no one would believe her that there was a
"second baby," a burial on the grounds. She claimed
Sherri Sexton had come to the library after her parents'
arrest and asked her, "Where's the grave?"

I knew authorities considered the strange aspects of her
story to be hysterical imaginings. Trying to calm her, I

asked the librarian to take a walk outside and show me the spot. As we approached the line of palmettos in the vacant field, she nearly collapsed. She had been afraid to visit there since the arrest.

Now, there was a hole in the ground—the size of the grave for an infant.

I called campus police, who seemed to dismiss the entire matter. I took pictures anyway. I chased the mystery of that hole for nearly a year.

Who'd dug up something? What? And why?

After I told Steve Ready and Otis Sexton of the discovery, other siblings began to disclose. Willie, from a phone at the mental hospital, said there had been a second baby, not Pixie's but Sherri's. It had been born on Treaty Road, then killed by Eddie Lee Sexton.

Skipper confirmed. He told me Sherri delivered the baby in the bedroom. His father took it into the bathroom, still screaming from birth. When his father emerged, it was dead in his hands.

"Then what did you do?" I asked.

"We went back into the woods, you know," he said. "You know what the old man was into. Sacrificed it, then buried it."

It all seemed to match the neighbor's news account of a baby screaming and finding a buried box behind the Sexton trailer. Sherri later confirmed the delivery and death to Steve Ready. The baby supposedly had been unearthed and moved by the patriarch, eventually ending up in Little Manatee State Park, said Willie in a fragmented account.

By late 1996, Pasco County cops were digging. They took Pixie Good out of jail to show them the site of the grave Sherri had shown her on Treaty Road. They found nothing.

They got Willie from Chatahootchee and returned to Little Manatee. Willie thought he could find the spot where the baby was buried. They dug at two locations, but found nothing.

Otis Sexton, who went to Florida for the excavations, was also hearing from siblings that the dead child had been moved again once more before the arrest in Little Manatee. Had that been what the FBI air surveillance saw when they spotted teens with a shovel in the forest?

Talking to elusive siblings for more details was often impossible. Just finding them, and trying to commit them to an interview, often took weeks.

Pasco County police decided they had spent enough time and resources. A detective marked the case inactive.

When I interviewed Pixie Sexton days after she was paroled, I carefully moved into the subject. Independently, she verified virtually all of Gail Novak's account. Yes, it was many weeks after Skipper Lee's death. "The first baby" was the miscarriage soon after she'd married Joel, she said. The "second baby" was Skipper Lee.

She admitted seeing her father burying something outside the library. I asked, what was it?

"It was Sherri's baby," she said. "Sherri told me after they were arrested Eddie had buried it at the library." Then later, dug it up again.

She claimed she didn't know it was in the trunk. "Eddie" would not let them near the trunk, she said.

"Novak said you wanted her to come out and see the baby?" I asked. "What about that?"

"I don't remember that," Pixie said.

Otis Sexton believes the child is still somewhere in Little Manatee, perhaps behind Ray Hesser's old Campsite Number 28.

And he, and others, believe there are fetuses and miscarriages buried around the property on the house at Caroline Street. One supposedly was buried under the statue of the handless Jesus.

Other things were ditched in the pond, siblings were saying. Stolen goods. Evidence. Bob and Edie Johnson complained about a thick infestation of surface algae they couldn't seem to stop.

"Hey, maybe bodies," Ready joked.

Then he stopped laughing. With the Sextons, anything was possible.

The investigation had no end.

One day, Steve Ready talked to Herb Schreiner of the Jackson Township Fire Department.

"Steve," Schreiner said. "You want to, I'll come over with a crew and we'll pump every drop of water out of that pond."

Ready thought about it. No longer on the case. No manpower. No compelling interest from the Stark County prosecutor.

He was burned out.

"They pump out that thing and what do I got?" he said. "I got a great big hole in the ground. And what am I going to do with it? Walk into it and start slugging through some bottomless pit?"

In a way, all of us already had.

In July of 1997, the worst fears of Steve Ready, Jay Pruner, and many others materialized. A Florida appellate court overturned Eddie Lee Sexton's capital murder conviction for the death of Joel Good, ruling some abuse testimony had prejudiced the Tampa jury. Sexton remains imprisoned in Florida on the conspiracy conviction. A new murder trial is being planned. Stark County Prosecutor Robert Horowitz still refuses to bring Sexton back to Ohio on sex abuse charges. And in both states, police and prosecutors wonder if the Sexton children are even capable of testifying again.

MORE MUST-READ TRUE CRIME
FROM PINNACLE

HORRIFYING TRUE CRIME
FROM PINNACLE BOOKS

Body Count
by Burl Barer   0-7860-1405-9   **$6.50**US/**$8.50**CAN

The Babyface Killer
by Jon Bellini   0-7860-1202-1   **$6.50**US/**$8.50**CAN

Love Me to Death
by Steve Jackson   0-7860-1458-X   **$6.50**US/**$8.50**CAN

The Boston Stranglers
by Susan Kelly   0-7860-1466-0   **$6.50**US/**$8.50**CAN

Body Double
by Don Lasseter   0-7860-1474-1   **$6.50**US/**$8.50**CAN

The Killers Next Door
by Joel Norris   0-7860-1502-0   **$6.50**US/**$8.50**CAN

Available Wherever Books Are Sold!

Visit our website at **www.kensingtonbooks.com**.